The Transparent Leader II

THE
Transparent
Leader II

Dwight L. Johnson

with Dean Nelson

**Executive
Books**

Executive Books has made every effort to trace the ownership of all quotes. In the event of a question arising from the use of a poem or quote, we regret any error made and will be pleased to make the necessary correction in the future editions of this book.

Transparent Leader II cover and inside page layout by Gregory Dixon *(Also special thanks to Koechel Peterson & Associates in Minneapolis, Minnesota for assistance in developing of the original cover concept)*

THE TRANSPARENT LEADER II
Copyright © 2006 by Dwight Johnson
Published by Executive Books
206 West Allen Street
Mechanicsburg, PA 17055
www.ExecutiveBooks.com

ISBN-13: 978-1-933715-11-7

ISBN-10: 1-933715-11-1

Printed in the United States of America

Contents

Dedication

The reason I am dedicating this book to Alma Harris is that she is a grateful, God-fearing, sold-out-for-Jesus Christian lady whose life mirrors those whose stories are in this book. She has taught me a lot about real faith.

Alma is less than five-feet tall, weighs about ninety pounds, and has the heart and beliefs of a giant. I have never known anyone or heard about any person who has a faith like hers.

My sister Ruthanne and her husband Dave met Alma and her husband Willy after they had purchased season tickets to the San Diego Chargers football games. Their seats were right behind each other, and they developed a close personal relationship. Alma shared with Ruthanne that she was losing her eyesight. Two years later, Alma was blind. The Braille Institute helped Alma buy a fantastic piece of recording equipment that made it possible for Alma to take cassette tapes and transcribe them as a way to generate income for herself and her husband, who had suffered a stroke.

When I shared with my sister that I was going to write my first book, Ruthanne suggested that I employ Alma to transcribe my tapes. That's what I did. Every time Alma would call me to tell me she finished another tape, she told me how the tape had ministered to her. She asked me to pray for her and for God to restore her eyesight. I found out that she had an atrophied optic nerve, which made it medically impossible for her to see again.

One time she called and asked me to pray, and I told her that it was medically impossible for her to see. That's where my faith failed. Alma told me, "Dwight, I'm not praying for or asking you to pray for a medical miracle – I'm praying for a spiritual miracle." What a lesson that was for me. I was looking for something that I could touch and feel, like a medical miracle to restore her sight, not a faith or spiritual miracle of healing her blindness.

Alma kept asking me to pray for a spiritual miracle to heal her, and chapter after chapter I changed my prayer for Alma. Two years after the first *Transparent Leader* book was published, Alma moved back to Colorado. A few months later, God healed her in a miraculous way. She not only has her eyesight back, but she is driving again and has driven to and through Chicago more than ten times.

She once was blind, but now, through God's miraculous healing, Alma and the rest of us can see!

Acknowledgements

The first Transparent Leadership book I wrote four years ago was a tremendous compilation of the stories of 19 men, most of whom I had known personally for at least 10 years. One of the men, former Congressman and Senator Hank Brown, and I go so far back that his mother and my mother were in each other's weddings 72 years ago.

The Transparent Leader II, 22 Men Who Have Lived Life With Character, Morals, and Ethics, is identical in format, and includes additional stories from men with whom I have had similar relationships, except for President Bush. When I listened to the DVD released by Focus on the Family about his life, I felt that his story of how his faith had helped him through 9/11 and his first five years of his presidency was so powerful that it needed to be told to the public at large.

One of my close accountability partners, Dick Darley and his wife, Norma, said they would help me get this volume published and distributed, as did the Issa Family Foundation, Art Garcia, Beth and Bill White, Peter David, Inc., Steve and Vicki Deal, Tyler and Diane Miller, Christian Catalysts, Inc., and Five Star Financial Consultants, LLC, Charitable Funding Solutions, Michelle and Tom Fox, and Doyle Young. Without these dear friends' support, this book would not have been possible.

Dean Nelson, the director of the journalism program at Point Loma Nazarene University, has been more than a ghost writer and editor – he has been a friend and colleague in this enterprise with his gifts and talents, as well as with his wise discernment.

I am very grateful to Charlie " Tremendous" Jones and his wonderful staff at Executive Books, in particular,

Greg Dixon and Jason Liller, for their wonderful cooperation in getting this book published.

My wife of 45 years, Betsy, has not only been an encourager, but she is also an excellent proof reader, and she knows most of the men in both books. Her knowledge of their spiritual perspectives and commitments has been a great help. Our three sons, Dwight Jr., Eric and Stephen encouraged me to include my story as a chapter, because they have such a strong appreciation for the effort I have made to be the father that they wanted and needed me to be.

Finally, and most importantly, putting this second book together has given me a tremendous resolve for how important friendships are and need to be in this incredible experience called life. The most important friendship that I have is with my Lord and Savior Jesus Christ, and it has been this relationship that has helped me through these last 50 years. I could not have made it without Him.

The title *The Transparent Leader II, 22 Men Who Have Lived Life With Character, Morals, and Ethics*, reveals the purpose being to love the Lord our God with all our heart, mind, soul and strength, and to love our neighbors as ourselves. May that be your purpose as you read. Enjoy!

Dwight L. Johnson
San Diego, California

Foreword

There are two ways to look at the present condition of the world. One is to concentrate on the scandals in business, politics, sports and entertainment and say, "What's the point in trying to live a Spirit-filled life? Look at how bad everything is! No one seems to care about character any more." It all seems so driven by greed that we can only believe we are in the end times.

Another way to look at the state of the world is to realize that there is more to the story than just the scandal and the ethical blunders we read so much about. Instead of giving up, we can say, "Show me the people who are living honorably, faithful to God and their families during these trying times. Those are the people I want to read about!"

That's what you're holding in your hand right now, put together by author, Dwight Johnson. This is a collection of stories of real leaders who have learned the eternal lessons of serving God in their work and their homes, who also work in the fields of business, politics, sports, and entertainment.

We need to know about people who are affecting industry and culture whose lives are committed to God, serving His purpose in the world through their businesses and families, through their successes and failures, through their questions and answers. The world is ready to see evidence of God's work as people make difficult decisions and face difficult circumstances.

This is a collection of personal stories of victory, failure, triumph, and loss, all shared by people who experienced these conditions. People just like you and me, and like Job or Moses, sometimes they wondered where God was in the midst of their experiences. Some of the people in this book asked where God was when they were being falsely accused. Some of them wondered why God granted them so much mercy when they didn't deserve it. Some of them never doubted God, but wondered how they would survive their predicaments. Some of them lost children to drug abuse. Some were confronted with what appeared to be unbeatable odds. These are the stories of individuals, but they are really all stories about God and how He works.

God has used some of the people in this book to change thousands of people's lives, like Josh McDowell as he speaks to standing-room only arenas, or like Tom Osborne as he inspires through his football legacy and his influence in Congress. God also has used some to change the lives of fellow prisoners in a federal penitentiary, like Bill Kennedy, who loves through his Christian witness. Dwight and I have been working for Bill's release from prison, for over thirteen years and we are amazed at his spirit of letting God use him even while in prison.

Some of the people in this book tell of buying up urban property and using it to glorify God. Some traded in their celebrity status to tell others about Jesus. But what I think is significant is that none of the people feels that his life is extraordinary. Every one of them points to the extraordinary work of God in their life and then pointed many others to Him.

Each story is different. Some deal with professional athletes, some with Hollywood, some with going to prison, some with family conflict, some with successful business ventures, some with bankruptcy. But they are similar in that all of them deal with real life issues and how God can use our circumstances to make Himself known. You'll recognize some of the names – some of these people are my friends, some I do not know, but all have a story of learning to know God. I hope you recognize yourself in this book. You and I have had many of the same temptations as these people. We are often tempted to look to our own strength, to be addicted to praise for our brilliance, to respond with anger rather than love, to worship success more than God, to believe that the world spins on an axis that looks a lot like us, to think that the Bible applies to people who aren't quite as smart as we are, to assume that the rules are a little different for us, to be impressed with ourselves, and even to ignore those who are less fortunate than us. And while you and I might respond to those temptations differently from the examples here, it is unmistakable that we are confronted with the same conditions of the human heart.

For instance, I think we are all tempted and sometimes seduced by power and accomplishment. We are all in a struggle with our egos, where our identities are determined by whether we win or lose. Sometimes it seems we measure ourselves by our accomplishments or our defeats. Self-serving leaders care only about gaining and maintaining power, status, and position.

That's what happens with each person in this book. Some had a rougher road than others in finding that security and meaning. I hope you will see the way God works through these transparent leaders. We serve a faithful, creative, and loving God. As we let Him shine through our lives, as these men have, we'll see a clearer picture of what we are put on this earth to do, and what God's plan is for us.

This book is the practical application of what living for Christ looks like in the present day. My prayer is that it will reveal to you how God can use your life to reveal His purpose in just as profound a way, to the people you live and work with. All of the men in this book faced some extraordinarily difficult circumstances. Sometimes they went to God, and sometimes God intervened. In all cases, God gave them an answer that was unique to their circumstances. Read this book and apply its lessons to your own life to see how God is working out the answer specifically for you. Then pass it on to someone who needs it, and watch God answer their questions in a way that changes the world around them.

I believe there is a struggle occurring today in regard to our future in general and our culture in particular. We all see the culture we are a part of, and yet we don't have to be overwhelmed by it or ruled by it. Once we truly see the activity of God in society and in our lives, we are free to create His world in our workplaces and homes. It is our task. It is our privilege! Reading this book will inspire you and challenge you to let God glorify Himself through your life.

Tim LaHaye
coauthor of the *Left Behind Series*

THE Transparent Leader II

Back in the 1970s I was appointed to the state of Colorado's Chairman of the National Business Consortium for Gifted and Talented Children. All of the state chairmen were flown to Washington, D.C. to meet with Vice President Bush and Barbara Bush, who President Reagan had asked to be directors of the special program. That is where I was introduced to George W. Bush.

The next time I met him was in San Diego at the Cinco de Mayo celebration breakfast, and he came to address our function. As he was greeting a number of us, I told him that my wife and I prayed for him every night. He took my hand, looked me right in the eye and said, "Thank you – your prayers are greatly appreciated and desperately needed."

Those of us who appreciate having a strong man of God in the most important position of leadership in the world, have an appreciation for his commitment. When I heard the DVD that was released through Focus on the Family and loaned to me by my confidant and accountability partner, Dick Darley, I knew this story of President Bush's faith had to be adapted for my second book so that more people could read it. President and Mrs. Bush have a huge responsibility, and many of us are grateful for their leadership and their willingness to be counted for Christ.

Tom Landry told me that he had watched George W. Bush grow up as a young man, and believed that if ever there was a man of faith who was going to be in a position of national prominence, it was this man. Thank you, George and Laura Bush, for your willingness to be transparent leaders.

Adapted from DVD provided by Focus on the Family

When God Changes a Heart

George W. Bush

THE QUESTION POSED TO ME BY THE moderator of the presidential candidate debate in Iowa gave me the opportunity of a lifetime. He was asking all of the candidates to name the philosopher that they most admired.

"Governor Bush, your philosopher figure?" he asked.

"Christ, because he changed my life," I replied.

The question was simple and straightforward, and I didn't hesitate to answer. But my answer seemed to send a shock wave through the halls of government. It seemed that all of Washington, D.C. was asking whether a candidate for president of the United States could fly in the face of political correctness and testify to his religious beliefs, which included a firm faith in Jesus Christ.

Pundits were quick to point out that I had committed political suicide. They asked. "Is this candidate out of touch with the American mainstream, or is he just a politician cynically pandering to the voters of the religious right?" The answer was neither. I was simply saying that my faith is a fundamental part of my being. You can't separate faith from who you are. I was simply willing to admit that I was guided by a moral purpose, which came from my Christian faith.

It turned out that it wasn't political suicide.

Only seven months into my presidency, the ruthless attacks on our country turned us away from our concerns about the economy, education, and care for our families and forced us to confront a more complex world in which America was no longer safe from attacks. It was a chance to show that my faith was not just paying lip service to the idea of God, but was a source of confidence and hope.

The moderator in Iowa asked me to explain my answer further and said, "I think our viewers would like to know more about how he has changed your life."

I said, "Well, if they don't know, it's going to be hard to explain. When you turn your heart and your life over to Christ, when you accept Christ as your savior, it changes your heart and changes your life. And that's what happened to me."

Some people seemed confused – even angry – about my comments. My expression of reverence for and deference to God struck a nerve in some. One magazine writer wrote, "It's one thing for a nation to assert its raw dominance in the world. It's quite another to suggest that this presidency my be a divine appointment for a time such as this."

I think many Americans are re-evaluating their spiritual lives. I also think that moral clarity, which comes from faith, is precisely what the public is looking for in a leader, regardless of what the pundits and other politicians say. It seems that mainstream America wants leadership with strong moral and ethical character.

After the attacks of September 11 there was an undercurrent of fear and doubt in America that could be felt from the most humble church pew to the highest level of government. It was a time when the nation needed strong moral leadership – leadership they could trust. From the outside we were under attack from radical Islamic fundamentalist groups. But we were also under attack from the inside. It was a struggle between those who regarded their Christian values as vital for our nation's survival, and those who viewed those values as obstructions to progress. The future of our nation depends on the outcome of this struggle, I believe. And this country has faced this struggle before. There are examples from our history of great leaders who found strength in prayer when they faced critical choices.

George Washington, our leader in the revolution, our first president, and "the father of our country," said, "It is impossible to rightly govern in the world without God and the Bible." I believe in the power of prayer. In addition to praying for the direction of this country and our world, I believe in the power of prayer for our co-workers and their families. Several times I have stopped what I was doing in the White House or on Air Force One and prayed for a member of our staff who was going through a difficult time. That's what people of prayer do. People don't seem to mind it. They seem to appreciate it. I don't see that as imposing my beliefs on someone. I see it as saying that I care for them and so does God.

As much of the world already knows, I have not always been a man of faith and prayer. I was just another hard-drinking young man caught up in the boom and bust of the oil business in Texas. I was my seventh-grade class president, got straight A's, played baseball and football as a boy and was known as a popular kid with a big mouth. I was arrogant, aggressive and sarcastic – not necessarily presidential qualities! My world was a combination of Texas bravado and the transplanted Ivy League of my father.

But in that environment, people accepted you for your word, your integrity and how capable you were in your job. Politics was something people talked about, but most of the men and women I knew were not interested in things outside of Texas.

My family's religion was an important part of my upbringing. My family was very involved in a Presbyterian

19

church, and I had plenty of examples of role models there. They emphasized being true to your word, faith, family and friends.

There were some dark days when I was a boy, particularly when I lost my sister, Robin, to leukemia. It is one of the starkest memories of my childhood. But I also felt my parents' pain, and would do whatever I could to try to bring joy to my mother's face. I wanted to change the mood in my home, and lift the depression from it. Perhaps it gave me the courage then to try to do the same for my country after we were attacked on September 11.

Still, it took me a long time to accept my church's faith as my own. I spent many years chasing "the good life" of smoking, drinking, cursing and carousing. But I was also calling myself a Christian. As Jesus said, "A house divided against itself cannot stand." Despite what I had been saying, I was far from God.

During our family vacations in Kennebunkport, Maine, we routinely invited Billy Graham to join us. We would all sit in the living room and ask him questions about religion and faith. It was a type of informal Bible camp for us. I could see God through Billy Graham's loving manner, and I was moved by it. I wasn't so moved by what he told us during those times as much as by his character.

One night, after a particularly moving discussion time together, he and I took a walk on the beach. He asked me directly, "Are you right with God?" I said, "No, but I want to be." My whole life I had been influenced by Christianity, but when asked this question, I could not say "yes." After this talk I was drawn to be different in my spiritual life. I wanted something real, and that's when my life began to change.

The night of my 40th birthday I had too much to drink, and woke up the next morning with a hangover. I went out that morning for my usual three-mile run, and decided that

I was never going to take another drink. I told this to Laura when I got back from the run. Lots of drinkers make promises like this and then go back to binge drinking relatively soon. But I had made up my mind.

My faith helped me have the strength to change, and helped me become much more disciplined about my life. It helped redirect my life where, instead of living for myself, I began to live for others.

My new faith was put to the test often. When I began working on my father's presidential campaign I was faced with the many temptations that are part of the ugly side of politics. But with God's help and the love of my family, I have tried to maintain my commitment to Christ in all aspects of my life.

As president, I make sure there is time every day for prayer, Bible reading, a physical workout, time to talk with my daughters, wife and parents, as well as going through the stack of briefing papers. Then there is the grueling part of all the meetings, appearances and decisions.

I try to show my respect for the Oval Office any way I can. It's a type of sacred place for me because I believe I have a sacred trust as the nation's leader. So I make sure I am wearing a suit when I go in there, even during the evening or weekends. We don't do casual-dress days. I also try to have staff members show respect for each other by being on time for meetings and getting their work done on time. I encourage them to pray for each other and to read their Bibles daily.

Some people say that my Christian commitment is a threat to our constitution and culture, but a person's religion is more than a church, a synagogue, a temple or a mosque. Faith is the framework for living. It gives us the spirit and heart that affect everything we do. It gives us hope each day. It gives us purpose to right wrongs, preserve our families, and teach our children values. Faith provides us with a conscience to keep us honest, even when nobody is looking. And faith can change lives. I know first hand because faith changed mine.

A congressman came to see me about a project he wanted my help with. He had a decent idea. But when he got to a part where he said, "There's something in this for you," I got out of my chair, helped the congressman to his feet and showed him the door. I thanked him for the good conversation, and told him I was very busy. I simply didn't want to be involved in something that could be perceived as unethical. My ethics are shaped by my faith. A person's faith should exhibit itself through kindness, truthfulness, self control, and a love for others.

My relationship with God, through Christ, has given me meaning and direction. My faith has made a big difference in my personal life and in my public life as well. I pray for guidance. I pray for patience. I firmly believe in the power of intercessory prayer. I know I could not do my job without it.

I am not interested in using my position as president to convert people to Christianity. I just want people to be better off. I want to serve them. This is why I have promoted what I call faith-based initiatives. A lot of religious groups and organizations serve the poor and indigent in their communities. I want to help them because I think our faith calls us to serve others.

I supported faith-based programs when I was governor in Texas. I supported Teen Challenge, a very successful drug rehabilitation program that used faith as a principle means for helping deliver people from their drug addictions. We helped get funding for 200 faith-based drug and alcohol treatment programs.

In Washington it has not been so easy. Interpretations of how to enforce the separation of church and state created a lot of opposition from people who feared that we were imposing religious beliefs on the public. I'm just trying to support effective ways to help people with their problems.

When I pray for God's direction, I do not see handwriting on the wall or hear an audible voice from God. I do sense the prompting of God in my heart, and I try to be attentive to those promptings. I want God's wisdom, and I need people to pray for me. We all need insight and counsel beyond ourselves. We need the direction of God in our thoughts and actions.

Prayer meetings are always occurring somewhere in the White House. I don't make them mandatory, but I do encourage them. It is common to see a person walking down one of the corridors carrying a Bible. I have a Presidential Prayer Team that prays for me and my staff. We call on the members to pray for our military around the world. Because of the Internet, I know that there are days when nearly 30,000 people are praying for a specific issue we need help with. More than 3 million people participate in this team. Some days we have more than 10 million visits to the Prayer Team website.

Three days before we went to war with Iraq, I met with a young man who had the deadly disease, cystic fibrosis. Laura and I talked with him and his family, and he told me about his life. Sam had chosen to deal with the disease by drawing closer to God, and he wanted me to know that. I gave him a baseball with the presidential seal on it, but he gave me an even better gift. He gave me a Bible with my name engraved on the outside. Inside was a bookmark to remind me to rely on God. He told me, "The only way to live is to rely on God." And even though there are rules about taking gifts on board Air Force One, I made sure that gift was with me when Laura and I flew out later that day.

Many people are worried and have expressed their concern that I am trying to promote a specific religion, and use taxpayer money to do so. I am not afraid to make my

Christianity part of my public life. Neither were many of our leaders before me. James Madison said, "The highest glory of the American Revolution is this: it connected in one indissoluble bond the principles of simple government with the principles of Christianity." He also said, "I consider a decent respect for Christianity among the best recommendations for public service."

The U.S. Congress voted a resolution in 1782 stating, "The Congress of the United States recommends and approves the Holy Bible for use in all schools."

God has been a participant in our nation's public life from the very beginning. Abraham Lincoln said, "I have been driven many times upon my knees with overwhelming conviction that I had nowhere else to go. My own wisdom and that of all about me seemed insufficient for that day." About 50 years ago, Dwight Eisenhower said, "Without God, there could be no American form of government nor an American way of life. Recognition of the Supreme Being is the first, the most basic expression of Americanism."

Every one of our presidents has referred to God in their inaugural addresses. Our forefathers were wise enough to lay a foundation that would sustain us for the long term. They unapologetically chose the Bible and its moral and ethical principles in that foundation.

John Kennedy, in his inaugural address, said, "The rights of man come not from the generosity of state, but from the hand of God." Harry Truman, in his speech, said, "We believe all men are created equal because we're created in the image of God."

My relationship with God, through Christ, has given me meaning and direction. My faith has made a big difference in my personal life and in my public life as well. I make decisions every day. Some are easy. Some aren't so easy. I have worries just like you. I have moments of doubt, moments of pride, and moments of hope, yet my faith helps a lot because I have a sense of calm, knowing that the Bible's admonition, "Thy will be done," is life's guide. In this hectic world, there is something incredibly reassuring in the belief that there is a divine plan that exceeds all human plans.

All of our presidents, in times of calamity, turned to God for guidance. All I desire is the courage to do what is right. Ultimately, I answer to Him.

I first met Gary Cuozzo at a Fellowship of Christian Athletes event with Tom Landry more than 20 years ago. He had just been elected to FCA's national board and was introduced as a dentist from New Jersey. It appeared to me that he was far more than a dentist from New Jersey. He was also a very good businessman who was interested in making a difference for the Kingdom of God through FCA.

Within a short time he was elected chairman of the FCA board, and he made a significant contribution to the organization's success. His wife, Peggy, also gave tremendous help as she traveled with him to as many meetings and functions as she could.

A few years later, Gary was very transparent when he shared that they had a family tragedy involving their oldest child. Gary and Peggy were devastated, and their first mission seemed to be how they could spend the rest of their lives trying to share their story with anyone who might be going through something similar. If they helped just one person avoid what they went through, they would be satisfied.

Gary had accomplished so much as an athlete, a husband, a father. But Gary felt he had been a total failure with his son, Chip, when Chip needed him the most and Gary didn't know it. Gary and Peggy's faith has helped them through this difficult time with a clarity and purpose that they had not had before. It was such a privilege to hear them both be so transparent about their own shortcomings and to lean so heavily on the support base of Jesus Christ, from whence comest their strength.

2

Letters From My Son

Gary Cuozzo

A LOT OF TIMES PEOPLE WILL ASK EACH other, "How are you doing?" And the typical answer is "Fine. Everything is fine." I guess it's just a polite way of not telling what is going on in our lives when we say, "Fine." I heard a speaker say, "I know I'm not fine. I know my life and I know what I'm going through, and if everybody is so fine, I came to the conclusion that 'fine' meant frustrated, insecure, neurotic and exhausted."

I related to his statement because I think sometimes you just assume that no one else is going through what you're going through. I know that was the case with the experience we had with one of my sons.

Life, it seems to me, is a series of going into a problem, being in a problem, and coming out of a problem. You can guarantee it. If you're a Christian, though, you know why. It's because we war against principalities and powers in the air. Satan simply does not want us to have a victory.

I grew up attending a church where we had varying degrees of sin. We had little sins and we had big ones. I was pretty much a guy who did the little ones. I didn't want to do the big ones. This was, of course, before I knew that all have sinned and that we have fallen short of the glory of God. Our church had a list of rules and regulations, and I kept them. I never missed formations! I really thought that was enough – Jesus died on the cross for my sin, but I thought I still had to do these things because I was constantly under the guilt of missing church or missing some little rule.

This all came apart for me when I was in the National Football League. It started with a mountaintop experience, where I came into a game to replace John Unitas, who had been injured. I threw five touchdown passes and set a record, which made me the NFL player of the week. Everyone in the nation, it seemed, tried to call me and talk to me that week. Three weeks later I had my shoulder separated and went to the hospital. The only person who came to see me was my wife. Other than my family, very few people seemed to care about what had happened to me.

It was a football god that I had been worshipping, and now someone else had the attention and everyone was cheering for him. It didn't matter that much. It was like what Bob Lilly said, after he won a Super Bowl ring with the Dallas Cowboys – "Is that all there is?"

Every time you climb on the ladder of success and find out you're on the wrong wall, it's disappointing. It was very disappointing to me, because from the time I was little, all I wanted to do was play football. And then my god of football was destroyed.

I met a couple of other guys in the NFL who called themselves Christian. It surprised me that they spoke of themselves that way because I thought Christian just meant you weren't Jewish. I didn't know the biblical definition of a Christian – to be born again and trust in the blood of Jesus Christ for our salvation. So these guys took Bibles with them wherever they went, and had prayer circles.

Through a variety of circumstances I ended up at a Fellowship of Christian Athletes camp, and the guys got together in a prayer circle in a gym, praying for the guy giving his testimony that the kids at the camp would really hear the message of Jesus. The only other time I had prayed in a gym was when I was taking free throws in basketball. So I was in that prayer circle thinking, "Why are we here praying?" My experience was so limited and weak that I didn't know about the sovereignty of God.

This encouraged me to open up my own personal life to one of the other athletes. We shared well into the night about the problem my wife and I were having. Peggy, my wife, was pregnant with our second child, Chipper. But our first child had the German Measles, which put our unborn baby at risk. The doctors recommended that we have an abortion, which we didn't want to do. My friend simply said, "Gary, I'll pray for you."

That was June. I got traded to New Orleans that year, and things got exciting for me again. I had my own television program and was the up-front guy again. Our season ended on time, but my friend was with Green Bay, and they were in the playoffs. We got a call from him during the playoffs asking us how our baby was. This convicted me, because I had been following rules, trying to serve God, and didn't realize how much more there was to being a Christian. My friend's call made me sit down and start reading my Bible, and I started in Romans. It became clearer to me that there was a God, that he was sovereign and that he is faithful.

It also became clear that the Word of God was our power – it was our sword and spear. The Apostle Paul wrote about it, that we need the armor of God to counteract the fiery darts of Satan. We need the shield of faith. We need the breastplate of righteousness. Standing on that power is all we have. It is the only place where we are going to find the peace of God. And what more do we want out of life than the peace of God?

I have been on the route of success through championships. I have been on the route of financial success. I'm telling you that they are empty without the peace of God. God used my friends to help me discover true salvation. What a relief it was to know that it wasn't about what I did, but what God did that was sufficient!

As I said, Peggy did not have an abortion, and our son Chipper grew up. He was a Pop Warner Scholar Athlete, an all-American, straight-A student, a model of a kid in regard to academics and athletics. He was also as strong willed as could be.

When he was thirteen he wrote an essay for a Pop Warner Scholar Athlete award. In it he said, "The things that turn me off about kids today are mainly smoking, drinking and taking drugs. I don't like kids that smoke and drink because most of them are deadbeats. They don't have much of a future by starting these things at their age. I found that most of the kids that do these things aren't athletic at all, and the few that are aren't very good. The kids who take drugs are just completely stupid. They're throwing their lives away. The drugs are messing up their minds, therefore ruining any chance of being very intelligent. These things turn me off because I want to be good at sports and I want to be intelligent."

This was our thirteen-year-old eighth grader before he got into high school and sports, before alcohol hit his life, before drugs hit his life, before peer pressure hit his life.

When he was 22, Peggy got a phone call from the police in Miami, saying that they had found a man – they didn't even say a young man – dead. They said he had two tattoos on his body. I wouldn't have even known this was my son because I didn't know he had tattoos. Peggy got off the phone and just cried out to one of our other sons, "Jeff, did Chip have tattoos?" Jeff said, "Don't tell me this body had two tattoos."

We had to go down to the morgue to identify his body.

We didn't know our son was a cocaine addict. We didn't

know he dealt drugs. We knew he had tried them, but had no idea the depths. How secretive he must have been to pull that off in a family. He had distanced himself from us, but we didn't have a clue.

Going through this was like having an out of body experience. I had always been the student council president, the president of this, the president of that, Phi Beta Kappa. I did everything. Now I was a drug dealer's father, with headlines in the local paper. My pride, which needed to be broken, was totally broken. On top of the greatest sadness of my life, I was also humiliated – embarrassed to walk into restaurants.

I began to pray that God would use his life in some way. I also prayed for assurance of his salvation. God answered those prayers within a week, because one of my kids went down to his room and found letters written to me that he never mailed. One described how he believed in Christ, but that he lived his life in misery, fighting the battle against the Satanic forces of the drug world. Once that's in your body, its beyond understanding. I have worked with a lot of people who have been on drugs since that time, and I know the battle that rages in them.

In one of the letters, he wrote, "God is the only thing that ever did, does and will ever matter. I never doubted God or his son, Jesus Christ. But no matter how hard I tried to remind myself of these things, I could not overcome my inferior, embarrassed, shy, negative opinion of myself."

This was hard to read because he was the homecoming king, quarterback on the football team, and had a football scholarship to college. He was a shy person who thought there was something wrong with being shy. Chipper was embarrassed to be shy. He called it his greatest secret. In one of his letters, he said, "This is the thing that has ruined my life. I'm afraid, I'm petrified of a conversation with a stranger."

I had no idea. I knew he was shy, but I didn't know the agony he was going through on a daily basis. The drug and alcohol thing came into his life as well as the peer pressure, while he was experiencing these other issues. Here he was, a kid trying to do right, fighting this substance, making bad choices. Some choices can be fatal. His were.

God has used this, though. He has used it in my life to change a lot of things about me that I don't like. His legacy goes on, which is an encouragement that God can use me through this. When I read in the Bible that there was nothing good in us, I almost had an argument with God. "But God, I did all that stuff. I studied hard. I tried hard." But the Bible says it's about Him, not us. I know that's discouraging sometimes. For me to try to share this about Chipper, just in my flesh, would make it impossible for you to get anything out of it. Other than the word of God, there is nothing that I can give that's powerful. My stuff is going to pass away, but God's words will never pass away.

We all get discouraged sometimes. But you know there is victory. If you read Romans, you know we win in the end. It's our victory. We've just got to claim it, live in his power, don't walk in our flesh, but walk in the Spirit. Chapter 5 of Romans says, "Therefore, having been justified by faith, we have peace with God through our Lord Jesus Christ; to Him also we have access by faith into his grace in which we stand and rejoice in the hope of the glory of God; and not only that, we also glory in tribulation, knowing that tribulation produces perseverance."

That word "tribulation" is a Greek word that means "crushing." How are we going to rejoice in crushing? Perseverance gives us character, and character gives us hope.

Have you ever grown from a mountaintop experience? I never have. I get very excited there, but I don't grow. It's when I get down in the valley and see God – that's when I grow. I hate it down there. But it's where I grow. God carries us through the valley of the shadow of death. I can't do it on my own. I tried for years.

I got so tired of walking in the flesh, trying to do things on my own. I hope we will all be able to see that Christ in us is the only thing that matters, and that when He died for us, he died for all the parts of us that we hate, so that we could have victory.

Eighteen years ago Dave Hentschel and I met at a mountain conference retreat where we had Bible study, quality spiritual messages, and recreation in the snow. Dave was the president and CEO of Occidental Oil and Gas, which was one of the largest companies in the world. I have seen few men have more fun with a snowmobile than Dave did that week!

I grew to admire his sense of humor and ability to laugh at himself. He had a huge job and a small ego. We went on several more retreats with the same results, and I asked Dave to speak at several different occasions. He did so willingly and effectively.

As I got to know his heart, I grew to admire and respect him even more. Few men have reached the level of success Dave has without becoming arrogant. I had the privilege of having dinner with Dave and his wife one evening and it was very apparent why he had been so successful as a husband and father of three boys. Dave's consistency about what he does and who he does it with says much about his heart for God and his desire to be available for God to use him

If we had more men like Dave Hentschel in positions of leadership and responsibility, we would have fewer problems in this country and around the world. He is truly a transparent leader.

Letting God Lead

Dave Hentschel

LIKE MANY PEOPLE, I CHOSE TO KEEP THE Christian side of my life sectioned off from everything else. It was fine for Sundays and other special occasions, if I happened to be in town, but not for the rest of the week. God was clearly *in* my life, but not *in control* of my life. I eventually became more open as a Christian, and certain events helped bring that about.

The first was after I had been with the Cities Service Oil Company for 14 years, and I was being considered for a promotion to the main office in New York. I had gotten to the point where the things that go on in major corporations – the politics in particular – no longer appealed to me. As I was cooling down from a run one evening, I thought about the prospects and the process I was going through. I asked the Lord to take over my business life. I committed it all to Him.

"Put me wherever you want me and I'll work as hard as I can and do whatever you want me to do – wherever that takes me is fine," I said. I got the job in New York and continued to be placed in positions with more responsibility. I had so many different jobs within the company that I decided there was no one in the firm who would be able to tell whether I was performing well in my jobs, because I was never there long enough to even understand it myself! I truly felt the hand of the Lord moving me through this process more rapidly than my own abilities would have allowed.

I was also aware that I had probably moved past the Peter Principal level of incompetence. But I discovered something in the process – if you get three or four levels above your level of incompetence, you become competent again, especially with the Lord on your side!

During that time I was not very open about being a Christian. Like many people, I chose to keep the Christian side of my life sectioned off to those particular days such as Sundays and Easter if I was in town. Then I was asked to give my testimony in front of three services at church. My immediate response was to find an excuse to avoid it. The idea caused me to think about my relationship with Christ, and what talking about it publicly might mean in how I conducted my life. As I thought about it, it became clear that what I was going to say, I had to be. What I said I believed, I had to live to the best of my ability. There is nothing that shows up faster and more harmful than a Christian who really doesn't walk the walk. I was 46 at the time, finally facing my responsibility as a Christian. Finally – I was beginning to mature as a believer!

I grew up in the oil fields, drilling wells. As a young man in West Texas, I had a nicotine habit where I smoked three or four packs of cigarettes a day. I finally quit, which was very difficult, but as I got up to give my testimony nearly 20 years later, I decided I had to take foul language out of my speech. That was harder to do than giving up smoking, believe it or not. The oil field was a pretty macho place, and talking that way was part of the life. But as a believer and follower of Jesus Christ, my language was an outward conflict with the commitment I made to how I wanted to lead my life. I wanted to be consistent with who I said I was.

My life had become very hectic because of pressures created by corporate raiders attacking the oil industry. Boone Pickens and a Canadian company bought large blocks of the shares of Cities Service in order to cause our company to be sold. Similar pressure was being put on another company, Conoco, so we entered into discussions with them to merge. But while the chairmen of the two companies were drafting an announcement about our merger, a hostile offer to purchase Conoco came out in the news media and that ended our discussions. But because our merger discussions had been made public, it was clear that our company was now in play. After that, the only question was who was going to buy us?

Twice we were able to sniff out deals where Pickens tried to buy us, and both times we were able to take measures to cause those deals to fall apart. One of those steps was to tender for the control of Mesa Petroleum, the company Pickens ran. It was one of those crazy things you do in a tight situation. You tender an offer to a company you have no interest in, and don't want in the worst way, but it appears to be the only way to save your own company. Shortly after our move on Mesa, Gulf Oil tendered for Cities Service, but that fell through. This put us in a very bad place. By then most of our stock was in the hands of arbitragers who had bought a large portion of the stock, hoping to make large profits when the Gulf deal was completed. As a result, the stock price dropped dramatically, putting the arbitragers in positions of losing big money.

During this time we also became aware of potential conflicts of interest with members of our board. A director of our company was the chairman of one of New York's largest banks, another director was chairman of one of the largest investment banking firms in New York, and another director was vice chairman of another large New York bank. What they needed to do, and what we needed to do were in direct conflict. The board's answer to this very difficult situation was to put up all the company's assets for sale, separately, collectively, or any way that any buyer wanted to configure it.

The next three weeks were crazy. The management of Cities Service had to tell the employees how everything was going to work out for the best, when in reality we had no clue how it was going to happen. That's when we were purchased by Occidental Petroleum, a company half our size, run by their chairman, Dr. Armand Hammer.

I can say that I knew the Lord was close, but to say I was comfortable during this time would be an overstatement of fact. To say that I knew at every moment that everything would work out wonderfully would also be untrue. I can say that I knew that whatever happened, I was still God's child, redeemed by the grace of God through his son Jesus Christ. I tried to focus on that during this period. At times, though, my focus was misdirected.

The first task I was given was to sell the refining and marketing division of Cities Service. I was running those businesses. But Occidental had no interest in these assets, so we sold them for more than $1 billion. Throughout that process I considered what I wanted to do after the Occidental takeover. I was the third man in line, and it appeared that only one would be staying.

No one was more surprised than me when I was offered the job of Chairman of Cities Service, which was to become the domestic arm of Occidental. As I thought about it later, it was just another time where God put me where I was supposed to be. The maturing process was continuing. A few years later I was named CEO of Occidental Oil and Gas Corp., the worldwide oil and gas operation.

During this maturing process, the Lord began to surround me with Christian friends. This may come as a surprise, but people at higher levels of corporations — especially if they have been at those corporations for some time – don't have many friends. The process of being CEO doesn't lend itself to being close to people in or out of the company. If I define a close friend as someone you can talk to about anything and not be fearful that your confidences would be breached, then my list would be two – in addition to my wife.

But that began to change, with amazing outcomes.

While I was running the domestic company, Dr. Hammer called and asked if he could send his grandson, Michael, to work in the company for about six months so he could learn something about the oil business. Michael had an MBA from Columbia and spent most of his life having a good time. He was still pursuing that interest when he came to Tulsa and we put him through the different stages, moving him through Houston, Oklahoma City, and Midland. About five months into his time with us, Dr. Hammer called and asked if I had ever heard of a person named Doug Mobley. I had lived in Tulsa three times and this time had been there for six years, and had never heard that name.

Finding out who he was led me to a friendship that I will always treasure.

Dr. Hammer read me a letter from Michael, where Michael had met a girl named Dru Mobley on an airplane and had fallen in love for the first time in his life. Dr. Hammer assured me that this was true, implying that Michael had a pretty good history of loving and leaving women.

He further stated that Michael wanted to bring the girl to Hammer's house in Los Angeles for him to meet her, because he was very serious. Dr. Hammer wanted me to gather information on her father.

What I found out was that he was the most undisputed witness for Jesus Christ that I've ever known, and that his presence in the Hammer family would change some of them in dramatic ways. He also quickly became one of my best friends.

Michael and Dru got married, but only after Michael had given his life to the Lord. You don't marry Doug Mobley's daughter without being committed to Jesus! They moved to Los Angeles.

Dr. Hammer had a brother, Victor, who ran portions of the Hammer business, such as his art galleries. Although he was born Jewish, Victor claimed no religion, but he understood there was something different about Michael and Dru. After a couple of years, Victor became ill and was in the hospital for a long time, and then moved to a Los Angeles hotel to recuperate. Doug Mobley was also in that hotel for a visit, and he felt a prompting from God to go visit Victor. During their conversation, he led Victor to Christ.

But as Doug walked out of the hotel, he wasn't completely sure about what had just happened. Victor was 84 and very ill. Did he know what he had just done? Doug said he spoke to the Lord as he left the hotel: "Lord, I need a sign about what actually took place up there, because dealing with someone you don't know well, and who is that age, and that sick, well, Lord, I just want to know that he understood what he was doing."

Later that evening, there was a message on Dru and Michael's answering machine from Victor who said, "Dru, I just want to tell you that your dad came up tonight and led me to the Lord. I now know what you and Michael have."

Victor went to the airport the next day and flew to Florida for some more rest, but he fell into a coma and died two days later.

This experience gave Doug a bridge to Armand Hammer, and the two of them visited frequently after that. Doug led Dr. Hammer into a relationship with Christ not long afterward. About a year later, when Dr. Hammer was on his death bed at age 90, our prayer group prayed specifically for him. One of the guys in the group said, "Lord, please reveal yourself to Dr. Hammer this evening as he struggles between life and death." He died that evening. At his funeral a few days later, his doctor told us that she had put a picture of Jesus on his night stand. He had been in and out of a coma, but that particular night he leaned up toward the picture, pointed at it and smiled – then he died. This occurred at the precise time we had been praying for him in Tulsa.

Six people spoke at Dr. Hammer's funeral: an attorney friend, a rabbi, a member of the Occidental board, a Catholic bishop, the mayor of Los Angeles, and Doug Mobley.

What I get from this is that God is working in many areas around us each day, and he really wants our help if we're willing to join him and make the necessary adjustments in our lives to serve him for his glory.

Doug was instrumental in bringing me into fellowship with five or six other people who love the Lord, and my life would not be the same without them. It was a small group of men in which there was no suspicion, where there was accountability, both of which were necessary if we were going to lead lives that were worthy of our relationship with Christ. We all had business problems where we needed consultation, comfort, support, and, most important, the prayers of each other. Every time something came up we could see the value of intercessory prayer and the interrelationships of men of like faith.

It was the support of friends like this that carried me through another harrowing experience. I needed to have some insurance forms signed by a local doctor, but because I had the good fortune of not being sick in Tulsa for 14 years, I didn't have a local doctor. I took my annual physicals in Dallas. But these forms needed a local doctor's signature, so I called a doctor friend and asked for the favor. He said he'd do it only if he gave me a physical. "I just had a physical in Dallas and will send you a copy," I said. No dice. So I went in to satisfy the requirement. That visit acquainted me with a test I had no previous knowledge about – a PSA test, which checks for the likelihood or presence of prostate cancer.

My results were mildly elevated, so I was sent to a urologist for more testing. Five biopsies were benign, but the doctor wanted to follow them up with more tests. I found out later that he knew cancer was there – he just hadn't been able to find it. Three subsequent tests came out malignant.

I asked the Lord to lead me to the person who should do the surgery. I wanted it to be His person, not mine. I visited four surgeons – one at Mayo Clinic, two in Tulsa, and one at Johns Hopkins. When the doctor at Mayo walked in the room, even though I had only heard of him a couple of weeks before, I had the answer to my question. For the first time in my life, I stood in a room with a man wearing the exact same tie as me! And I had just bought mine two days before in Amsterdam. Coincidence? Not at all. Assurance? Definitely.

The surgery had some complications and concerns, but there are very few guarantees in life. I relied on what had gotten me to that point in my life so far: my relationship with Jesus Christ, and my like-minded friends. I knew I was covered in prayer, and it gave me the assurance that regardless of the outcome, God is sovereign. There is much I don't understand in the world, but I do know that for sure.

I retired from Occidental after 37 years, and I can honestly say I became busier than when I was working full time. I got involved with a program where communities across the country are being asked to support recommendations to improve the school systems of those communities. A lot of the recommendations were easy to achieve, but we're still working on reducing crime and violence in schools. That's a problem in every community in the country.

I have also gotten involved in programs trying to eliminate sexual abuse of children, physical abuse of women, substance abuse and domestic violence. When my wife and I chaired the Tulsa United Way campaign, we saw 11-year-old girls walking around with babies when they should have been playing with dolls, and 6-year-old children who had been molested by three or four members of their families. These are things that require changes that can't be imposed by government. They have to be imposed by us as individuals as we work in these communities.

What disturbs me about this is that in Tulsa, Oklahoma, there are churches on almost every block, for 20 miles in any direction. They are good churches. They are great churches. They operate very well inside the confines of their buildings. But for some strange reason, all these things are happening, and the churches don't seem to have an impact. There has to be a unity of purpose among these churches, behind the presence of Jesus Christ, if we are going to see some of these problems solved. More government programs aren't the answer. More prisons won't solve the problems.

My life is very different now than it was when I was in the oil business. But this is where the Lord wants me. He wants to be in control of my life, not just in my life. That's what I want, too.

Forty years ago in Estes Park, Colorado at the Fellowship of Christian Athletes summer conference camp, Tom Landry and his wife Alicia came to our dinner table, introduced themselves, and sat down to eat with us. Six years later, Tom was chairman of the FCA board and I was a board member. Tom and I became close friends, and when he came to Denver without his family or the Dallas Cowboys, he stayed in our home with us. You get to know someone pretty well when you spend four weekends together, and we had many wonderful discussions.

I asked Tom to come to Denver in 1971 to be the keynote speaker for our Governor's Prayer Breakfast. When I picked Tom up at the airport the day before, I told him that the media would like to have a press conference, and he said he would rather go to our home and relax. My wife and I had two sons at the time, Dwight Jr. and Eric, and they raced home from school to see the world famous coach. I'll never forget Tom sitting there on the couch with a nine- and six-year old, sharing with them about the quiet time he has in the morning and in the evening before he went to bed. He made such a powerful impact on the boys that they still have their quiet time every day because Coach Landry cared enough to share that with them.

It was Tom who first encouraged me to write a book about the importance of being transparent. "If you will put a book together, I will write a foreword for it," he said. To have a foreword of a new book written by Tom Landry was fabulous. Tom wrote it and sent it to me. However, he became ill with cancer and died before we were able to get the book published.

Instead of using his foreword in that first volume, I wanted to make his story its own chapter, and include other things he has talked about. The portions of his chapter on leadership and character are the strongest words on the subjects that I have ever heard. The Dallas Cowboys, under Tom's leadership, were not only America's favorite team, but Tom was also America's favorite coach. He is greatly missed by all who knew him, especially his wife of more than 50 years, Alicia, and his daughter and son. Tom truly was a Transparent Leader.

Faith That Overcomes Doubt

Tom Landry

I HAD ONE THING ON MY MIND, GROWING UP in the Rio Grande Valley, an area I had never been out of through my senior year of high school: climbing the ladder of success. The great thing about our free enterprise system is that we get that opportunity, and I wanted to climb that ladder. Once I did that, I thought, I would have happiness, fulfillment and everything that life had to offer me.

The University of Texas had a great football team. We went to the Sugar Bowl and beat Alabama. We went to the Orange Bowl and beat Georgia. What I discovered with these huge victories, though, was that after these great achievements, in my mind there was an emptiness and a restlessness that stayed with me after all the excitement had passed. I didn't understand it, but I assumed that if I were able to reach the top of my profession that I would finally find what I was after. So I went into professional football.

I played on some great teams in New York, and loved living there. We had great success and won the world championship. I achieved everything football could offer me. But I still had that emptiness and restlessness inside. Eventually my wife and I moved back to Dallas where I decided to go into business. Since I hadn't found fulfillment in climbing the ladder of success as an athlete, I figured I would find it in business. I told all of this to a friend of mine who was a Christian, and he immediately knew what was wrong. He knew I was a church goer, and not a Christian.

My family went to church when I was growing up. I didn't have much choice, since my dad was the Sunday School Superintendent. We didn't pray or read the Bible at home, but we were church attenders. I didn't know there was anything beyond that.

My friend, Frank Phillips, invited me to a men's prayer breakfast at a local hotel. He said it would be a few guys eating breakfast and studying the Bible together. I wasn't at all interested. But I couldn't think of a gracious way to decline his invitation, so I went. When I got there, I saw about 30 or 40 businessmen at tables gathered for that week's study on Jesus' Sermon on the Mount in Matthew 5-7.

I had never studied the Bible. I had hardly even read it. I found it confusing and irrelevant. But that morning, as we read those chapters and the men began discussing the meaning of Jesus' words, two passages jumped right off the pages at me. The first was Matthew 6:25-34, which says, in part, "Take no thought for your life, what you shall eat, what you shall drink; nor for your body, what you should put on. Is not life more than meat and the body than raiment? But seek first the kingdom of God, and his righteousness, and all these things shall be added unto you. Take therefore no thought for tomorrow, for tomorrow shall take the thought for the things of itself."

The second passage was Matthew 7:24-25: "Therefore, whoever hears these sayings of mine and does them, is like a wise man who built his house on a rock: And the rain descended and the floods came, and the winds blew, and beat upon that house; it did not fall, for it was founded upon a rock."

In the middle of my personal struggle to find direction and security in my life, here were Bible verses talking about those very issues. I was so surprised and intrigued that I went back to that Bible study the next week, and the next and the next. I wanted to understand what else the Bible had to say.

Using the same sort of scientific, analytical approach that enabled me to break down and understand an opponent's offenses, I read and studied and discovered the basic message of the Christian gospel.

We've all sinned and can't measure up to God's standard. Our failure stands between us and God. Jesus took the punishment for our failure, and his salvation was offered as a free gift to anyone who accepted it. We can't do anything to earn it – we just have to believe. God wants us to turn our lives over to him and let him direct us and provide for all our needs.

I realized that, even though I had attended church all of my life, I had never understood Christianity. I had been a spectator, when God wanted me to be a participant. I had always been a good person, but here was the Bible saying I was as much a sinner as anyone in the world. I had based my life on the idea that if I worked hard enough and learned enough, I would succeed and be a winner. But the Bible was telling me that it wasn't knowledge or works that made the ultimate difference – it was faith. All of my life I had made my football career the number one priority and let it dictate the direction of my life. But the Bible was saying I needed to make God and his will first and follow his direction for my life.

So the crossroads I faced when I was done playing football was really a spiritual crossroads. I had to decide whether or not I believed what the Bible said. All my other questions hung on that one. The more I read, the more it made sense, and the more I wanted to believe. And yet the analytical part of my nature kept asking questions and having doubts.

Then I came across a short passage of a poem by Robert Browning that said: "You call for faith, I give you doubt, to prove that faith exists. The greater the doubt, the stronger the faith, I say, if faith overcomes doubt." Something clicked in me when I read that, and I began to understand faith in a new light.

I can't point to a specific moment or a specific time when I had a sudden "born-again" experience. It took place over a period of months. But I finally reached a point where faith outweighed the doubts, and I was willing to commit my entire life to God. The decision did not make an immediate visible difference in my life, or immediately transform me into a better person. But what my new Christian experience did was place football behind the priorities of my faith and my family, and gave me a sense of confidence and peace about the future, whatever it would be.

It was the same discovery most people make when they accept Christ: they realize that life is really about priorities. Whatever you consider most real and valuable in your life is your religion. It doesn't necessarily have to be God. It can be football, as it was with me for so many years. I was in my thirties when I accepted Christ in my life. And when God became first, my family took on a completely different dimension than it ever had before. As I began to understand what the Bible taught about loving God and my family, it helped me put football and winning and losing into perspective. It didn't make me want to win any less, but I realized that whatever I did or didn't accomplish as coach of the Cowboys wasn't the most important thing in my life. That helped take some of the pressure off.

After I made my commitment to God, I looked for ways to incorporate my faith into my daily work and life. Soon after taking over as head coach of the Cowboys, I appointed Christian players to lead voluntary chapel programs, and to invite guest speakers for a short morning service before our Sunday games. I also encouraged the beginning of a weekly husband/wife Bible study for players as a means of building spiritual and family values. While some of my assistant coaches and their wives joined the players at these Bible studies, I didn't attend them for the same reason I didn't lead or speak at the team chapel services: I wanted to be careful not to abuse my authority as head coach to push my own beliefs down the throats of my players.

At the same time, I never tried to hide what I believed. I regularly shared appropriate Bible verses in talks during team meetings. And every year at training camp when I met with incoming rookies for the first time, I would share the story of my own spiritual pilgrimage, including what I'd learned about priorities.

The first time Bob Lilly heard me say that as a Christian I believed my relationship with God and my responsibility to my family came before football, his reaction was to think I'd misspoken myself and gotten the order mixed up. When he realized I'd meant what I said, he thought, "Oh no! We're never gonna win a football game!" Bob went on to make his own commitment to the Lord after he retired from the Cowboys, but when he joined us, he didn't understand how I could say such a thing.

I'm sure many other players never understood. And some who did couldn't agree with my beliefs. Yet it was as important for me to tell my players what I believed as it was to try to live it.

I found that the only way to make my family the priority I wanted it to be was to give it priority in my regular routine. I was able to watch my son play football and my daughters do cheerleading. My wife, Alicia, and I went out as a couple one night every week. I tried to eat breakfast with my children every day before they left for school. And no matter what was going on at the office, no matter how much preparation remained to be done before Sunday, I always came home for dinner with my family. A lot of nights after dinner I disappeared into my den to watch more game film, but whenever one of my daughters knocked on the door and asked, "Are you busy, Daddy?" I'd turn off the projector and say, "I'm never too busy for you, Sweetheart."

I was not a perfect father or husband. But I was a much better person to live with than I would have been if God hadn't shown me the need to reorder things in my life I counted as most important. Fortunately, God was as patient with me as my wife and kids were when I would succumb to a serious case of tunnel vision and temporarily lose sight of everything but football.

Another important aspect of my spiritual life was my involvement with the Fellowship of Christian Athletes, which presents the message and biblical teaching of Christ and challenges athletes to put those life-changing values into practice in their own lives. My being a professional football coach gave me a platform to speak to thousands of young athletes about their physical and spiritual needs.

My exposure during my early Cowboys' days to the great people working in Christian organizations like FCA and the Billy Graham Evangelistic Association provided me with an invaluable spiritual boost. The more experienced Christians I met there inspired and challenged me to grow spiritually to become more consistent in applying Jesus' teachings to my life. It was through the influence of these people that I became convinced of the importance of establishing the habit of setting aside a daily time for Bible reading and prayer.

When I was fired from the Cowboys in 1989, after the new owner had his own coach in mind, I thought about the low points I had experienced as a player and a coach. I'd suffered numerous gut-wrenching losses in big games. This was the biggest. Worse than any playoff loss marking the sudden end of a season. After this, there were no more seasons.

I couldn't help thinking about the past forty years in professional football. Even a quick mental review of the important people and events in my life made me feel very thankful. My teammates, my friendship and rivalry with Vince Lombardi, the Super Bowls, all those Cowboy comebacks, the twenty straight winning seasons, so many great players. But I couldn't think only about the past. I immediately had to face the hard adjustments of an as-yet-unimaginable future. For that I knew I would need and could ask God's guidance and help – as I'd learned to do so many times before. I could never have imagined – at sixty-four years of age, standing at the sad, sudden involuntary end of a long and fulfilling career – that the weeks and months to come would hold the most satisfying, most rewarding, and most incredible days of my life.

The restlessness I had at the beginning of my career was long gone. Saint Augustine said, "Our hearts are restless, Oh God, until they find their rest in thee." Perhaps the highest praise I have heard was from a player who said, "I'd rather see a sermon than hear one any day. I'd rather one would walk with me than merely show the way. That was Coach Landry's method. He lived his Christianity."

Tom Landry On Leadership

Coaching and leadership have the same basic rule in common. Their purpose is to get people to do what they don't want to do in order to achieve what they want to achieve. The challenge of any great leader is to get the absolute best out of people.

The first requirement of leadership is knowledge. A leader doesn't have to be the smartest member of the group, but he does need to demonstrate a mastery of his field. Mastery means more than just knowing information and facts; it requires an understanding of the information and the ability to apply that information.

If I had to pick my greatest strength as a professional football coach, I'd say it was innovation. But it started with preparation and knowledge. As a leader you have to understand the present system, situation or problem you're faced with before you can react effectively – before you can be a successful innovator. If you're not one step ahead of the crowd, you'll soon be a step behind everyone else.

Every organization and every leader must have a clearly understood philosophy. It is simply an abstract statement of what you believe. It can provide a powerful sense of unity for everyone in the organization. And it is the leader's responsibility to make sure everyone buys into that philosophy.

Out of that philosophy must come shared goals. I don't believe you can effectively manage people without helping them understand where they fit into the goals of the organization.

Motivation is part of leadership. Vince Lombardi used fear to motivate his players. I always felt that fear motivation was risky. It can quickly backfire. I always believed that knowledge could motivate a person. The better prepared you were, the better you felt and more confident you became in your ability to perform.

Leaders must learn to live with demands. Two major factors explain my long survival. The first is my faith. Knowing your job isn't the most important thing in your life relieves a lot of the pressure. And because I felt I was doing God's will for my life, I knew that I didn't have to do it all in my own strength; God promises the necessary strength to those who follow him. Also, doing my job for the Lord gave me an extra incentive to keep going. The second factor was the leadership style of the Cowboys' owner. He constantly attempted to reduce the pressure for me with his encouragement, patience, confidence and security.

Leaders face adversity. It is so much a part of leadership that your reaction to adversity will determine your success or failure as a leader. It is partly a matter of attitude. William James said, "The greatest discovery of my generation is that human beings can alter their lives by altering their attitude of mind." Difficulties and adversities are challenges to overcome rather than problems to worry about. Leaders can't afford to look back and get too upset about their past mistakes. They have to focus on what they will do differently next time. Leaders always have others watching to see how they react when things go bad.

The way leaders stay in control of themselves is by having confidence in their basic philosophy. Leaders have to be able to think clearly under pressure, which means they depend even more on their preparation. Leaders will be criticized for making both the right decisions and the wrong ones. They must be willing to listen to criticism and make changes. Or not. The trick is in deciding which to do when. Perhaps the most important step in dealing with criticism is realizing it's part of the job.

Leaders must be committed to excellence. Vince Lombardi's famous line, which he borrowed from an old John Wayne movie, is "Winning isn't everything, it's the only thing." I'm sure it worked well in a rousing pep talk, but I don't think it's true, and I don't think Vince believed it, either. If winning is the only thing that matters, then you'd do anything to win. You'd cheat. You'd sacrifice your marriage or your family to win. Relationships wouldn't matter. People wouldn't matter. Winning would be worth any price you had to pay. I don't believe that.

We had our own quote on a sign in our Cowboys' locker room: "The quality of a man's life is in direct proportion to his commitment to excellence." That means you get up every morning and say to your self, "Today I'm going to do my best in every area. I'm not going to take the easy way; I'm going to give 100 percent." That doesn't mean we'll reach our goals. Some of the time we'll fall short.

The apostle Paul is one of my favorite biblical characters because he was such a competitor. He explained some of his motivation in his first letter to the Corinthian Church. He was stoned, shipwrecked, imprisoned, and still wouldn't quit. "In a race, everyone runs, but only one person gets first prize. So run your race to win. To win the contest you must deny yourselves many things that would keep you from doing your best. An athlete goes to all this trouble just to win a blue ribbon or a silver cup, but we do it for a heavenly reward that never disappears. So I run straight to the goal with purpose in every step. I fight to win. I'm not just shadow-boxing or playing around. Like an athlete I punish my body, treating it roughly, training it to do what I should, not what it wants to. Otherwise I fear that after enlisting others for the race, I myself might be declared unfit and ordered to stand aside."

That kind of commitment to excellence – the kind of will to win Paul wrote about – is absolutely essential to successful leadership.

Tom Landry On Character

When things were going badly for my team and me during a particular season, I read this quote from Harry Truman: "The way in which you endure that which you must endure is more important than the crisis itself." He was talking about the need for character. Horace Greeley once said, "Fame is a vapor; popularity an accident. Riches take wing; those who cheer today will curse tomorrow; only one thing endures – character."

I've seen the difference character makes. Give me the choice between an outstanding athlete with poor character and a lesser athlete of good character, and I'll choose the latter every time. The athlete with good character will perform to his fullest potential and be successful, while the athlete with poor character will usually fail to play up to his potential and often won't even achieve average performance.

In my opinion, character is the most important determinant of a person's success, achievement, and ability to handle adversity.

Most of a person's character is developed as a child, the result of values learned from family and other significant people early in life. That's what makes our role as parents and coaches so important.

We also learn character by going through adversity. The apostle Paul says "We know that suffering produces perseverance, perseverance character, and character, hope." But the only thing I have seen that can radically change a person's basic character is a relationship with Jesus Christ.

I think there is a lot of confusion in the world today about what it means to be a Christian. Unfortunately, a lot of well-meaning Christian athletes contribute to that confusion. I think it's important for Christians to speak out and explain what they believe. But I have to admit that I'm troubled a little and have very mixed reactions when I see a football player kneel down in the end zone and thank God after a touchdown. I have the same feelings of misgiving when I hear from winning locker rooms the excited testimonies of happy players who say, "I just want to thank the Lord because without him this victory would not have been possible."

Athletes should feel gratitude for their God-given abilities. I think we all ought to regularly give thanks to our Creator for our blessings, our opportunities, for life itself. But I'm afraid these little "God helped me score a touchdown" and "God helps me be a winner" testimonials mislead people and belittle God. I don't think God plays favorites like that. Neither do I believe God cares who wins a football game, despite the old joke in Dallas that the reason Texas Stadium was designed with a hole in the roof was so God could watch his favorite team play every Sunday afternoon!

While I don't believe God helps Christian athletes run faster, jump higher or hit harder, I do believe a personal faith in Christ can be a very real advantage in life – as a football player, a surgeon, a business executive, a teacher, a student, or a parent. Because a personal faith in God can change and improve anyone's character.

A person who is trying to put the teachings of Jesus Christ into practice in his life every day should begin to take on some of the character – the integrity, the patience, the truthfulness, and so on – of Christ. That's what being a Christian is all about.

As a football coach I have seen two common barriers that most often prevent people from performing to their fullest potential. The first is a pattern of past failure and past mistakes. The second thing holding people back is a fear of failure.

Christianity addresses both of these problems and removes those barriers. As a Christian I believe my past is forgiven; I can start over with a clean slate. The mistakes of the past need not hold me back. Neither does my fear of failure, because as a Christian I believe God is in ultimate control of my life. While that doesn't mean I'll always win the championship or never get fired, it means I can believe the promise of Romans 8:28, which says God can bring good out of every experience for those who trust in him. So I don't need to worry about failing.

Without the burden of past mistakes or anxiety about failing in the future, I'm free to concentrate on doing my very best in the present.

The most important lesson I've learned in my life is that God is so gracious that he accepts me, my failures, my personality quirks, my shortcomings and all. Believing that gives me the greatest sense of peace, calm and security in the world.

It is that belief, that faith, more than anything else, that enabled me to last twenty-nine years on the sidelines of the Dallas Cowboys. It's that faith that allowed me to keep my perspective and not feel devastated or bitter about being fired. And it's that faith that gives me hope for whatever the future holds for me outside of professional football.

Fifteen years ago I was attending a meeting of Christian leaders, and one of the men I met was Ron Walters. He was extremely friendly and outgoing, and I was pleased to find out that he was the general manager of the local Christian radio station. Prior to that he had been the senior pastor of a large church in Santa Barbara.

I asked Ron to serve on the board of a local organization of Christian business leaders, and every time I was around him I was amazed by his enthusiasm and high energy level. It didn't make any difference what I asked him to do or when I asked him to do it. He always accepted the responsibility and did it well. I so appreciated his positive mental attitude.

Ron was so successful with the local Christian radio station in San Diego, KPRZ, that Salem Broadcasting, the parent company, promoted Ron to general manager of their large station in San Francisco. He had such great success with that station that Salem asked him to join the parent company as vice president in charge of relations between Salem and 365,000 churches in the U.S.

As he was in everything else, Ron was enthusiastic and optimistic about the new responsibilities. Salem has grown a lot in the last several years and is the largest Christian radio company in the U.S., with stations in more than 38 cities. Ron and his wife live in Fremont, California, just south of San Francisco.

5 Living With
The Law

Ron Walters

ALL OF LIFE IS GOVERNED BY LAWS. IF YOU drove anywhere recently, you probably observed a few of them. But we have laws that govern everything in life, such as the law of gravity, which we don't even think about. When you sit in a chair or walk around, you don't think that you are abiding by that law, but you are. And  it's a good thing. There are laws of thermodynamics. There are laws everywhere.

Some laws don't even have names, but you know they are true nonetheless. For instance, there is a law that serving coffee on an airplane will cause turbulence. It's a law! It happens!

Another law is that the one who snores, always falls asleep first. There is a law that says you never hire an electrician with singed eyebrows. There is a law that says the colder the X-ray table, the more of your body you're required to place on it. These are laws! They govern your life as we know it!

Here is another law. It's one that God spoke in II Chronicles 16:9: "The eyes of the Lord look to and fro throughout the whole world to find those whose hearts are completely His, that He might show Himself strong on their behalf." That's a law!

There are two implications in there. The first is that in

order for God to scope you out on a daily basis, and to make Himself strong, He must find two things – that your heart is completely His – that He is your top priority, that He is the one you are obeying. That's the first thing.

The second implication is what often gets overlooked, but it is there: the Lord is making Himself strong on your behalf. The implication is that you are weak and He will show Himself strong. He will provide the mighty muscle of omnipotence to raise you up. The theory behind this is that you will be put in a situation where you find yourself weak.

That's a foreign concept to a lot of people who consider themselves leaders. We pride ourselves on being in control, being in charge. But God says, "That's not the way I work. I've got to have you under the load in order to make you strong." Are you starting to see how God works?

This played out for me when I was involved in a traffic accident. It was partly my fault, which I claimed from the beginning. And it was a great deal the other guy's fault, which I also claimed. Then, I was delivered a summons to appear in court. I was being sued for more money than I had ever heard of, and far more than I was ever insured for.

I met with a friend and shared this with him. We prayed over it right away. For months I had this enormous lawsuit hanging over me. I felt that I had been unjustly accused, and I was standing on the brink of disaster. Just before my court appearance, I met with some men and told them what I was up against. It was difficult for me to verbalize what I was facing, but I shared my struggle with them and they prayed with me.

In court I met one of the dirtiest attorneys ever. I will never understand how anyone could treat a human being the way he treated me. I kept thinking, "I've done nothing wrong." But that didn't matter to this guy. He grilled and grilled and grilled, but the constant thought in my mind was that I had spent time in prayer with men who had prayed me through this. It was as if one day in that court-room, the eyes of the Lord looked to and fro throughout the whole world and scoped out a little guy on a witness stand, and God chose, through His mighty muscle of omnipotence, to lift him up and to hold him securely in His hand. The jury, thank the Lord, saw in my favor. This lawyer was making my life miserable, but I never forgot those prayers.

The truth of it is that the Lord will allow these things to happen to us. While I was going through those three years of agony in that lawsuit, I saw how often the Bible talks about these kinds of things. Everywhere I turned I stumbled across instances where the Lord saw His people through difficult times, and how He kept comparing those times to something in life that we prize.

For example, in I Peter 1:7 it says, in my paraphrase, "I know you're going through tough times. I know it, and it's okay because I'm allowing this to affect your faith, just like gold being tested by fire." When I read that, I thought, "I can't read this right now – I'd better move on to something more encouraging." So I turned to the book of James. Did you ever read the Bible and laugh? What I read in James said, "Consider it all joy when you go through trials." I mean, who writes this stuff?

I can't speak for others, but I know that I do not volunteer for trials. I look for any way to get around them. But the Word says, "Consider it all joy when you encounter various trials. It affects your faith, which produces endurance." This produced a panic in me. "But let patience have her perfect result that you may be perfect and complete, lacking in nothing." Incredible. I couldn't get into that. So I read in Job, "I know when God tests me, I will come forth as gold."

Sometimes, it's just hard to read the Bible.

In both the Old and New Testaments, God talks about you and me as a chunk of gold that He wants to refine for

His purposes. Whatever gold goes through, your life will go through. This made me wonder how gold is refined, so I looked it up. Think about the process as what your life goes through when God uses it. First, gold is found only after a great deal of pressure is exerted. It's found in the middle of a mountain or at the bottom of a river, and it has to be pounded down to break it free from its comfort zone. What an appropriate analogy! This is what God allows us to go through – great pressure to break us loose from our comfort zones.

Then it has to go through the amalgamation process in order to be refined. This process takes the gold in its big chunk and puts it in a vat, like a huge mixing bowl. The refiners lower drills from the top and the side and they pound on the chunk to pry loose all the impurities. The friction makes it so terribly hot that they have to constanly fill it with water, which quickly evaporates. When the water isn't enough to protect the gold, the refiners pour in mercury. When this process is finished, they pull out the gold piece that has most of the impurities taken away and it has all this mercury stuck to it. So they take the chunk and put it into an oven and crank it up hotter and hotter until the mercury melts away.

They're still not done, though. They throw it on a table and a guy with a hairy arm takes a gigantic mallet and starts pounding on the gold until finally the gold is the size of one thousandth of a millimeter in thickness. The gold is exhausted by now – just like you and me, right? But there's more. The guy with the mallet now takes a sharp blade and makes long strips so the gold can be used to decorate something – to make something beautiful. That's how gold is refined.

When I look at the analogy of how gold is purified, and read that God says, "And that's what you'll go through," quite frankly, that frightens me. But I think it proves the point that life is what happens to you while you're making other plans. God has the ability to take you through circumstances, and He says it's for your betterment. It's what makes you. And you can never get to your class A gold status until you have gone through that process.

My guess is that there are a lot of people reading this right now who are in the fire right now.

When we go through this, we typically ask two questions. The first is, "Why me?" The answer is that God has made it clear that you can't get there without this process. Romans says, "It is God's desire to conform you to the image of His dear son." How much change will that require? Whatever it takes to conform you to His son, Jesus.

The second question is, "How long?" The answer is, until the Father is finished

We might want say, as a follow-up statement, "But I didn't do anything! It wasn't my fault!" Think about this: When David was still a shepherd – not a king, but a shepherd – no one had ever heard of him. In I Samuel 16, David is minding his sheep, and minding his own business. But his father says to him, "Your brothers are up there fighting the Philistines. Would you run some refreshments up to them? They could probably use some home-cooked food." David says, "You bet." In Chapter 17 he arrives on the scene. But instead of fighting the Philistines, the people aren't fighting at all. There's a gigantic guy at the bottom of the ravine named Goliath, and he's challenging anyone who would face him, and he's shouting obscenities at the God of Israel.

David arrives, hears this, and says, "This guy can't talk to our God like that! Why doesn't somebody take him on?" To which his brothers said, "He's a giant. You can't hit a giant!" I can hear David saying, "You're kidding. You can't *miss* that giant!" Then David killed Goliath. That's Chapter 17. Chapter 18 says that David is the topic of the number one song on the Jewish hit parade – "Saul has slain his thousand, and David his ten thousand." Chapter 19 shows Saul saying, "Kill David."

For the next 11 years, David runs from Saul. Why would this happen? Why would God ever allow him to get into the oven and turn up the fire like this? Why would he have to go through this onslaught of trials? And consider it all joy? Yeah, right. Does that make sense to you?

Except that 11 years later, when David is crowned king, he has an understanding of suffering. He had an understanding of what it means to rely only upon God that he never could have had if he stayed those 11 years out herding sheep.

Here's another example of refining – Job. Here's a guy who would have fit in with any leadership or executive group. He was the big deal maker in his town, terribly successful, and everyone in town knew his name. He had everything. Best of all, he loved God.

But in one of the courts of the throne room of God, in a situation I can't explain, God and Satan have a conversation. God says, "have you been out there scoping things out?" Satan says, "I have. And, by the way, no one out there loves you." But God knew better because, remember, the eyes of the Lord go to and fro throughout the whole world to show himself strong on behalf of those whose hearts are right with Him. So God says, "Have you considered my servant, Job?" Satan says, "Listen, God, the only reason that Job loves you is that you give him everything. You take away what you've given to him and he'll curse you to your face." God says, "No he won't. I know this man. As a matter of fact, I'll allow you to prove it. You may do whatever you like to him, but don't touch him."

From that moment on, Satan did everything he could to ruin Job's life. Everything Job had was burned to the ground, rained away, stolen or killed. Even his own kids died. He lost everything. And when it was all over, Job said, "Naked I came into the world, naked I'll leave this world. The Lord gives, the Lord takes away. Blessed be the name of the Lord."

So that's the answer, right? That's the secret. That's all we have to do is say that line and we're home free, right? Well, it's just the end of Chapter 1.

Chapter 2 begins with more conversation between God and Satan. God says, "So how did Job do?" Satan says, "I didn't expect him to cave in that easily. But you wouldn't let me touch him. We played games with his possessions, but if you let me touch him, he will curse you to your face." God says, "No he won't. I've been scoping out and I know. I'll even prove it. You can touch him, but you can't kill him.

The rest of the chapter shows what Satan did to Job. He hit Job with a sickness that we can't even imagine. From the top of his head to the bottom of his feet, he was covered with boils. There was not one part of his body that didn't have boils on top of boils. He was the most disgusting thing imaginable. The Bible says he even sat down in an ash heap to show how he felt about his personal worth. He took broken pottery pieces and scraped the sores because his body was so full of infection and pus. It's disgusting. Sick.

His wife says to him, "Job, can't you get it? God's had it with you. Why don't you just curse God and die? Why not just call it quits? Commit suicide. Tell God off. He'll strike you with a lightning bolt. Just curse God and die." But Job says, "You foolish woman. Are we to love God in times of prosperity and not times of adversity?"

So Job is home free now, right? But guess what! That's only the end of Chapter 2! In Chapter 3 we meet Job's friends! I think we all have some of Job's friends in our lives. They never die. They're like the doxology: "As it was in the beginning, is now and ever shall be." They never go away, these people, and they are sure there is sin in Job's life. That's the reason he's going through what he's going through. They give him every possible argument – entire chapters of the book – as to why he must be suffering. He must have done something wrong.

Job's answer was, "I don't know of anything I've ever done. But even if God chooses to kill me, I will continue to trust him." Even then God doesn't release the pressure. That doesn't happen for another 34 chapters. How would you tell Job to get out of this mess? Listen to this sermon, watch this video, tune into this radio station, talk to this counselor, read this book, it will get you through this? That's not how it works. The refiner puts gold in the oven and turns up the heat. He knows how much you can stand, but also knows how much it will take to wipe out the impurities.

In the middle of my lawsuit I wondered, "God, are you even hearing these prayers? Where are you?" And the heat just kept going up, making me stronger.

As I look back, it was good that I had that experience, because when I moved to the Bay Area, running a Christian radio station, I was an open target to people who thought it was funny to destroy reputations and call me every name in the book. When Promise Keepers came to town we supported it, and other stations railed about how Promise Keepers was full of men who batter their wives. The interesting thing was that wives started calling those stations and saying, "You've got it all wrong. My husband didn't leave me at home all by myself – I sent him!"

But I couldn't have withstood what I had to face there had there not been that previous pressure, where the oven was turned up and I felt the fire refine me.

There is one other passage in the Bible that I find helpful on this topic. I have held on to Hebrews 12:1-2 for a long time. It follows the phenomenal chapter 11 of Hebrews, that bible hall of fame, and hall of faith. Chapter 12 begins with,

"Since we've been surrounded by such an incredible company of believers..." And who are those believers? They are men and women who had gone through the refiner's fire, people who had been shot through with the arrow, driven through with the sword, sawn in two because of their faith. And with that as a backdrop, the Word says, "Cast aside every encumbrance to sin that so easily besets us, and let us run with endurance the race that is set before us."

That word race has its root in what gave us the word "agony." Run the race. It's not a sprint. It's a marathon. It's an agonizing thing we go through. Run the race with endurance that is set before us, "Fixing our eyes on Jesus, the author and perfecter of our faith."

My track coach in high school was Mr. Foster. He ran the hurdles with us, and I was always tripping over them. I just couldn't get over them when I ran. He would always say, "Walters, look over the hurdle. Don't look after. Look over the hurdle." When you do that, somehow you just seem to clear it. So it is in life. Don't look at the trial. Look over the trial, fixing your eyes upon Jesus, the author and perfecter of your faith. And what will happen? You'll qualify, for the eyes of the Lord they look to and fro throughout the whole world to find those whose hearts are completely His that He might make himself strong on their behalf.

Sixteen years ago I was introduced to Peter Ochs who had come to San Diego from Orange County to share an unusual success story with a group of business leaders. Peter pointed to his employees as the reason for the Fieldstone's success. It was the largest residential builder in the U.S.

The highlight of the story for me was a small card about the size of a credit card, which listed the six objectives of the company. Each employee was given a card to carry with them at all times. These cards served an accountability function.

At the ripe young age of 50, Peter and his wife Gail decided to retire and spend the rest of their lives serving the Kingdom of God. They started the Fieldstone Foundation as a vehicle for the company to give its profits to the Kingdom. Peter and Gail have taken that role of giving the biblical tithe of their time, talent and treasure.

I have had the privilege of attending several functions for Christian families to come together to discuss the pros and cons of different outreach programs. Some of us have had a few unfortunate experiences with several organizations, but I was impressed with the way Peter handled his part of the discussion, never in a negative way. Gail was also very positive and supportive. I appreciate the way Gail and Peter complement each other in a wonderful example of how business and its profits can contribute to the larger community.

6 Creating A Christ-Like Environment

Peter Ochs

IN THE UNITED STATES, ABOUT 150 MILLION people are employed full time, and they each spend at least 50 hours per week in the work world – especially if you include meal breaks and commuting time. It's the number one time commitment most of us have. The two other major time commitments are the hours  we spend with family, friends and common interest groups, and the time we spend watching television.

I think about the time we spend in these various places, and then I think about the most obvious place a person could see a Christian in action and find it an attractive enough life that he or she would also want to become a Christian.

If you look at the time we spend with neighbors or families or community groups, unless someone in those groups is a Christian and has an active witness, it's likely that a person is never really exposed to the Christian possibility. If you look at the time we spend watching television, there is even less likelihood of seeing someone's active Christian faith at work.

Our work places, then, are significant opportunities for people to see Christian faith in action, don't you think? Some pressures exist that run counter to many Christian principles, such as ambition, hurry, anxiety, time away from loved ones, anonymity and hoarding of wealth. These things can work against the message of Christianity.

But most people come to know Christ by seeing models of Christian behavior and being attracted to them. It is the result of the way most people learn anything – they see it in practice. Children learn from what they see their parents do, not from hearing parents say what they should do. Ideas are caught, not taught. Joe Aldrich, at the Multnomah School of the Bible, said, "Not many non-believers are reading the revelation of God's grace revealed in Scripture. Many are reading the revelation of God revealed in your life and relationships." But a lot of people say that the reason they don't believe Christianity is relevant is the hypocrisy they see in Christians. They see Christians living differently from what they say they believe.

If people are spending most of their time in the workplace, though, it is the most obvious source of where authentic Christianity can be modeled and "caught." The place where people spend more than half of their waking hours could be where people come in contact with some form of Christian testimony, which has the potential to be a very powerful interactive kind of modeling of the faith.

The question I want to explore is whether it is possible to create an environment for running a company that would be positive for the promotion of the Gospel, and at the same time is viable from a business perspective. If it's only good in promoting the Gospel and doesn't work from a business standpoint, then ultimately the business realities will choke it out. It won't have staying power. And if it's only a viable business model, then it's irrelevant as far as Christianity is concerned – it has lost its reason for being a witness in the secular culture.

The challenge for the Christian in the workplace was best articulated by Os Guinness who said: "The problem is not that Christians are not where they should be. When you think about where Christians are in our country today, they're in every walk of life. They're in business. They're in politics. They're in education. They're in everything. The problem is that they are not *what* they should be right where they are." That captures a very critical concept.

Any kind of organization has a culture – whether it's a business, a non-profit, a political party, a church. Any group of more than three or four people develops a set of values, which defines their culture. And no business practice can be successful in the long run that is in opposition to the organization's culture. In fact, if an organization has a strong culture, it's going to spit out a person who tries to change it, or tries to work at cross purposes with that culture.

Cultures simply *are*. They exist. You can't say, "Gee, I'd like to have a business that had a culture." The culture is there. My premise is that business needs to develop a set of basic Christian values, out of which the organization's culture will emerge. These values can be expressed in secular terms as well as in Christian terms, and they can be justified from either a Christian perspective or from a business perspective. They can create a framework, or a culture, within which an organization can run successfully, *and* be a testimony to the people who are in it and to the people who come in contact with it.

At my company, we created what I called "Fieldstone Values." We put them on cards, and employees know that if I see them at work I'm going to ask to see their card. Some laminate the card and hang it in their office. But they all have it with them, whether it's the receptionist or a superintendent in the field or a senior manager. It's a visual symbol that these are the core values on which our company is run. They are so central to who we are that, when we decided to change one of them, we spent about a year talking about it, and then another six months talking to people in the company to make sure that there was almost universal concurrence before we made the change.

We put the values in secular terms, but I have a biblical reference for each of them, which I did not put on the cards.

1). *Excellence in everything we do.* Everyone can identify with this, whether you're a Christian or not. It's a powerful concept because it calls people to the best that's in them. Proverbs 22:29 says, "Do you see a man skilled in his work? He will serve before kings, he will not serve before obscure men." That's a statement about excellence. Colossians 3:23 says, "Whatever you do, work at it with all your heart as working for the Lord and not for man." That's also about excellence. There are many others in the Bible. This is a biblical model expressed in secular terms, eliciting a powerful response from the secular culture.

2). *An environment of teamwork and trust.* Who doesn't want to work in a company that has an environment of teamwork and trust – one that really has it and isn't just talking about it? It's a powerful model for people. People want to be in a place where they feel safe, where they feel they can be open and trust the people around them. They want to be where the others will help them. Every now and then I run into people who are Lone Rangers and don't want to be in that kind of a model. We simply won't hire them.

The great majority of people respond well to this value. Proverbs 14:21 says, "He who despises his neighbors (the people in the office next to him – my translation) sins, but blessed is he who is kind to the needy (or helps the one who needs help)." Proverbs 17:9 says, "He who covers over an offense promotes love, but whoever repeats the matter separates close friends." The person who says, "Well you tried hard but it just didn't work," or "Let's all take some of the blame for that because we're all in it together," promotes love. Proverbs 15:22 says, "Plans fail for lack of counsel, but with many advisors they succeed." That's the idea of team-work – working together. Proverbs 18:1 says, "An unfriend-ly man pursues selfish ends. He defies all sound judg-ment." The first part of that is an objective statement: An unfriendly man pursues selfish ends. Unfriendly people do that. They're self-centered. The second part is a commentary on the objective statement: He defies sound judgment – it's a pretty stupid way to live your life!

3). *The value of each individual employee.* Valuing people as individuals is in part seeing them as Christ sees them. Proverbs 3:3-4 says, "Let love and truthfulness never leave you, then you will win favor in the sight of God and man." People respond when they know you love them and know you care about them. If you're truthful with them, they know they can trust you and they respond to that. People want to be valued. They want to be loved. They want to be in safe settings. Everyone in a secular culture responds well to that concept, but it's a biblical concept. I John 4:7-11 says, "Dear friends, let us love one another, for love comes from God. Everyone who loves has been born of God and loves God. Whoever does not love does not know God, because God is love. This is how God showed his love among us, he sent his one and only son into the world that we might live through him. This is love, not that we love God, but that he loved us and sent his son as an atoning sacrifice for our sins. Dear friends, since God so loved us, we also ought to love one another." That speaks emphatically to the value of each individual employee.

4). *Commitment to our customers.* We are in the home-building business. Lots of what is in the management liter-ature these days is about being customer driven, customer oriented, putting the customer at the center of the business. It is essentially a biblical principle. Proverbs 16:11 says, "Honest scales and balances are from the Lord. All the weights in the bag are of his making." Proverbs 11:1 says,

"The Lord abhors dishonest scales, but accurate weights are his delight." It's talking about giving fair value. It's talking about not cheating. It's talking about being committed to the customer you're dealing with.

5). *The importance of profitable operations.* We had this value in at the very beginning, but then we took it out for a while because we thought, "Well, maybe profit comes when you do everything else right." Eventually we realized that a business can do everything else right and still go out of business, so we put it back in. We looked at Proverbs again. Chapter 24, verse 27 says, "Plant your field first, then build your house." I think it's saying, "get your business in order, then go have fun." Proverbs 14:23 says, "All hard work brings a profit." The result of hard work is profit. Proverbs 10:4 has the same principle: "Diligent hands bring wealth." The idea of wealth creation is embedded in diligence and hard work. Anyone in a secular culture instantly responds to that. They know that a business has to make money to stay in business. They know that if the business doesn't make money, their livelihood is in jeopardy, their job is in jeopardy, their families are in jeopardy, so they want the business to make money.

6). *Integrity is the conduct of our business.* Again, people in a secular culture respond to this without question. People want to be in an environment of integrity. They may not know how to carry it out, but they want to be in that kind of place. It makes them feel good about themselves. A fear that people have in coming into the business world is that they will be asked to do things that they don't think are right, but they will be powerless not to do them. That's a hard place to be when it happens, and people don't like it. It grinds on you internally if it happens. So, if you can be in a place where the expectation is this value, that the culture is that this is a place of integrity, what a great place to be! And integrity is just strewn all over Scripture. There are whole sets of verses on gaining financial resources in a way that lacks integrity, and the result is always bad. That's a constant throughout Scripture. Proverbs 10:2 says, "Ill gotten treasures are of no value, but righteousness delivers from death." Proverbs 13:6 says, "Righteousness guards the man of integrity, but wickedness overthrows the sinner." Proverbs 11:13 says, "The integrity of the upright guides them, but the unfaithful are destroyed by their duplicity."

We're dealing with a situation as I write this, where we're trying to buy a piece of land, and there's a competitor who is also trying to buy it. It's a real cat and mouse game going back and forth, and it is unclear how it is going to turn out. In some ways, our competitor is acting without integrity in the process, and we're being challenged to make decisions on the basis of integrity over profitability. Proverbs 21:6 says, "A fortune made by a lying tongue is a fleeting vapor and a deadly snare." It's not just that it's not going to last – a vapor, but it's also a deadly snare. It's going to trap you.

These are the values we operate from. They are values everyone can believe in – Christian, non-Christian, atheist, it doesn't matter. They all want to work for an organization that talks this game. But the challenge is, can these values really be implemented and the company be successful? Our goal is to take these values and use them to shape the culture of the company, instead of letting the culture happen – which it will do – and then reacting to it. We see the culture as a business variable that we can work on.

It doesn't matter if you're a builder, running a non-profit, a sole proprietor, an attorney – there is relevance to having biblically based values define your culture.

The Fieldstone Company started in 1981, a severe recession year. That first year was a profitable one for us, with sales of $10 million. Ten years later, when southern California was in the third year of another severe recession, our sales were about $130 million, and our operations were profitable. Professional Builder Magazine listed us as one of the largest real estate developers in the U.S. We were the ninth largest privately owned building company in the country. But those rankings don't describe us that well. There are other descriptors that I think are more important.

One is that we have never laid off an employee. I have never, in my entire business career, laid off an employee. I don't think there is anything evil or wrong necessarily with laying people off – it's the reality of many businesses. But we have tried to run our business in such a way that we wouldn't have to do that, and it's part of the value that we see the importance of each employee.

Peter Drucker said, "A great mistake of the 19th Century, and we inherited it, is that people are a cost. In tough times we cut costs. The result is highly unproductive people." I think he is absolutely right. I think people are an investment, not a cost, and when you begin to look at them that way, when you run your business that way, it changes your mind set. But the view of people as investment has to come out of some basic value that says, "I value people, and I value people by valuing every one of my employees. If I do that, I'll see them as an investment, and if I see them as an investment, they are not a cost. And if they are not a cost, but an investment, then I don't want to cut my investment when times are tough. That's what's going to help me be successful."

When this company started, we said in our mission statement that we would build at least 1,200, but not more than 1,800 units a year to provide stability of operations and growth for our people. When the market turned south, we stuck to our statement and reduced margins in some cases, cut prices, adopted a different mind set, doing everything we could to avoid layoffs. As we look back now, we are convinced that doing what we did for the reasons of not wanting to lay people off, was also the most profitable way we could have run a building company in a recession. We didn't do it to maximize profits, but that was the result, which was pretty amazing.

Another descriptor of our company is that we have a highly pro-active charitable giving program, focused on the communities where we build. We developed the largest single urban project in the United States for Habitat for Humanity – 48 condominiums in Orange County, which we delivered for less than half the normal price, with 20-year zero-interest rate mortgages to people who were the working poor. These were people who had solid families, were hard working, but because their salaries were too low, would never in their lives be able to own a home if it weren't for this kind of alternative.

We do this for one reason: We're grateful. One of the ways to show gratitude is to invest in communities.

We've done some other things, such as develop a part-nering program with our subcontractors, which dramatically reduced our costs to build. It took at least a dollar off per square foot. For us, in one year, that was about $2.5 million out of our costs, with no change in quality, just by talking to the subcontractors earlier in the process. It was a cooperative relationship instead of a competitive one.

We do focus groups in our company. A focus group is a gathering of people who are there because they see a problem, they have something to do with that problem, and they want to help fix it. Every person in the company is trained in how to be a member of a focus group. Sometimes it's superintendents, or customer service people seeing a problem, they get a group together to define the problem figure out what it means, come up with a solution, and people in management will never know that the problem existed. They don't even have to ask permission to form the group. They don't have to ask permission to implement the solution. You can do this when you value people, when you believe in them and invest in them.

There has to be a way to measure these values in action, though. Anyone can talk a good game, but if the people don't believe it, which is often the case, it's not worth very much. After we had had these values for several years, I wondered if anyone really believed them. I talked about them all the time, and had people show me their cards, but I still wondered if the people really believed them, and if they thought the management team really believed them, and if they REALLY thought we were putting the values in action.

So we hired an outside consultant and we developed a survey with 60 questions, mostly related to the values, and we sent them out for the employees' anonymous replies. The company never saw the individual replies – only the aggregate results. I thought, "This is great. This is going to tell us where we really are and then we can either feel good about it or..." and I didn't know what the "or" was. I just hoped we'd feel good about it. The problem with doing this, with developing a "feedback loop," is that you have to listen and learn and change, which can be a challenge for managers. But if you don't have a feedback loop, you're just guessing. And if you're guessing, you're going to get it wrong at least part of the time.

One of the areas I especially prided myself in was in how we compensated our people. We were trying to be in the top quarter of our industry in pay, benefits and longevity of employment, areas where I was sure we were better than our competitors. That was an easy question to put in the survey. But 42 percent of our employees said, "Wrong." Our compensation was a problem. What would your reaction be? I had two reactions. One was, "They don't understand clearly, and I'm going to get them together and tell them so that they will understand." The other was, "We've got a bunch of troublemakers out there and let's get rid of them and get some people in here that do understand." I was pretty annoyed, and despite the forms promising anonymity, I wanted to look at them. The consultant said "No way." But then he said, "Let's try something."

We formed a focus group of employees, for the sole purpose of telling us what people meant by that answer. We had about eight people from all parts of the company, and no members from management. They weren't out to fix anything. They were there strictly to explain to us. I thought it would be good to have someone from management in the group. They voted and said that we could do that as long as the manager did not talk unless he was needed to answer a question.

I hit the ceiling again, and after I got calmed down I said, "All right, we'll try this once." The focus group met twice. That's all it took. "The pay is fine," they said. "No problem. Vacation, holidays are great. Profit sharing, wonderful. Medical benefits, lousy." Now we had isolated it to a single issue. But I still didn't believe it because I knew how much we were paying for those medical benefits. But at least we had it focused – we knew it wasn't the pay or vacations, so we had some validation there. Still, I was bothered because of the amount we were spending and the enormous amount of time we had spent developing those programs.

It was easier to take the next step, though, since we knew what the problem was. We decided to survey our competitors, and I knew that we could then say to our employees, "Here's what they do, here's what we do, and here's why your attitude is wrong." That was a good participative management technique, I thought!

We did the survey, and, sure enough, we found we were spending just as much or more than our competitors. The problem was that we weren't spending it as well. Their programs were all better than our programs, which is just what

79

our people had told us. It's really a blow to the side of the head when you realize, "You know what? What they said in that meeting was right and totally different from what I had thought for years." This had come out of the grass roots of our organization, and all we had to do was ask. It had been there the whole time – we had just never asked. We immediately went to work and rebuilt our medical plan. We reduced our cost by 20 percent and put that 20 percent savings back into the benefits program. We set up 401-K programs that we'd never had before, with a company contribution to it that added some favorable employee tax treatment that had been available all along, but we just didn't know it.

We unveiled the new package to the employees and they were blown away by it. We asked and listened. We responded to what they said. It said to them, in the most tangible way possible, "We are serious about these things. We really do value you, and if we work together, we can be better than what management working alone ever could be." This unlocked a floodgate of change that continues today. It gave people the vision that they could act on ideas that no one had listened to before.

One group of employees challenged one of the ways we did things and finally got a group of architects, subcontractors and code enforcers together and came up with a better way of doing the same thing, which saved us at least $700 per house. We deliver more than 1,300 homes a year. That's a big savings for us, simply because we had a person willing to challenge an accepted way of doing things and a group of people on a team that said, "Yes, this is the culture of this company. We really look at these things and make changes."

Some of the advantages of running a company this way is that people became very loyal to us, particularly during recession years. They believed in the values we claimed.

That created a willingness in employees to work harder and have high morale, even during the difficult years. This came home to me when I was going to different regional offices of the company to deliver my "State of the Company" address. Employees came in from all areas and they asked me questions and I solicited their comments. It was a time of shared vision and direction. At the end of a meeting, one of our hard-bitten field superintendents came up to me and said, "Peter, I got a comment for you." I thought, "Oh no, here it comes – he didn't have the courage to say it in the big meeting, but I'm going to get blasted."

"The other guys and I were just talking," he said, and then he began to cry. I put my arm around him and tried to turn him away from the others to save him some embarrassment. It took him a while to regain his composure. When he did, he said, "All I can say is, Thank God I work for Fieldstone." He knew how bad it was in our industry during those years, and he saw his friends out of work and losing their homes. Guys in construction know how brutal a bad economy can be. He saw the value of having a job, of being able to work, and it created this emotional response.

Talk about being a testimony. Talk about being a Christian witness to something. How are you going to reach a guy like that field superintendent? You're probably not going to reach him when he goes out drinking beer with the guys after work. You're not going to reach him through television. You have to reach him where he spends most of his life, and that's at work. How? By telling things? By yelling at him? By sending him memos? That's not going to touch him. You have to do it by example. It's what he sees modeled in your life. He's drawn to it, because it's so attractive.

I have to be honest in telling you that building a values-driven company is not easy. It has plenty of obstacles. And if these obstacles are too great for you, then don't even attempt this, because you'll raise expectations, and if you don't produce, you'll be worse off than before.

The first obstacle is in how we view people. If your basic view of people is that they need to be tightly managed and controlled, then none of what I just described will work. A values-driven company has to flow from a view of people that sees them through God's eyes as having great capability, a desire to do their best, and a willingness to learn and contribute. You have to see people like that. Not everyone is equally capable, but they are all equally valuable. It doesn't mean lack of accountability. Poor performance is not acceptable. We have a slogan in the company that says, "We're soft on the people but hard on the issue." There has to be accountability and performance, but within a context of valuing people.

In the book of Genesis, right in the beginning, in the first chapter, God creates man in his own image. If we are made in the image of God, then how can you look at people as those who must be controlled, watched and tightly managed because they're going to screw up if you don't? How can you look at them that way if they are created in the image of God? They have to be viewed as people of great value and great potential, with great optimism, and we have to provide a climate within which they can act out that potential.

The second obstacle is this question: Who knows best? Me or them? This is a tough one, particularly for those who own their own businesses. You can operate from a "Father knows best" kind of paternalism. But our surveys say over and over that people want a say in things that affect them. They don't want to be told what to do and what's going to happen to them no matter how good it is. In our problems with the compensation issue, the people didn't understand the process and they weren't sure it was fair. The people knew more than management did, and when they were offered a chance for input they pointed us in the right direction quickly.

Letting go of this control, though, for many executives, can be very threatening.

A tangent to this obstacle is the Big Brain Theory, which says, "All decisions need to be funneled up to me and I'll make them. You're a good person. You do your homework. You prepare the material, but I'll make the decisions." A lot of companies and divisions and departments are run that way. But what it really says is, "I'm more important than you. I don't value your ability to make those decisions." On occasion, of course, there are decisions that are inappropriate to be made other than by the CEO, but most can be delegated throughout the organization.

Philippians 2:3 says, "With humility of mind, consider others better than yourself." That's a verse that I have skipped for years. I didn't like it. But finally, I started to allow God to speak to me about what it was saying. It's a tough concept, but incredibly valuable.

A third obstacle to running a values-driven company is the emphasis on power. You can value people and still say, "I don't always know best, but I have the power, and I like it that way, and I'm going to keep it. I know you could make good decisions, but it's my company and I'm going to make the decisions." But you don't really value people when you do that. It degrades them. It takes a lot of self confidence to give people a stake, a voice, and allow them to make critical decisions for the company. It's hardest on middle managers. They've spent their whole careers learning how to manage and make decisions. It's hard for them to shift to being more of a coach, or a person who helps people learn how to make their own decisions. That takes retraining.

But think of the model in Ephesians 4, which is a model for the Body of Christ. It's a model of people working together. It says that a healthy organism, or healthy organization, has people fitted together, each in his or her own area of giftedness, doing what they can do to cause the whole organization to grow and thrive. That's the concept of sharing power, of delegating authority, of letting other people have a piece of the action. It's a very powerful and motivating concept.

The last obstacle is perhaps the toughest one. When the chips are down, when things are really tough, how deeply do you own those values? When integrity would say one thing and survival would say another, how deeply do you hold those values? If you adopt these values, you will be tested. And it's not fun. It's painful. You have to know how far down the road you're willing to go before you even start down the road.

Matthew 6:24 says, "No one can serve two masters. Either he will hate the one and love the other, or he will be devoted to one and despise the other. You cannot serve both God and money." So you have to decide who your master is.

You'll need some people in your life if you're going to try this. I meet with a group of guys who are not developers every Friday morning for two hours. It says in Proverbs that "Iron sharpens iron, so one man sharpens another." That's what they provide me and I provide them. Think carefully about the kind of person you want in your life to help you think about these things. Perhaps it's a spouse. But you have to have someone to live through this with you.

What is the result of all of this? I told you the business results. Other results I'm excited about is that two of our top management team members have accepted Christ. Members of their families are accepting Christ. We have some Bible studies that go on in the office. They are completely voluntary, and they happen outside of working hours. Being a Christian is in no way grounds for hiring or promotion in our company. That's based on the job you do. But we want to provide an active witness for people, and people find it attractive.

Christians are called to put their faith out on the line, for the world to see in action. Talk is cheap. Action is where it counts, and not just action outside of work. Sitting on church committees and non-profit boards is fine, but action is needed where we spend most of our waking lives. It's all about being what we should be, where we already are.

One of the companies I had consulted with had just entered into a relationship with an accountant who was going to help them get their books up to date and bring some additional investors to the company. The president called me and asked if I would join him and this accountant for lunch. It was fascinating to meet a professional who was actually interested in learning all he could from everyone he met.

Rich has a fascinating background of not only serving as advisor to his clients, but also having a servant's heart for making a contribution to the Kingdom of God. No matter what organization he is involved in, Rich wants to contribute everything he can to making it better.

Despite his desire to give all that he can to his clients, one investor decided he wanted control of a company Rich introduced him to. This created a disaster for Rich and the company. After years of confusion and lawsuits, Rich has continued to be confident that God would see him through this extremely difficult time. Rich's faith is so strong that it is an encouragement to all of us.

Rich and Pam have three married daughters and live in Costa Mesa, California. He continues to operate his accounting and consulting business full throttle!

7

"What Do You Need?"

Rich Boyer

I BEGAN MY ACCOUNTING CAREER MORE than 30 years ago with a desire to serve the Body of Christ. After forming my own CPA firm I tried to understand the meaning of Romans 12:2, "Do not be conformed to this world, but be transformed by the renewing of your mind, so that you may prove what the will of God is, that which is good and acceptable and perfect." My accounting training definitely caused my thinking to be conformed to this world. What I wanted to learn was how to have my mind transformed by God to really know His perfect will. I had no idea that this desire would lead me through one of the most contentious personal and legal challenges imaginable!

My accounting practice consisted primarily of Christian ministries and Christian clients. While serving on numerous ministry boards I became weary of the lack of financial resources that so many ministries faced. It just didn't make sense to me. I had 300-400 non-profit groups as clients, and all of them seemed to waste so much time on seeking contributions, and spend too little time on the rewarding work of sharing the faith, leading people to Christ, and ministering in Jesus' name. They never quite had enough time to truly fulfill their vision.

I prayed about this frustration, and felt that if God

would allow me to have access to unlimited funds I would do my best to channel those funds into various Christian ministry projects. For whatever reason, my wife and I have always felt instructed to pray very specifically. In fact, when I was single and felt that I was ready for a serious relationship, I prayed that God would send me a person with a certain kind of personality, with brown hair, and whose birthday was the same as mine. Within a few weeks I met the very person I had asked for, and we got married! She and I would write out our vision for our lives each year, and pray over it, and watch God work. As I got started in my career I prayed that I would be able to help my very first client to be used by God in a profound way. When my first client came to me, she was also just getting started and was trying to grow her business. She was trying to get broader exposure for a young psychologist named James Dobson.

So when I prayed for this kind of access to funds for ministry efforts, I felt that all along God had been telling me that I could trust Him, and that I could ask Him for anything.

Sure enough, I was introduced to a company that had several breakthrough technologies in the communication and energy fields. The communication technology had the potential for changing the telecommunications industry worldwide. I was brought into the company to perform some tax planning services, but was soon intrigued by the magnitude of these technologies and their potential impact on society. It was a system that could greatly multiply the world's bandwidth needs, while substantially reducing the power requirements for such a system. Not only could this technology produce the financial resources greatly needed for various ministries, but it could also be the means to spread the Gospel more efficiently throughout the world. It appeared that this company and its technologies were going to be an answer to prayer and provide the funding for many Christian ministries.

The company was in a start-up phase and, like most start-ups, had not attended to their legal and accounting compliance needs. During the process of reviewing the company's operations, I told a Christian friend, who was also a client, of the technologies to get his opinion of them. He met several times with the owner and chief scientist of the company, and became interested in becoming an investor in the company. His interest became so great that he decided to make a substantial investment in the company and move his family to San Diego where he could participate in the day-to-day management of the company.

But because of the narcissistic tendencies of both the owner of the company and my Christian friend, and because of the astronomical profits that were at stake as a successful prototype of the communication technology emerged, they began to clash. I continue to be amazed at what happens to people when confronted by greed and power. My Christian friend saw an opportunity to take over the company, and I saw him manipulate negotiations that dragged us all into a bitter and acrimonious conflict.

My Christian friend had convinced the company owner and the chief scientist to let him loan them money for them to put down payments on homes in the San Diego area. None of us realized this was part of his scheme to take over the company and its assets. He had already made the company dependent on his capital for maintaining the operations of the company. Then he began withdrawing that money, and filed lawsuits aimed at bankrupting the company and anyone associated with it – including me. His lawsuits were filled with lies regarding the operations of the company, including the characterizing of his loans as theft and tax evasion. His lawsuits were designed to prevent the existing management from raising any capital to continue the research and development and marketing of this technology. He then hired several unethical lawyers to initiate criminal proceedings against the management of the company, to ensure his ability to buy the technologies out of bankruptcy for pennies on the dollar.

I was overwhelmed by how corrupt my Christian friend was, and also by how corrupt our legal system is. I had no idea that it was for sale. Until this experience I had believed in our legal justice system, trusting that the truth would win out every time. I was appalled to find out that you could pay a former U.S. Attorney a substantial amount of money to use his influence to get a group of people indicted. I was likewise appalled to learn that U.S. attorneys, the IRS and the FBI routinely lie and provide false information to the courts to make sure indictments turn into convictions. They are allowed to take your property. Their job promotions occur when they convict people, regardless of innocence or guilt. I had no idea that a U.S. Attorney's office could tamper with and intimidate witnesses. But that's what happened.

My Christian friend was successful in putting the company into bankruptcy court to approve an auction for purchasing all the technologies. Of course, he put himself in the position of being the qualified bidder. Given the difficulties and expense of fighting several lawsuits and false criminal accusations, it seemed impossible for any of us to raise the capital needed to participate in the bidding.

On an airplane coming home from a meeting with another client, I considered what was happening. I had four lawsuits against me. I had attorneys coming after me on criminal charges of fraud, tax evasion and money laundering. The legal costs were staggering. This was the bleakest possible time in my life. I was devastated by what was happening. What I had been working for, with the intent of providing funds for the advancement of God's Kingdom, was all going to be gone in 30 days, and I was going to be ruined legally and financially. I might even be headed for jail.

Strangely, though, I was not worried. I never went to the Lord in complaint. I constantly said, "I don't like what's going on, but I know I can trust You completely." Despite the bleakness of the situation, God gave me peace. I knew that worry was not in God's plan for me. When we worry, we boldly go into the throne room of God, shake our finger at Him and say, "I don't trust you." This breaks God's heart. Worry is an act of disobedience. It is sin.

On that airplane I sensed God say to me, "How will you spend the money?" I wondered what that meant. I kept getting that question, though, so I wrote up a business plan for how I would spend the money that I did not have, in order to get the company out of bankruptcy. Two days before the sale of the assets, I sensed God again, this time asking, "What do you need?" My initial reaction was, "That's too simple." But for the next seven hours I wrote out what I needed in order to buy this company back. I needed an immediate $760,000 for the deposit and working capital to be able to bid in the bankruptcy auction, a $6.5 million total commitment for the final development and marketing of the technology, a completed business plan and a completed plan of reorganization to be submitted to the bankruptcy court.

The following morning I met with a top bankruptcy law firm in San Diego to review the plan that I had written the night before. They told me my plan would probably work, assuming that I already had the working capital and the $6.5 million capital commitment. I was politely escorted to the door when I told them I didn't have the commitment, and that I had written up the plan the day before.

While I was in the lobby thanking the attorneys for their time, my pager went off. I could tell by the number that it was from someone I had asked to help fund this plan. I asked the attorneys if I could use their phone to call this potential source before I left their offices. Sitting in the attorneys' library, I returned the call and gave him the details of the plan and of what had just happened with the attorneys. He said he liked the plan and said he would give me the $6.5 million and could wire the working capital directly into the attorneys' account that day.

In that moment the Lord reminded me of James 4:2: "You do not have because you do not ask," and John 16:24: "Until now you have asked for nothing in My name; ask and you will receive, so that your joy may be made full." Needless to say, I was overwhelmed with joy! The lesson I learned early on was that I could trust God. That continued to be the lesson during this ordeal.

On the day of the bankruptcy auction there were only two bidders – my Christian friend and me, and I outbid him. He continued to pursue me in both civil and criminal court, though. The civil suit was designed for me to forfeit all of the technologies to the government. The criminal suit charged me with tax evasion. When someone is indicted, one of the tactics of the government is to try to bankrupt the person so he can't pay for good legal counsel. In my case, the government even threatened my attorney with an indictment unless he dropped me as a client.

Throughout this portion, though, I kept sensing God saying, "Do you still trust me?" I would always reply, "God, I trust you completely." Every time this happened I was in perfect peace.

At one point, when some significant attorney fees were due, I simply did not have the money to pay him. I had $25,000 left, but the fee was $125,000, which was due immediately or he would drop me. I did something I have never done before or since. I woke up that morning at 4, and had a lengthy quiet time with the Lord. Then I called the attorney and said, "I am wiring you $25,000 now, and I will wire the rest of it to you this afternoon." I had no idea where the rest of it was coming from. That was at 6 a.m. One hour later, I got a call from a friend I hadn't talked to in months. He said, "Rich, I got up this morning and felt impressed to pray for you. God told me to give you $100,000."

My trial lasted eight weeks. Even though it was clear that the government attorneys were coaching their witnesses to lie and telling them what to remember from seven years before, my attorney was able to bring out the truth in cross examination. It was clear that the government was losing its case. They created some false evidence about tax evasion and submitted it to the jury, over our objections because they were false documents. The jury acquitted me of all counts except the one that depended on the false evidence. They found me guilty of that one, and I am appealing that conviction.

Throughout this period of difficulty I found myself asking this question: "God, are you allowing this to happen or is this the work of the enemy?" I am well aware of the fact that when we anticipate a great work of God, we can expect spiritual warfare. The enemy doesn't want it to happen. So I wanted to know what was behind this seven-year conflict. Why would a Christian man do such despicable things to others? The owner of the company had gotten cancer and had died. Who was behind this?

When I thought Satan was behind it, I became angry. When I considered that God was behind it, I saw it as a way for God to use this is a tool to help me learn to trust Him more and experience His peace despite the dire circumstances. James 1:2-4 says, "Consider it all joy, my brethren, when you encounter various trials, knowing that the testing of your faith produces endurance and let endurance have its perfect result, so that you may be perfect and complete, lacking in nothing." In my profession, the definition of wealth and riches is expressed in dollars. I have found that being wealthy or rich is when I "lack nothing." God helped me count it all for joy while I was going through these trials and continue to go through them. We had to alter our lifestyle considerably during these difficult years, and my daughters now say they are so glad we went through it. Our culture is so inundated with material things that bring us comfort. When we have to trust God for everything, we realize how shallow the culture's provision really is. In my family, we thought we had to go someplace in order to have fun. During these trials, we couldn't afford to go anywhere. We would stay home and play games. It didn't cost us anything – and my daughters say that those were the best family times.

God was allowing this difficult time for our good. Because I knew God was in it, I could extend forgiveness to the man who was trying to ruin me financially. I watched other people suffer greatly because they couldn't forgive. But we are commanded to forgive, just as Christ forgave us. How can we do otherwise? I also continue to pray that God will give my Christian friend a Godly conscience.

Before he died, the owner of the company accepted Christ. I am so grateful that he didn't think Christianity was represented well by the actions of my Christian friend.

For seven years I have been embroiled in this conflict. All I wanted to do was provide income for ministries that were trying to advance the Kingdom. But I have learned some things in this process. When we try to do something for God, pride rears its head. Sometimes we want *our vision* more than we want God. We want to see good things happen. What we should want is that, above all, God will be glorified.

During these seven years I have also found out what the perfect will of God is for our lives. Jesus gave us the answer to this question by telling us in Matthew 22:37-40: "You shall love the Lord your God with all your heart, and with all your soul and with all your mind. This is the greatest and foremost commandment. The second is like it, You shall love your neighbor as yourself. On these two commandments depend the whole Law and the Prophets." Love is described in I Corinthians 13:4-8 as being patient, kind, not jealous, does not brag, is not arrogant, does not act unbecomingly, does not seek its own, is not provoked, does not take into account a wrong suffered, does not rejoice in unrighteousness, rejoices in the truth, bears all things, believes all things, hopes all things, endures all things and never fails.

I am still going through this trial, this time in the appeal process. I will continue to pray, "God, I trust you completely." Nowhere in the Word of God does it say that we should trust our government, trust our president, or trust in any man or woman. Whether I remain free or go to jail, I will continue to trust God!

Thirty-eight years ago, God introduced me to a fascinating man who was making a name for himself in the somewhat seasonal restaurant industry. Jim had the largest restaurant chain in the world, and the largest steak house chain in the world, Mr. Steak, with 278 free standing buildings.

Jim has a great heart for God, and it seemed as if we were constantly working on Kingdom projects together. One of the most enjoyable times was when we formed a partnership with 14 other businessmen to purchase land for a local Christian university.

Jim and his wife of 47 years, Dottie, were advised by some of their young MBA management team to take the company public. With a great deal of concern, Jim agreed to do an IPO, which was very successful, followed by a secondary issue which was also successful. But they eventually lost $60 million.

Jim and Dottie were very disappointed, but neither of them were bitter or angry, which said a lot to us about their faith and how grounded they were in the things that matter.

During the success of the company they had one of the largest construction companies, one of the largest meat companies, and one of the largest trucking companies. Through all of this success his resolve as a Christian businessman was evident. He always wanted to put more back into the community than he took out.

Jim lost Dottie more than 12 years ago, and God led him to Linda several years later. Their interest now is in missions work, and has been for the more than 10 years they have been married. He continues to give back to the Kingdom of God, which he has done all of his life.

8
What the Restaurant Business Learned from the Israelites Jim Mather

WHEN THE MISTER STEAK RESTAURANT franchise business was at its peak, we had 286 restaurants and used nearly 2 million head of beef each year to supply those restaurants. The success of the company made me the top retail sales person in the United States, and it seemed that nothing could stop the company from growing to even more success.

The company ultimately failed because of something we did that was similar to what the Israelites did as described in I Samuel.

I confess that in my private Bible study, I became annoyed with the Israelites – angry, even. It may seem childish to feel that way, but that's how I felt. They were led by a pillar of cloud by day, and a pillar of fire at night, and they could hear Him speaking to Moses. They could see and hear the direction of God.

In I Samuel 8, though, the Bible describes how Samuel was getting old and that he appointed his sons as judges for Israel. But the sons followed their own flesh instead of God, and things got messed up.

They accepted dishonest gain and bribes, and perverted justice, it says. So the elders got together with Samuel and demanded that he appoint a king so that they could be like other nations.

This disturbed Samuel and he went before the Lord with his concern. But the Lord told him, "Listen to all that the people are saying to you. It is not you they have rejected as their king, but me, as they have done from the day I brought them up out of Egypt until this day, forsaking me and serving other gods, so they are doing to you. Now listen to them, but warn them subtly, and let them know what the king who will reign will do to them."

So Samuel told the Israelites, "This is what the king who will reign over you will do. He will take your sons and will make them to serve with his chariots and horses. And they will run in front of his chariots. Some he will assign to be commanders of thousands, commanders of fifty, and others to plow his ground and reap his harvest, and still others to make weapons of war and equipment for his chariots. He will take your daughters to be perfumers and cooks and bakers. He will take the best of your fields and vineyards and olive groves and give them to his attendants. He will take a tenth of your grain and take your vintage and give it to the officials in attendance. Your men servants and your maid servants and the best of your cattle and your donkeys he will take for his own use.

"He will take the tenth of your flocks and yourselves will become his slaves. When that day comes, you will cry out for relief from the king you have chosen and the Lord will not answer you that day."

But the people refused to listen to Samuel, and still demanded that he appoint a king. Once again, Samuel took his concern before God, and the Lord said, "Listen to them and give them a king. Obey me and follow my commands and I will bless your lands with honey and it will be a great blessing. If they don't, I'll scatter them all over the face of the earth."

I think we all know what took place. That's why I was angry with the Israelites. They had a perfectly good system going, but they wanted to be like other nations, and things fell apart.

When the Mr. Steak business started, I told everyone who would listen that the Lord owned our business. It was God, family and business, in that order. The Lord owned our business and blessed it.

I had a concept that included starting a restaurant business, but then broadening it into developing businesses that provided services to the bigger restaurant industry. That meant we would expand and diversify, while serving our core business and the business of those also in our industry.

It began with developing a computerized accounting system. The price of food changed so rapidly that it was best to stay on top of those prices. That system served Mr. Steak, but we also sold it to restaurants throughout the country.

We also knew that restaurants had a difficult time providing a quality product consistently to their restaurants, so we started our own beef production company. We provided beef to our own company and sold it to other restaurants and companies. At one time we had the contract to provide all of the hamburger for all Safeway stores.

But the meat has to get to its location, so we started a trucking company to get the beef in 36 states and Canada. We also moved product to other people as we were moving around the country. Then we started a restaurant equipment business that sold product to our company and to others.

Then I fell prey to Wall Street.

No one knew anything about Wall Street back then. They were the mysterious ones, way before they were exposed for their own corruption. They began wooing me, telling the world that we could become the McDonald's of the steak house business in the United States. Our growth had been fantastic so far, and I made the mistake of believing them.

During this time of intense flattery they told me I needed to take my company public.

"Why do we need to go public?" I asked.

"You need the extra money," they said.

"We have a few million dollars in the bank – why do I need extra money?"

"You need it to buy equipment."

"We finance our equipment purchases any time we want to."

"But you need to lease the equipment in order to buy land."

And so it went. We talked like this for hours. It was when they said "You don't understand," that I should have turned and run.

I have a high school education. They were CPAs and attorneys and seemed so wise in this. I think they were trying to say to me, "You don't have the background or education to understand all of this, and you *really* don't understand what we're about to do to you."

But I got caught up in how romantic it sounded to become a public company. All of the executives liked the idea because they would have stock in the company. So we went public. In about a year a company that researches companies that go public found that a contract that should have been in our prospectus wasn't included by all these smart attorneys and CPAs, so we were named in a potential class action lawsuit. That went on for nine years.

Remember, our company had been growing like crazy, starting new businesses, with what appeared to be an unlimited future. But now we were told to act like tortoises, to pull our heads in and be on the defensive. We had to use all of our money to defend ourselves. Finally, the company investigating us said that it was an accounting question, and not a question of the company's integrity. So there was no action taken against us. But it had drained us of our impetus to do what we wanted to do. We became inferior in our thinking.

When this died down a little, I attended some religious services, and the Lord revealed to me my anger at the Israelites. It was as if God was saying, "Mather, look – you have done exactly what made you angry at the Israelites for doing. You claimed that God was blessing you and your company, and then you asked for a man king when you took it public." When we were a private company we could say or do whatever we wanted, and what we did was take our profit and give much of it to Christian organizations. But when we went public, the world owned our company. What had made me so angry at the Israelites is the same thing I had done. I wanted to be like the other kingdoms. And I couldn't undo it.

It was very bad judgment, and the Lord revealed it to me through his word.

A few years later I decided to retire, and brought in a guy I thought was a good Christian. I told him that, when he was ready to run the company, I would resign from all committees and let him run it. In two years he said he thought he was ready, so he took over and I left. I had been gone for about two years, and my wife Dotty and I went on vacation to Hawaii for a month. When we got back, one of our franchise owners talked to me and mentioned something about Chapter 11. In a very short period of time, my replacement filed for bankruptcy protection. We had no bank debt and owed no back taxes. He did it to get out from about $600,000 in annual leases where the properties were not meeting expectations.

So I made another bad judgment. I guess I didn't hear the Lord in that, either. The result was that the 1.3 million shares of stock I had in the company went to zero.

My wife and I kept being involved in as many ministries as we could, because we wanted to contribute as much as we could during our retirement. Dotty became ill, though, and what the doctors thought was a gall bladder problem was really pancreatic cancer. She lasted a month and a half after that diagnosis.

She was the same angel in the hospital as she was during the rest of our 47 years together. She didn't have one complaint while she was there, and even told me not to make the doctors and nurses feel badly about anything. Even when we brought her home for the final days during hospice care, she didn't want me to call people and have them come over. But when she knew the end was near, she told me to call our family and friends. One by one they came in the room, and she came out of what looked like a coma and greeted each person by name. As they left she went back into a state of semi-consciousness. When the next person came in she became alert again.

She died early in the morning, after we had one more time where we said "I love you," and "Goodbye." My daughter in law observed, "I don't know anyone whose feelings were hurt by her, or who was angry with her." She was right. I have hurt nearly everyone in my family and have had them mad at me at some point. But not Dotty.

I miss her very much. Sometimes I even talk to her. To fill the void I got involved in some ministry groups and ended up going to Russia to teach courses in Christian ethics and morality as a foundation for society. We brought nine and one-half tons of materials with us. Each person in the course got their first Bible, and they all got a copy of *The Jesus Film*. They all got curriculum they could teach in their own schools. One of the school district leaders said to me at graduation, "We are so grateful you have brought Jesus to us." Can you hear your school superintendent in America saying that?

What the Restaurant Business Learned

I learned some difficult lessons in business, and learned that I am a lot like the Israelites in the Bible. But throughout those times I learned something – the same lesson the followers of God learned in the book of Samuel: whether I would have kept the Mister Steak company or not, God loved me the same. He didn't love me less when I took the company public. He didn't love the Israelites less when they demanded a king. He doesn't abandon us when we make bad decisions. We can't escape their outcomes, but one thing we know for sure: Nothing – *nothing* – can separate us from the love of God. Not attorneys or CPAs or replacement executives. I am grateful that I have been able to continue to serve him even though I didn't listen to Him as closely as I should have. Praise God for that!

In 1957, my good friend James Jeffrey brought his two-year-old son Neal to the Fellowship of Christian Athletes summer conference in Estes Park, Colorado. From that time, I knew that Neal was destined for greatness no matter what area he chose to pursue.

Jeff mentioned that Neal had a speech impediment, which made one-on-one conversations with him challenging. But Neal used that difficulty as a means for focusing his efforts early in life. Jeff told me how Neal would come home from school and throw a football for hours at a target, and he would get it in the bull's eye 99 out of 100 times. That's consistency.

Neal was an accomplished athlete in high school, and received a scholarship to his dad's alma mater, Baylor University. He was a college all-American quarterback for Baylor. His coach said that Neal was one of the most focused, dedicated men he had ever coached. Neal then played for the San Diego Chargers for three years and developed a desire to use his speaking gifts in some capacity. After graduating from seminary, he realized that his speaking talent exceeded his expectations. People listened to him, and were helped by what he said.

Motivational speakers are abundant throughout the world, but few of them have had the lasting impact Neal has on an audience. His compassion and heart for the Lord are very evident in all that he says and does. He and his wife have two daughters and a son and live in Dallas. Neal continues to conduct motivational workshops and he also works with the Prestonwood Baptist Church.

9

Stuttering Well

Neal Jeffrey

WHEN I WAS A KID I HAD A TARGET SET UP next to my garage, and as soon as I got home from school I would practice throwing a football at that target. I would do this for hours until I could throw one hundred out of one hundred through that target. Then I would go up to my room and work on something that was maybe even more important: calling signals.

I needed to practice calling signals because I am a stutterer. I'm a really good stutterer, too! I don't want to brag, but I've always stuttered well! But being a stutterer is really no big deal, unless you're trying to say something! Then it can be a factor. And all my life it has been a factor. If anything, my stuttering has made my life exciting, because I never know in any situation I'm in if I'll be able to say something or not.

As a kid, our home phone would ring and, thousands of times, I would answer it and get stuck. I'd start stuttering and not be able to say anything, so I'd just have to hang up. It had a big impact on me as a student, too. In a high school speech class our first assignment was to stand in front of the class and speak for three minutes about our lives. I was up there for about 15 minutes and wasn't able to say much of anything.

In Spanish class we had to do dialogues. If you can

imagine me stuttering in English, you should have heard me stutter in Spanish!

You can imagine the impact this had on me as a football quarterback. The person in that position has to be able to talk – at the least he has to call plays in the huddle and yell "Hut!" at the line of scrimmage. And what if he has to call an audible once the teams are lined up? That was exciting. In high school, a team was allowed 30 seconds to call a play. For me, that wasn't always enough time. I'd be in the huddle calling the play and get stuck. I'd begin stuttering, and time would run out. The referee would throw a flag and we'd lose five yards each time. I cost us a lot of yardage.

So my coach devised a system where he had one of the receivers stand next to me in the huddle. If I got stuck calling the play, the receiver would finish it, say the snap count, and then say, "Ready, break." My coach just said, "Neal, you be on one knee and act like you're doing something, but don't open your mouth because it confuses everybody. So the receiver would say the play, we would break and hustle to the line of scrimmage. The fullback who always lined up behind me would call the "huts" for me. It was great to start a game against a new team and watch the reaction of the defense when the fullback called the "huts." They didn't always know where the voice was coming from!

What I want to tell you is similar to what a coach would tell you before you go out to play a game. Mostly a coach simply reminds you of things so that you'll go out and play the game of your life. I want to remind you of six things.

The first is that you only play the game for so long. Every game is precious. But there is an end point. I played a lot of football in my life. I started playing flag football in third grade, then tackle in fourth grade. I played all the way through grade school, then junior high, then high school, the four years at Baylor and three in the NFL. That's a lot of football. But the fact is that I'm never going to play it again. If I was going to improve, make a difference, be the player I wanted to be, it had to be done while I was playing. My time is over. Done. I will never walk on the field again.

It's amazing how many high school athletes say in their minds, "Oh, I'll play this game forever. I've got fervor to play this game!" And then a very subtle thing happens. Over time, that athlete begins coasting a little. He just doesn't give everything he needs to give. He just doesn't work as hard as he ought to work, and he's kind of loafing, yet he's thinking, "One of these days I'm going to get serious about this, and start doing everything. I'm going to find out how good I could be."

The problem is, though, he never gets there. Then before he knows it his career is over and he's thinking, "How good could I have been if I had just given my best every day?" It would affect an athlete's life if he played every game as if this were his last, if he did every drill as if, "I'm not sure how long I've got, but I'm not going to waste a game." Every practice. Every drill. "I'm going to find out how good I could become."

This is a life lesson as well. The reason this day is such a precious thing is that you and I get to live it one more time. The day will come when we won't get to do this anymore. You've heard the saying that any day you awake, stretch out your hand and don't feel the side of a coffin – that's a great day! But it is true that one of these days we will not open our eyes again. So maybe we can adopt that athlete's position of, "I'm not wasting a day. I'm not wasting an hour. I'm not wasting an opportunity. I'm making this day count."

One of these days I'm going to kiss my wife for the last time on this earth. That's why it ought to be done today. I've heard Zig Ziglar say he never leaves his wife without kissing her. Not a peck on the cheek, either. I'm talking a long, juicy, wet kiss on the mouth. Because he knows that one of these days it will be his last, and he wants each of them to go into eternity with that last kiss on their minds.

One of these days I'm going to tell my wife how precious she is to me, how my life has been enriched, has been blessed, has become wonderful as the result of her love. That ought to be said today.

One of these days I am going to play catch with my boy, because it may be the last time. He always wants to play catch, and I love playing catch. But there are some days where there is a bunch of stuff going on, and he wants to play catch and I'm thinking, "I have too much to do." But I must always remember, "Neal, you only have so long. Play catch with the boy today."

There will be a time that will be the last time you and your wife will have a chance to kneel by your bed together to pray. How many men ever do that with their wives? Most Christian men never do it. But God intended that we be intimate with our spouses, not just physically, but also spiritually. The oneness of praying together binds your souls and spirits, and you become deeper and more intimate than imaginable. Pray with your wife today.

There will be a day when you'll have your last chance to share Jesus Christ with another person. We're surrounded by people who are lonely, wounded and hopeless. They're asking, "What is the meaning of life? I've got everything as far as money and possessions, but my life is empty." Make this one day count. We only have so long. Tell someone about Jesus today.

If you've ever been surfing, you know what it's like to sit on your board in the ocean, looking for the wave you are going to catch. You see it forming, and you say to yourself, "This is the one." As it nears, you can feel it building around you and the undertow pulling you. You watch it curve and you get up and hit it just right and ride it all the way to the beach. It's incredible. It's dynamic. It's a rush. But if you miss the wave, nothing happens. You just sit there. Today is my wave of opportunity, and I don't want to waste a day, an hour, a minute or a second. I want to make this day count. We only have so long. We can't waste it.

The second point is one that athletes already know: You are always being watched. When I played at Baylor, there were a lot of reasons for me to play well on Saturday afternoons. My family was up in the stands, the fans were there, and so were the sports writers. Every athlete knows that whatever he does on Saturday on the field is being captured by someone on tape in the press box. Whatever he does on Saturday will be seen again on Sunday, with commentary. So he knows that if he blows it or makes a great play, it's all being scrutinized.

The important point is simply that we are being watched.

In the recent Olympics, one estimate showed that about 2 billion people watched the track events. If you're a sprinter lining up, and you see the camera pointed your direction, you're thinking, "The world is going to watch me do this. I'm going to give it my best. I'm going to leave it all on the track and give it everything I have."

We have to recognize that what we do every day in life has a powerful effect on the people around us – we are literally shaping lives. I've got three kids who watch their daddy, and they are probably going to go the same route as their daddy did.

My dad, James Jeffrey (one of the founders of the Fellowship of Christian Athletes) was raised by his father, who was an alcoholic. His father was a good man, but he just drank too much. His dad's side of the family drank, and his mom did, too. All of them were alcoholics. They worked hard and were good people. When my grandfather would be gone on a drunk for days at a time, sometimes weeks, my grandmother never allowed the doors to be locked, just so her husband could have an easy time getting in the house when he came home.

One day my dad's father left on a drunk when my dad was in high school and never came home again. My dad never saw him after that. It was one of the deep hurts in his life. He always hoped and prayed that he'd get to see his dad one more time. He never did.

Experts say that my dad should have been an alcoholic, too. Everybody else was. I should have been raised in a home of an alcoholic. I could have been one just as easily. But when I was at Baylor, my dad met Jesus Christ and it changed his life forever. He started following Jesus, and everyone who was following my dad, ended up following who he was following. My brothers and their spouses all ended up going the same way, because my dad did.

How does a boy learn how to become God's man? He watches his dad be God's man. Where does a boy learn how to live life? He watches his dad live life. Where does a boy learn how to love a woman the way God wants a woman to be loved and treated, honored and respected? He watches his dad love his mother. Where does a boy learn how to love Jesus Christ? He watches his dad love Jesus Christ. Where does he learn how to love God's holy book, and memorize it and hide it in his heart? He watches his dad do that.

Every day matters. And every action matters.

We only have so long, so let's live today as if it's our last day.

Also, the tape is rolling, and someone is watching. Give today your best.

Carey Casey is one of the greatest expositors of the Christian faith that I have ever heard. Several years ago he came to San Diego for a conference and I asked him to speak to a group of Christian business and professional men. Many said it was one of the most powerful messages they had ever heard.

In 1990, Carey was asked to be the chaplain for the Olympics in Korea. He spent several weeks reaching out to the competitors, officials and volunteers. It was one of the highlights of his career.

Carey's experience with the Fellowship of Christian Athletes in Kansas City was so powerful that FCA asked him to be president of the FCA Foundation, a position he still holds. Thank God for men like Carey, who have been so faithful to continue to break down the color walls. And as he says, "Let's just make a difference for the Kingdom of God, no matter what color we are. It's not the Fellowship of Colored Athletes, but the Fellowship of Christian Athletes! Let's just make a difference for the Kingdom of God, no matter what color we are."

The Three R's of Our Calling

Carey Casey

I REMEMBER A NIGHT WHEN MY DAD WAS called a nigger. It was a very scary night when my brothers and sisters and I were in the family car, and my dad ran out of gas. He had to walk about a mile to a gas station, and when he got there he saw several white men sitting on stools drinking beer.

"I need some gas," my dad said.

"Nigger, we're not going to give you any gas," said one of the men.

It was in situations like this where I saw my dad put his feet to his faith. His Christianity was not just in the Baptist church back home. His faith included his mind and his heart. He was able to negotiate with that man, without it becoming a physical confrontation, and we got gas that night. His response set me on my own course to act in a similar way.

My dad was smart about things like race. When I was a young athlete, he got me involved in the Fellowship of Christian Athletes. He told me it wasn't the Fellowship of Colored Athletes, but Christian Athletes. When other dads were telling their kids, "don't get on that bus, because it's white," my dad had the vision to have his children schooled cross culturally. He saw that it was all about relationships.

10

With FCA, you take a black kid from the inner city and make him roommates with a white kid from the suburbs. They start out the week thinking, "I'm rooming with a nigger," or "I'm rooming with a honky." But they compete together, they eat together, and they hear the Gospel of Jesus Christ together, and that message goes from their brains to the hearts, and the hearts get changed. Then they become new creatures, and the world around them begins to change.

Black, white or whatever color you are, God is asking you, "What are you going to do with what you have?" People around the world know what a great country this is. People are trying to move here from other countries by the millions. But if we don't do something about the problems in this country, where people are truly hurting, we're going to be in trouble. Other kingdoms have fallen, and America is not exempt. We are to be stewards of this country and the world. How is Christ calling us to do that?

I believe he calls us through three Rs. The first R is Relocation. That means, on the one hand, that we are to be in relationships with people other than those who are just like us. For me, I felt that the call to Relocate was literal. I moved from the suburbs into the inner city because I think God wanted me entering into relationships with the world around me. If you look around to our inner cities, you will see that a cancer is spreading. There is a cancer where our young people live – where I live. And when you have cancer, you have to do surgery. You can't put Band-Aids on wounds that require surgery. Eventually that cancer will spread. Our children and grandchildren will not survive in society if it keeps going the way it is going. The bottom line is that we cannot be in this life for ourselves only. We have to enter into relationships into parts of society that make us uncomfortable. This is not a problem that can be solved by throwing money at it. The surgery that is needed is invasive surgery, where we physically move to the area that needs us most.

Where I live, there are drug dealers on the street corners. They think they can make it in this world by selling drugs. When I walk outside my house, everyone asks me for money. It's a neighborhood where conflicts are resolved with gunshots. But I moved from the suburbs to the inner city because I believe that we have to be there with people, and that people have to *see* a sermon, and not just *hear* one.

My daughter asked me one Sunday morning, as we were getting dressed for church, "Daddy, are you going to be a sermon today?" That has stuck with me. When I talk to men's groups I tell them to be strong, to run their businesses with integrity, to be smart, to stay on top of the trends. But what it really gets down to is that they must be sermons to their wives, children, and people they work with. I tell them that if they don't have their families, they don't have a ministry. The greatest blessing that children can see is when their fathers and mothers love each other, and love the Lord Jesus Christ. The relationship we must be in is with those close to us and those who are not like us at all.

When we moved to the inner city, the biggest drug house was right next door. I saw more drugs sold out of that house than at any Walgreen's store. Little kids would come out of that house and ask my wife what she had on her finger.

"It's my wedding ring," she said.

"You're married to him?" they asked.

"Yes, Pastor Casey is my husband."

They hadn't seen a married couple. They hadn't seen a family.

That drug house isn't there any more. Our church bought it and tore it down. Now we own two blocks of the street. We have gymnasiums. We have a medical clinic that sees 2,000 people a week. If you can't pay the medical fees, then you sweep the gym or pick up the paper around the neighborhood. No one loses their dignity. We have a development corporation, making it possible for people to lease a home, then purchase it.

The way things have gone through government programs is completely backwards. You don't get anywhere if people are waiting around for someone to give them something without working for it. The work ethic doesn't have a color label on it. Some white people are lazy, as are some black people and some Hispanic people. What they need is to be taught from the Word about how to be a Christian, and how to work.

It isn't easy living in this neighborhood. We had bullets go through our front window. I was out of town, and talked to my wife on the phone. I was sure she was going to say, "This is enough – we're out of here." But she didn't. She was more committed than ever.

Some people feel that we are being dumb, living in this kind of environment, that we are putting our family in danger. Everyone is not called to do things exactly as we do. But as Dr. Martin Luther King said, "If you don't have something that you're willing to die for, you're not fit to live."

Jesus doesn't call us to be comfortable. He calls us to be *conformable* to His will and to himself. For many of us, that means we have to Relocate to where He can use us with the most impact. Some people who feel they want to become missionaries don't need to leave this country. They just need to move to the city.

The second R of our calling to live out the Gospel in this culture is Reconciliation. We are called to be reconciled with God and with each other. Do you have a friend who is another color than yours? Is there someone in your life from whom you can learn something about another culture? Do we hear their hearts and trust them and do they trust us? That's a kind of racial reconciliation that can change the world.

The third R is Redistribution. People need to get in their communities and make an economic difference. We have to bring in businesses to our community. There is not one place to buy a pair of shoes there. For years there was not one place to sit in a restaurant and have a nice meal. Then we went into business with a pizzeria. At first people said, "You can't do it – it's in the inner city. It will lose money. It will be broken into." But eventually the company agreed to take the chance. They connected their test store to our church, and hired our people.

There hasn't been one break in. No one has robbed it. It helps that we got guys from our prison rehabilitation program to work there washing dishes and busing tables. They'd been lifting weights in prison for years. Even a person with a machine gun would have second thoughts about taking them on!

All of us are blessed to live in this country. The things it will take to make it better don't cost a lot of money. I think it will take God getting in the minds and hearts of the churches, where the people in them will begin to say, "What can my church do? What can my family do? What can I do personally?" There is enough money in churches in America to do what needs to be done in our cities and to respond to what God is calling us to do. If we lived according to the three Rs of what God calls us to: Relocation, Reconciliation and Redistribution, that would mean we were using our resources the way God wants us to use them, and the government would be coming to us and asking for a loan.

I mentioned that I remember when my dad was called a nigger, and how his response to it affected me. Not too long ago I was driving down the street and a car pulled up behind me, with its lights blinking and horn blowing, as if to say, "Get out of my way." There was plenty of room for the driver to go around me – there were open lanes in both directions. Eventually he pulled alongside me and used some sign language in my direction. The driver was white, and he was not suggesting that he loved me. I saw his lips moving, and they were not saying, "God bless you – I look forward to seeing you in church Sunday."

His car pulled in front of mine and he rolled down his window. Then he spit out that window so that it hit my car. Suddenly I felt the same way I did when I played football at the University of North Carolina. My foot went down on the accelerator. Everywhere his car went, I followed him. We went through school zones speeding, because he was trying to get away and I wouldn't let him. Then he pulled into a gas station and I pulled in next to him. His wife jumped out and ran into the station to call the police, while I got out of my car and banged on his window, saying, "Sir? Sir?" I could see him inside his car shaking.

Here was this big black guy standing outside his car, banging on his window.

Finally, he got out of his car, still shaking.

I didn't want to say it, but the first words out of my mouth were, "God bless you and I love you!"

I know for a fact that Jesus can change a person's heart. Your worst enemy can become your friend. Satan comes to steal, kill and destroy. But Jesus comes so that we might have life and have it more abundantly. The abundant life, I believe, is the life that acts like Jesus, crossing boundaries and barriers, and living the sermon that He preached wherever we go.

At the Estes Park, Colorado summer conference for the Fellowship of Christian Athletes, I had just checked into my cabin when a tall, thin redhead came up to me and asked if I knew where he might find Dwight Johnson, his assigned roommate for the week. We spent the rest of that conference together and had a wonderful week.

We kept in touch through his successful career as a football coach for the University of Nebraska under the leadership of Bob Devaney, one of the greatest coaches in history. Tom eventually became head coach, and everyone could see that one of the most significant aspects of Tom's personality was his character. It was evident on and off the field.

In 1972 Tom and I were both elected to the National Board of the Fellowship of Christian Athletes, which meant I got to see him every year. He struck me as a clear thinker and he made a significant contribution to the board. His character and reputation for having the courage of his convictions was evident as he spoke from his heart on serious and controversial issues.

After his career as a successful football coach, Tom was elected to the House of Representatives from Nebraska, as a way to give back to the state that had given him so much for so many years. After several terms in Congress, he has been asked by Nebraskans to run for governor. Most people would consider retiring at this point in their lives. Not Tom. He's ready for a third career! He and Nancy are continuing to carry on for Jesus.

Living Life For Others

Tom Osborne

ONE OF THE MORE DIFFICULT THINGS ABOUT coaching is calling the right plays at the right time. It was the hardest part of the game for me. I remember our team playing in the Liberty Bowl in Memphis many years ago, and we weren't doing very well. We were trailing 17-14 with two minutes left in the game. North Carolina had the football, and it looked pretty desperate for us.

But they fumbled, and we fell on the ball. We had to go about 70 yards to win the game. The quarterback came over to me on the sidelines and said, "Coach, what do you want to do?"

I said, "I don't know. I can't think of anything. We've tried everything tonight. What do you want to do?"

He said he couldn't think of anything either.

Our trainer was standing there and he heard this conversation. It began to worry him. He thought maybe we weren't going to do anything at all. Finally, he spoke up and said, "Why don't you run play number eight to the right, and number seven to the left?" I didn't even know he knew anything about our plays. "That sounds good to me," I said to the quarterback. "Run an eight right and a seven left."

So the quarterback went out there and ran an eight to the

right and we went 12 yards. He called a seven left and we went 10. Eight to the right, another good gain. Seven left, more yards. We were going right down the field, eight, nine, ten, twelve yards a crack. It was better than we had done all night.

Then we had a first down at the five yard line, with time running out. The other team started seeing the pattern. We ran eight to the right again, and the defensive end broke through the line and we lost two yards. Seven to the left, and that defensive end broke through and we lost another two. We go eight to the right again and lose a yard. Now it's fourth down and 10 at the 10 yard line. Our quarterback began to realize that the eight and seven plays were no longer working. So he looked to me at the sideline. Those who have been in coaching know what I did next. I looked up in the stands and pretended not to see him. Eventually he realized he was going to have to do something, so he pulled the boys into a huddle and called a play. I began to watch again, because I was interested in what was going to happen.

I could have sworn that he handed the ball off to our tailback, who went to the line of scrimmage and about eight guys from North Carolina piled on top of him. But then I saw that the quarterback had made the greatest fake I've ever seen. He had hidden the ball on his hip. He raised up and hit our wide receiver, who was standing all alone in the end zone. We won on the last play of the game. Everyone was excited, and again, anyone who has been in coaching knows what I did next: I took full credit for the victory!

But later on in the locker room, after the media and everyone else had left, I saw our quarterback still in front of his locker. I went over to him.

"That was the greatest call I've ever seen," I said. "How in the world did you come up with that play at that time?" There was a play in our play book that very few people knew about, and after about the middle of the season we hadn't even practiced it because it hadn't worked very well. In fact, I had forgotten all about it.

"Well coach," he said, "it really wasn't that hard. We had run eight to the right and seven to the left."

"Yes," I said.

"Then it seemed like it wasn't working very good," he said.

"Yes, I noticed that, too."

"Well, I didn't know what to do, so on fourth down I got in the huddle and added eight and seven together and I came up with 14, so that's the play I called," he said.

"Now wait a minute," I said. "Eight and seven isn't 14. It's 15."

"Coach, if I was as smart as you, we would have lost the game tonight," he said.

That gives you an idea of my play calling in my early years!

We had some good football teams at Nebraska, and as you can see, there are certain things a coach can't take credit for. But something I have emphasized throughout my career is the character of my players. Character is in short supply in our country, in my opinion, and it's something that we all need to think about.

The famous publisher Horace Greeley said, "Fame is a vapor. Popularity is an accident. Money takes wings. Those who cheer you today will curse you tomorrow." I know all about that. The only thing that endures is character. At the end of the road, when everything is over in your life, it's not going to be very critical how many games you won, what kind of an athlete or coach you were, how much money you made, or what kind of jobs you've had. The most important thing will be your character.

In my years as a coach, I tried to instill four elements about character in my players.

The first thing I wanted the players to understand was the importance of discipline. I'm not talking about the kind of discipline where parents would take away the car keys, or spank their children. I'm talking about the discipline that has to do with the work ethic. Bobby Knight, the basketball coach, has a great definition of discipline. I can't say that I agree with everything Bobby does, but I like his definition. He said, "Discipline is doing what needs to be done when it needs to be done as well as it can be done, and doing it the same way every time." Bobby is a drill guy. In basketball he has his players doing certain drills in passing, shooting, dribbling, and repeats them over and over until they become automatic. That's what I do in coaching, too. We repeat, repeat, repeat, and do it right each time so that when the heat's on, and the game is on the line, the team will perform correctly.

After each fall season, we have winter conditioning, spring football and summer conditioning. Before the season starts, it is 75 percent determined, based on how well we stuck to the discipline of those off-season workouts. We don't make a lot of changes after the season begins, so that work ethic and discipline is critical.

The same is true academically. The way the requirements have become more stringent, it is no longer possible for a student to just coast along for years and step it up for his senior year. If players aren't on track by ninth grade now, we have to tell them that they simply aren't going to make the requirements by their senior year. So that work ethic and discipline is important on the academic and athletic side.

But discipline is also crucial in our spiritual lives. Without it, a good spiritual experience will last about four days, and then will become only a pleasant memory. Several years ago I visited the country of Haiti. The most meaningful thing I did was visit one of Mother Teresa's homes for children that her Sisters of Charity had opened. The children were two years old or younger, and about 90 percent of them were going to die because of their critical illnesses. Most of them had AIDS or drug addictions because of the condition of their mothers when they were born. I talked with one of the Sisters of Charity – a young lady perhaps 30 years old. She had worked nine years as an apprentice, and had just taken her vows.

"We work seven days a week, and we know that most of these children will die," she said. "We lost 38 of them last month. We get to go home once every 10 years."

"How do you do that?" I asked. "I know what it's like to lose, but how do you lose seven days a week, 14 hours a day, and go home every 10 years? How do you endure that?"

"Well," she said, "we get one hour a day of personal devotion. That one hour of prayer and meditation and worship is what rejuvenates us. That's what causes us to hang in there."

That suggests to me that if you're in a good place spiritually right now, it's because your discipline has carried you through. Discipline is what makes a good football and basketball team. The work ethic is crucial. One of the reasons for our success in Nebraska over the years is that, at times, we will outwork everybody.

If you want to bench press 300 pounds, you can't go to the weight room just on Easter and Christmas and do it. But that's what we try to do spiritually. It has to be steady. Daily.

Paul said in Corinthians, "Those who compete in the games go into strict training. They do it to win a crown that will perish. We do it to win a crown that will last forever."

Paul knew that the Greeks set themselves aside to prepare for the Greek games. They went to a training camp. They didn't see their families for nine months. They worked unbelievable hours to win a wreath of olive branches that, within two days, would turn brown.

Paul knew that if people worked that hard for a wreath that would last two days, it would take work to gain a wreath that would last forever. In II Timothy he said, "For God does not give us the spirit of timidity, but the spirit of power and of love and of self-discipline." I told this to our players just before a bowl game. In my opinion, the self discipline comes before the spirit of power and the spirit of love. If you discipline yourself, if you pay the price spiritually, you'll begin to experience those fruits of the spirit that will result in power, will result in strength, and will result in your ability to love other people.

The second thing that I think is important about character is perseverance. This is in short supply in our society. We live in a culture of the quick fix. One of the most difficult things I had to do with our players was deal with their desire for instant gratification. Or if it wasn't instant, they wanted it within a week! They wanted to be stars after eight or nine days of practice. That's just not the way life is. Nothing is that easy. Thomas Buxton said, "With ordinary talent and extraordinary perseverance, all things are possible." I'd qualify that and say, *almost* all things are possible.

Each year I would meet with a group of about 30 young men who were at the University of Nebraska for the first time. I would say something like this to them: "Fellows, look around the room, because in two or three years, only about 75 percent of you will still be here. The things that will determine who's still here and who isn't won't be the ones you think they'll be. It's not going to be height and weight. It's not going to be how many scholarships you had, or how great a player you were in high school. Those factors won't be critical at all.

"The single most important factor that will determine who is still here and who isn't will be the level of perseverance one player has over another. It will be the player who has a bad practice and gets demoted from the second team to the third team and comes back with more determination. It will be the guy who has an injury and rehabilitates. It will be the guy who has a bad season and rededicates himself in the off season. It will be the guy who hangs in there and has staying power."

I think the same is true in a person's spiritual life. It's easy to live at a high spiritual level when you're at a retreat with great scenery and great speakers and great music. But that's only one week out of the rest of your life. Paul said that five times he had 39 lashes. Thirty-nine lashes was often a fatal punishment. It often left your ribs and spine exposed. Three times he was beaten with rods. Three times he was shipwrecked. He spent a day and a night in the open ocean. He had gone without food. He was stoned and left for dead. And remember what he did each time? He went out to the corner and started preaching again. He had great courage. And perseverance.

I have noticed that the differentiating factor between people who are successful and people who are not, is how they react to failure. Every person is going to experience discouragement, disappointment and failure, but the successful people will look at failure as a temporary setback. They will look at it as a learning experience and say, "I'm going to get better because of this situation."

In the book of James it says, "Consider it pure joy, my brothers, whenever you face trials of any kind because you know that the testing of your faith develops perseverance." How many of us actually do that – consider something pure joy when a bad thing happens to us? I saw it in a young player that we had recruited from Texas. He was a really good player, and almost a fanatic in the weight room. He couldn't wait to get to the University of Nebraska to play football. He told me he had his bags packed two

127

months before it was time to report. He came to town within days after his high school graduation. I had never seen a player so fired up about playing, three months before the season. I knew how much he was counting on this. The first day he was here he was practicing on his own, and popped his ACL – a huge injury.

And I couldn't believe what he said to me.

"You know, Coach, this will probably make me strong because this kind of adversity, in the long run, will make me better," he said.

That guy had the right attitude.

The third thing I think is important about character is how important it is to be a team player. This became a more difficult concept for players during my later years of coaching, because our culture increasingly teaches us to ask "What's in it for me?" and to look out for number one.

There were essentially two kinds of players who started coming into our football program. One group that we recruited would say right away, "Well, I'm glad to see you coach, but I wonder if I might make the traveling squad as a freshman?" The next time I saw players like this they were asking if they might be All American as freshmen. Pretty soon we got around to talking about the Heisman Trophy. This would make me uneasy, because it was clear what was happening. These were players who wanted me to build the program around them. It doesn't work very well that way. You can't build a program around 20 different freshmen players. So I would get worried when all I heard was, "What's in it for me? What am I going to get out of this?" Yet, that is the message I think we receive from the culture over and over again.

The second kind of player was the kind that was important to me. This was the player who operated out of the question, "What can I contribute? What can I do to become a better player? What can I do to make this team a better team?"

One year we had a receiver from California, and we were in the middle of two-a-day practices, workouts that lasted about 14 hours a day. I was very tired one night at about 10 o'clock, and I heard voices down the hall in the locker room. I thought everyone had gone home. I went into the locker room and there was this receiver, standing at the blackboard. He had all 10 of our freshmen receivers there, going over the pass patterns with them. These were the players who were trying to take his job away from him. He was tired and he knew the stuff cold. He could have gone home an hour earlier. But he was a guy who was interested in what he could contribute. There were so many players in our program like that.

There is a spiritual parallel to this. In I Thessalonians, Paul says, "Therefore, encourage one another and build each other up just as in fact you're doing."

Are people around you encouragers? Are you an encourager? How many of us build others up instead of tearing them down? Our society can be so negative. People are cut down by the news media. They're cut down by their peer groups. They're cut down by their coaches. But Jesus says in Matthew, "Whoever wants to be great among you must be your servant." Can you imagine a TV commercial saying, "Don't look out for number one. Be a servant."

But Jesus lived his life for others, as a servant. Mother Teresa said, "Unless a life is lived for others, it's not worth living." I believe that.

The final point about character is that it is important for each person to have a sense of balance in his or her life where body, mind and spirit are all given equal treatment. As a coach I saw so many people who were only one-dimensional. And when only one dimension is emphasized, people set themselves up for failure.

A lot of my players thought the ultimate goal was to play for the National Football League. But in the NFL, according to the players' association, the average career of a player is 3.1 years. Fifty percent of the players leaving the NFL leave broke. The divorce rate of those who enter the league married is 80 percent coming out. What happens? These guys have the American dream. At age 22 they became instant millionaires. They had name recognition. They had celebrity, youth and talent. If you believe the television commercials, they had everything anyone could want. Yet so many of them come out the other end as broken people. Why?

The reason is that they were one-dimensional people. They knew how to tackle. They knew how to block. They knew where the weight room was. But they had no spiritual depth. I never felt good about a player of ours who left our program without a spiritual commitment. The messages that are out there constantly tell us: 1). Things will make us happy. If you have the right kind of car, the right kind of job, the right kind of clothes and shoes, you'll be happy and successful. That's a lie. 2). Promiscuity has no consequences. You can live a promiscuous lifestyle and nobody will get hurt. That's also a lie. You end up breaking yourself when you're engaged in this activity. It's a no-win deal. 3). Violence doesn't really hurt anybody. Once you've seen 30,000 people blown away on the screen and nothing much happens as a result, people get the idea that it really doesn't hurt anything. Another lie. It hurts us all, and it's destroying our country.

Jesus was interested in balance and in perspective. He said, "If any man would save his life, he will lose it." It sounds paradoxical. But he's saying that whatever occupies most of your attention, time, energy and thoughts is really number one in your life. When I was young, I tried to save my life with football – with being a good athlete. I was insecure and felt that if I was a good enough athlete, enough people would pat me on the back and then I could feel good about myself. That's how I was going to save my life.

But then I couldn't play any more. I went into coaching, and I tried to save my life through my won-loss record. You can't win enough games to please people. No matter how many wins, it's never quite enough. When I had heart surgery I started wondering if I had enough money in the bank – I wondered if I could save my life through my financial resources. Jesus never said that there was anything wrong with being a good athlete, or being a good coach, or wanting to win football games and make money. But he seemed to say that if we're counting on those things, if these things are number one in our lives, we're going to be disappointed.

That's why the other half of what Jesus said is so crucial: "If any man will lose his life for my sake, he will find it." All that means is that He must be first in our lives. On the one hand that's a very hard concept, but on the other, it's very clear. There's no middle ground. We can't have it both ways. When we're willing to give the talents we have and are willing to serve Him with those, and put Him number one in our lives, then life will take on a new dimension.

I have one goal, and that is to honor Christ. I remind myself of that, and I fail miserably at times. I wanted to honor Him in the way I recruited, in the way I stood on the sidelines, in the way I talked to players, in the way I dealt with my wife. Everyone can hold onto that goal in all areas of our lives – to honor Him when we are on a date, when we play in a game, when we have the opportunity to cheat.

When we lose our lives for His sake, I think three things happen to us. The first is that we are given the strength to serve others. Isaiah says, "Those who wait upon the Lord will renew their strength. They will mount up with wings like eagles. They will run and not grow weary, and they will walk and not faint." When we commit to serve Christ, we are given whatever strength we need to serve Him and others.

The second thing that happens is that our lives take on a purpose and sense of meaning that did not exist otherwise. If you can say at the end of your life, "I wouldn't do it any other way," then that's all you can ask. In the book of Hebrews we read, "Therefore, since we are surrounded by such a great crowd of witnesses, let us throw off everything that hinders and ascend what is reasonably attainable, and let us run with perseverance the race marked out for us. Let us fix our eyes upon Jesus, the author and perfecter of our faith, who for the joy set before Him endured the cross, ignoring his sin, and sat down at the right had of the throne of God." The writer says that life is like a race, so strip off everything that holds us back. It might be friends or habits, things we read or watch. But get rid of all the unnecessary things and run the race and keep our eyes fixed on Jesus. If we do that, our lives will have purpose and meaning.

Another thing that happens when we honor and serve God is that we are given a sense of stability. So many come from disrupted families or horrendous neighborhoods. School and the workplace can be scary. But the Gospel of John says "In the beginning was the Word, and the Word was with God and the Word was God." Jesus always was, is, and always will be. He will not change. So when we base our lives on what is solid and unchangeable, something that has always been and always will be, it doesn't mean you won't get hurt or won't lose a game, or that if your family has trouble you won't feel the pain. But you'll be supported by something very powerful and strong and stable and will not change. You'll be held by something you'll always be able to count on.

Stay in this race for the long haul. There are all kinds of

people who are motivated to play on Saturday afternoon. When the balloons go up, they'll do anything to get out there and play. But when it's January, you have to be lifting weights. And when it's hot in July, you have to practice. Not many people are willing to do that. So when you make your commitment, don't look back or even turn away. Pay the price and follow God.

Eighteen years ago I helped organize a conference for businessmen and their wives in San Diego. Kevin Jenkins and his wife Helen attended. He was the president and chief executive officer of AirCanada, one of the largest airline companies in the world, and he was the youngest president of any airline company in the world.

I found him to be not only bright and engaging, but also very sincere and humble. What a blessing to meet a young man, then 35, who has accomplished so much and has his priorities so correct. As he shared his testimony, it was very apparent that his love for God was the most important priority, closely followed by the love for his wife and family, with love for his job coming in a distant third.

I had the privilege of being in several small group discussions with him and was impressed by his ability to think outside the box and get to the heart of the issue we were discussing. I have never seen anyone do a better job of keeping the discussion on target and yet get everyone in the group to contribute. It's a real gift of his, and that's what leadership is all about. He has the ability to balance his career and faith.

Kevin wants to make a difference in the Kingdom of God and do it through his professional relationships in his community. Observing and getting to know Kevin in these different arenas of life has been a privilege for all of us who have had the opportunity to watch him in action. Because Kevin is so transparent, he tells it as it is, and what you see is a lot.

More Than One Journey

Kevin Jenkins

I BELIEVE THAT EACH OF US IS ON AT LEAST three journeys in our lives – a physical journey, an intellectual journey, and a spiritual journey. And my favorite line on what direction we are headed in these journeys is from Lewis Carroll's *Alice in Wonderland*, where the Cheshire Cat says to Alice, "Any road will get you there if you don't know where you're going."

On all three of these journeys, it's important to know where we're going.

The most tangible of the journeys is the physical one. It is marked by periods of good health and bad. In all cases, the physical journey takes us to the same destination regardless of the road we take. All physical journeys end in death.

The intellectual journey is also pretty tangible, and it has a high profile in society. There are recognized benchmarks for this journey, including university degrees, success in endeavors, and ability to express one's self clearly.

But the spiritual journey is different from the other journeys. Unlike the physical journey, which in many cases is beyond our control, the spiritual journey involves a great deal of choice. Whether we are aware of it or not, every one of us is on a spiritual journey. It may be on hold, or it may be progressing at a snail's pace, or it may be in a period of

12

acceleration, but the journey is underway. This journey is a search for purpose, for meaning, for fulfillment, for peace. It may take the form of asking, "Is there a God?" "Who was Jesus Christ?" "Why did He come?" "Does my life have significance?" "Is there life after death?" "Is this all there is?"

Some of us chose to stop exploring spiritual things when we were old enough to pressure our parents into no longer taking us to Sunday School. There are a lot of people with university degrees, which mark our progress on the intellectual journey, but have third-grade educations when it comes to their spiritual journeys. If our spiritual journeys were abandoned while we were children, and our physical and intellectual journeys continued into adulthood, then it is no surprise that God plays such an insignificant role in society today.

Why do we pay so much attention to our physical journey, which includes accumulating material possessions, and to our intellectual journey, and so little attention to our spiritual journey? It can't be from lack of need.

A famous cartoonist in the United States left this note pinned to his pillow before taking his life: "I have had few difficulties, many friends, great successes. I have gone from wife to wife and from house to house, visited great countries of the world, but I am fed up with inventing devices to fill up 24 hours a day." Each of us feels empty from time to time. Pascal, the French philosopher, said that there is a God-shaped vacuum in the heart of every man and woman which can only be filled by God through Jesus Christ.

In my favorite play, *Les Miserables*, there is a touching scene where the main character, Jean Valjean, has just been given a new life by the Bishop from whom he had stolen. Valjean is overwhelmed by the forgiveness the Bishop has shown him – no one had shown him that kind of kindness before. In expressing his gratitude he says, "He told me I had a soul. How does he know?"

Have you ever wondered about that? Why don't we spend more time on questions like that? In part, because we think we're too busy. Most of us are too busy "living" that we don't take the time to seek a peaceful moment when we can find a special place from which to view our own lives. Ken Blanchard and Norman Vincent Peale, who wrote *The Power of Ethical Management*, said that our inner self takes longer to wake up in the morning than our outer self. Many people would be surprised to discover that they have an inner self in the first place!

A lot of people leap out of bed and they are off and running. They're into their morning routine – turn on the radio or TV, brush their teeth, get the coffee going, shower, look for clean clothes, go to the office, and so on. All of this is getting the outer self awake while our inner self is still on snooze. Many of you have heard the poem, "This is the age of the half-read page, and the quick hash and the mad dash, the bright night with the nerves tight, the plane hop with the brief stop, the lapped hand in a brief stand, the big shot in a good spot, and the brain strain and the heart pain and the cat naps til the spring snaps and the fun's done."

Like many others, I had a life like that. I am president of a company that serves five continents. I took care of two of my journeys, but not the third one.

I was brought up in a mainline church. But, like many, as soon as I was old enough to pursue other things as a teenager, I lost interest. I pursued my purpose and fulfillment through applying a personal philosophy to life, which was to excel at my work and have a disciplined life of physical fitness. The books I read for my intellectual journey included *Looking Out for Number One*, and *Winning Through Intimidation*. It was good reading, and they had interesting ideals, but ideals are abstractions, and it is difficult to maintain a passion for an abstraction.

Neither God nor Jesus played a role in my life during

this period. I respected Christ, but hadn't considered him or his claim seriously since I was a child. Furthermore, my childish concept of God had no relevance to my adult mind. I was still stuck on the saying, "Gentle Jesus meek and mild, look upon a little child." The Jesus of that ditty was too placid for the passions of red-blooded humanity. He was uninspired and uninspiring. I outgrew that Jesus and needed to find my heroes elsewhere.

As a lawyer in the 1980s, I got a call from a man who wanted me to help him incorporate an oil company in Texas. He paid me a lot of money per hour, and one day he asked me if I ever thought about spiritual things. He told me that his faith in Jesus Christ changed his life. I listened politely, which was easy to do since he was paying me a lot per hour! Then he gave me a book called *Born Again*, by Chuck Colson, who had been special counsel to President Richard Nixon.

Two things stuck in my mind about that book. One was that Colson said that, after he left the camaraderie of the university, he had never found close, open relationships with other men. Every time he met a friend or acquaintance or neighbor there was a jostling for position, he said. "How big are the deals you're making? Where are you flying to? Are you an officer or just a middle manager?" they asked each other. Everyone was trying to peg themselves and see where they fit in the hierarchy. There was always an underlying tone of competition.

It was very hard for them to let down the masks everyone wears and say, "I have weaknesses, too." Colson found intimacy for the first time in a Bible study with three other men, where the purpose was to understand what the Bible said. It was in that group that he felt comfortable and loved. When I read that, I understood exactly what he meant about the competitive nature of guys when they are around each other.

The second thing that got my attention in the book was he wrote that he pursued fulfillment primarily through his job. He was a very successful man. Special Counsel to the president of the United States is the highest position you can have as a lawyer. But he discovered that he could not satisfy his deep longings through his job. Every time he reached a new rung on the ladder of success he would say, "Well, now that I'm partner in the law firm, I can have all these associates do the work, so I can have more time and just make policy decisions. That will be more fulfilling."

But then he wanted to start his own law firm. Then he wanted to be special counsel. He found that, as he blasted through his career, he was always stuck with one fact: That Chuck Colson always had an ambition for more. As you and I blast through our careers, we have the same fact to confront. Even though there is a significant amount of fulfillment available in one's job, it will never satisfy as the primary source of fulfillment. Colson said that the first time he found the fulfillment he was seeking was when he committed his life to Christ.

In his book *The Screwtape Letters*, C.S. Lewis addresses the same topic as Colson when he writes, "Prosperity knits a man to the world. He feels that he is finding his place in it while really it is finding its place in him. His increasing reputation, his widening circle of acquaintances, his sense of importance, built up in him a sense of being really home on earth. You will notice that the young are generally less willing to die than the middle aged and the old. Often a search for fulfillment, primarily through visible success, is an attempt to gain self worth and acceptance." The pressure never ends.

Colson realized that the pressure came off when he entered into a personal relationship with God. He loves us. We don't have to prove anything to Him.

This was a great revelation to me. But there was only one

problem. Chuck Colson wrote this book from jail. I couldn't relate to being in jail. So I continued my search at a Bible study, which met once a week at noon. Studying the Bible cleared up a number of issues that I had on my mind. The first was what I call, "Good News, Bad News." The good news was that the Bible offered purpose and fulfillment that I had been seeking earlier in my teens. When I read Jesus' words in John 10:10, "I come that they might have life and have it more abundantly," I was very attracted to having an abundant life. But then came the bad news. In order to get this life, I had to submit my life to Jesus.

That contradicted everything I believed. I had built a philosophy on getting control of my own life, at excelling at physical things, at excelling in business and law. And now I come to a belief system that says, "If you want this fulfillment that you are seeking, you need to submit your life, not take control of your own life." It was totally upside down.

I also had a problem with the language I found in the Bible. It said that believing in Christ meant I would be forgiven of my sins. I hadn't murdered anybody. I didn't feel a burning need for forgiveness. But then I learned that the word "sin" is an archery term in Greek that means "missing the mark." In Biblical terms it meant missing the mark that God had set for us. The fact that I had been indifferent to God, that He played no role in my life, qualified me as a sinner. For that I needed forgiveness.

Studying the Bible also taught me that Christianity is much more than a philosophy or a code for leading a good life. It is completely centered on the life and teaching of one man, Jesus Christ. In many ways, Jesus was like a street person. He had no home, and no net worth. Yet he changed lives, more than any other man in history. I continued to read the Bible, not to learn about a religion, but to learn about Jesus. Throughout the New Testament, Christ claims that He is God – not a prophet or a good moral teacher. No other man of credibility has made that claim. If in fact he was God on earth, I had to deal with it.

I also learned that the Bible is the Word of God, and that no one denomination has exclusive rights to it. No one can put God in a box. And the word "mild" that I associated with Jesus? That did not accurately characterize him. J.B. Phillips, in his book *Your God Is Too Small*, said, "This word 'mild' is apparently deliberately used to describe a man who did not hesitate to challenge and expose the hypocrisies of the religious people of his day. A man who had such personality that he walked unscathed through a murderous crowd. A man so far from being non-entity that he was regarded by the authorities as a public danger. A man of such courage that he deliberately walked to what he knew would mean death despite the earnest pleas of well-meaning friends. Mild. What a word to use for a personality whose challenge and strange attractiveness nineteen centuries have by no means exhausted."

In the midst of my searching, Chuck Colson happened to be speaking at an event in my city. I wanted to go, and suggested it to my wife. "Are you kidding?" she said. "That's a Christian gathering. I've heard about those Christian gatherings." She came with me anyway, and I was impressed with what Colson had to say. It had been several years since Watergate, and it was clear that Colson had a sustained, deep-rooted faith. His conversion was not a foxhole conversion or a flash in the pan. His conversion had clearly changed the course of his life and the purpose of his life. Listening to him excited me.

On the way home I said, "This is going to change our lives."

"That is exactly what I am concerned about," my wife said. "I don't want to be dishing out porridge in Africa. I don't know where you're headed."

Isn't the spiritual journey an interesting one?

Two months later we were at a dinner and the speaker explained that we were all sinners and were separated from God's love and plan. He explained that we could accept Jesus Christ as our Lord and Savior that night.

On the way home, I asked my wife what she thought of the evening. To my great surprise, she said that she had committed her life to Christ. *I* hadn't even done that!

"How did you come to that conclusion?" I asked. "How did you get all the way from not wanting to dish porridge in Africa to making a commitment?"

"It's like when I married you," she said. "I don't know everything about Christianity. I don't know everything about Jesus Christ. But I know enough. I didn't know everything about you when I married you, either. I know enough things now to know that He is a dependable object of my trust and faith, and that I can commit myself to Him going forward as I lean more about Him."

It dawned on me that we exercise faith in a lot of areas of our lives. I regularly closed business deals by using a fax machine. One party was in London, another in Calgary or Vancouver. I sign in Canada and someone else signs in England. On the basis of that, airplanes and money go all over the world. That is faith. I don't know why his piece of paper ends up in Vancouver, and my piece of paper ends up in London. So as I thought about my wife's analogy to marriage, and I thought of the number of areas of our lives where we aren't able to logically explain every step, what I considered to be a leap of faith turned into more of a step of faith. I, too, submitted my life.

Unlike my own efforts at finding fulfillment, the Christian life provided a peace and purpose beyond my understanding. I won't mislead you and say it has been without trials, but through it all I have had the energy to press on.

My temperament today is more of a thermostat and less

of a thermometer. A temperament that is like a thermometer is dependent on how stressful things are, on the heat of the moment. It goes up and down with outside circumstances. A thermostat is set and stays there regardless of what is going on outside.

My relationship with Christ changed my outlook on relationships, especially my marriage. The Bible says a lot about marriage, and can be summarized this way: Approach every issue by putting your spouse's best interests and preferences ahead of your own. Can you imagine a marriage where both partners are putting the other's self interest ahead of their own? It's almost unfathomable. And without Christ, it is impossible. The intimacy is great when you attempt to submit your self interest to that of your spouse's.

Christ also gave me a new perspective on my life, my family and my work. He gave me an eternal perspective. It's tough to have an eternal perspective living in North America today. We can get instant cash, instant hamburgers, instant everything. To think a week ahead is almost impossible, let along thinking ahead to eternity. But perspective is very important. An educator gave this illustration about perspective: During the Middle Ages, a dispatcher went out to see how laborers felt about their work. He went to a building site in France. He approached the first worker and asked, "What are you doing?"

"Are you blind?" the worker replied. "I am cutting these impossible boulders with primitive tools and putting them together the way the boss tells me. I'm sweating under this blazing sun. It's back-breaking work, and it's boring me to death."

The dispatcher approached a second worker and asked the same question: "What are you doing?"

"I'm shaping these boulders into usable forms which are then assembled according to the architect's plans. It's hard work, and sometimes it gets repetitive, but I earn five francs a week and that supports my wife and kids. It's a job. It could be worse."

Somewhat encouraged, the dispatcher went to a third worker. "What are you doing?" he asked.

"Can't you see?" the worker replied. "I'm building a cathedral."

Now *that's* the right perspective!

Thirty-five years ago, one of my tennis partners, Harold Williamson, introduced me to his office roommate, Art Shingler. I found Art to be a very engaging person with a tremendous propensity to be involved with many people in all walks of life. His wife, Ginger, is a very outgoing lady with tons of energy and enthusiasm for life. She helped Guy Boyer and I host the Billy Graham movie, *Time To Run*.

That was a great opportunity for me to get to know Art and watch him interact with his life partner. I was impressed then and have continued to stay impressed with Art's commitment to his family and friends.

In spite of an impressive time in the savings and loan industry, Art was extremely happy and grateful for his time as chief financial officer of Point Loma Nazarene University. I would meet Art for lunch on the campus and as we walked to the cafeteria and back, Art greeted students by name and told me how thankful he was to be there. His background in accounting and finance made it possible for him to do things for and with the school that were simply amazing.

Art calls problems "opportunities," never complains about them. His positive mental attitude and his faith were so strong that time and again Art would handle the ups and downs in great stride. It is a pleasure to know someone who, no matter what the circumstances, or the insurmountable odds, gets through them with a smile and a grateful heart for the experience. Art and Ginger have retired to Boise, Idaho.

In Whose Hands Would We Rather Be?

Art Shingler

I DO NOT HAVE A "TURNAROUND" STORY. I was not headed down a path that was about to end in jail or death or other trauma where only at that point I found that I needed God. What I have learned, through some dire circumstances involving my career and my family, is that the following statement is true: "We cannot judge God's goodness or His activity in our lives by our circumstances." When a lot is happening, good or bad, God is at work. Conversely, as my friend Reuben Welch often says, "When nothing is happening, something is happening." All the time, in good circumstances or bad, or even in the midst of neutral circumstances, He will finish what He has started in us.

Remember the old television commercial where the frustrated girl says, "Mother, please! I'd rather do it myself"? I don't remember what product was being advertised, but I do know that it is a statement of our nature when it comes to trusting God. It seems unnatural to put our trust in anything other than ourselves.

We tend to buld our security upon friends, family, power, prestige, intellect and influence – or at least I did. Then when circumstances come that strip all of those things away, what are we left with? We'd better have something else in our lives, or else we are adrift. The absence of something else is what drives people to jump out of skyscrapers when their empires fall.

As a young man, when my comfort levels were stripped away in my own life, I knew I had a choice – I could either have a breakdown, or I could trust God. I could trust that God was at work and could be trusted even when it seemed like only bad things were happening.

What I learned was that I had to distinguish whether I believed more in my circumstances, such as my past generations of Christian heritage, my education, my wife and family, my intelligence, friends and career, than I believed in the identity, integrity and personhood of God Himself. Was I believing in God, or was I believing in the good gifts I assumed He had been giving me? Did I truly love God or was I just attached to the benefits of loving God?

Unfortunately, it seems that we can only learn to distinguish these things the hard way.

During one particular downturn in my career when I was in my late 20s, a friend and I began discussing the heart of man. I told my friend that I had never turned my back on God, that I had tried to find His will for my life, that I went to church, that I prayed and kept as many commandments as I could, that I was basically a pretty good person. I did steal some comic books when I was in the fifth grade, but I thought that was pretty small change when it came to revealing the heart of man.

My friend quoted Jeremiah 17:9 to me, but I knew that the deceitful heart described in that verse applied to bad people – the real sinners – surely not to me.

The next day I was in church, about to take Communion, and I asked God to show me my heart. He did, for about 1.5 seconds. He just cracked open the door. It was the single worst experience of my life. My heart was a dark, ugly, awful, terrible, indescribable mess. It was an overwhelming evil. It didn't reveal past sins – there weren't that many!

What it revealed was a condition. And I remember it as vividly today as when it happened almost forty years ago. All of a sudden I was one of the "real sinners." I was just as guilty of nailing Jesus to the cross as any of the really "bad guys." This was a devastating experience. I couldn't even eat lunch after church.

But that evening, my agony turned into sweetness. It was as if God was saying, "Now that you understand you are a sinner, you can understand that my Gift of forgiveness is for you personally." That evening was the most intimate time I have ever had with God.

It became the foundation for enduring the circumstances that were to come.

I was the chief financial officer for a savings and loan institution in northern California during a time when our company went through astronomical growth. Our company acquired another very large savings and loan, and before long I was the president of the largest savings and loan corporation in the world. Our company was listed as one of the 50 best-run publicly traded companies in America.

But the savings and loan industry started experiencing great turbulence. Our company never did anything dishonest or that was contrary to state or federal regulations, but, like many S&Ls, we were investigated twice by the Securities and Exchange Commission.

During the first investigation they told us that they believed we had misstated our financial representations. In other words, they accused us of making misleading and fraudulent financial statements. We, along with our certified public accountants, believed that their understanding was incorrect, and set out to show them their misreading of our statements.

If we could not find an acceptable compromise with the SEC, a restatement of earnings would have probably resulted in crippling class action lawsuits and failure in our attempt to acquire the other S&L.

During the first investigation I flew to Washington, D.C. with our accountants several times to plead our position and defend the company. Toward the end, when it looked like we had come to an agreement, I worked around the clock from Monday through Thursday. I slept a total of five hours that entire week. Ultimately we reached a compromise with the SEC and there were no negative consequences.

This experience and what followed were the most intensely stressful times of my life. It seemed like the weight of the world was on my back, as I tried to deal with all the issues of the acquisition along with the SEC investigation.

After resolution of the first investigation, we completed the acquisition of the other savings and loan. I was in charge of putting the two companies' operations together. Our little S&L of about $1 billion in assets with 450 employees, where I had started, was now a $20-plus billion in assets company with approximately 5,500 employees.

Over the next year we grew to $33 billion in assets with more than 7,500 employees. Those with operational backgrounds can appreciate the stress such growth places on leadership. I was on the ragged edge of exhaustion most of the time. I knew that no financial institution had ever grown at a rate approaching ours without serious operational failures. The stress of handling these issues was greatly compounded when the SEC launched its second investigation.

The second one lasted several weeks. It centered on a narrow technical accounting issue regarding security transactions. At the conclusion of their investigation, they changed the accounting rules and informed me that if we did not retroactively apply their new rules, they would indict our senior management for fraud. This was the first and only time the SEC forced a company to restate earnings based upon retroactively applying new accounting rules. Also, no other S&L was required to restate their earnings this way. The unfairness of the SEC's dealing with us increased my level of stress to its absolute limit.

As a result of the forced restatement of earnings, our customers withdrew more than $6 billion in savings deposits. In addition, the regulators forced a change in senior management and we were sued personally in many class action lawsuits to the amount of $.5 billion. The market value of the company's stock plummeted, and the value of my personal stock account lost several million dollars.

As an insider I couldn't sell the stock I had in the company without triggering an SEC indictment. So I was broke, unemployed, and faced many lawsuits. My dear wife, Ginger, remained supportive, as did my family and friends. In the midst of all this trauma, I could not see how God was acting on my behalf. What was he trying to teach me? My faith was not challenged, but I sure had a lot of questions.

After leaving the S&L, it dawned on me that there is a subtlety to success that is somewhat addictive, but operates at a level where we are largely unaware. I noticed that I missed the perks that came with a powerful position. My influence was gone. I was no longer useful to other powerful people. Influential people in government and business stopped returning my phone calls. I realized that I had come to expect the prestige and authority that crept in along with my job.

Fortunately, I never confused my job status with my spiritual status. I learned that from my own father when I saw him go through some rough times. He never confused God and his own circumstances. I never got caught up in the faith and success stories. They didn't ring true then and they don't now. That's not to say things weren't stressful. They were.

About six months after losing my job, one of my sons was riding in a car to a school function and was hit by a drunk driver. The two girls my son was riding with were killed, and so was the man who hit them. My son was in a coma for days, critically injured. I knew God was not doing this to us. My faith wasn't that shallow. But emotionally it was devastating. He survived his serious brain damage and was healed. He and his wife and children are now going as missionaries to the Ukraine.

During this difficult financial and emotional time I worked in real estate development and investments, and got back on my feet. Then my good friend from college days, Jim Bond, called and asked me to be chief financial officer of Point Loma Nazarene University in San Diego, where he had just been elected president. Both of us are alums of the institution, when it was Pasadena College. The school prospered. All of my business experience and hard times in the S&L industry prepared me for my time at that university. It was the most fulfilling professional experience I had in my entire life. I had more satisfaction and joy in helping run an operation that educated young men and women to serve Christ in the world, than in all the places where I had power, prestige, authority and influence.

As I look back, I see the truth of the statement, "When nothing is happening, something is happening," even more clearly. Just because it looked like bad things were happening didn't mean God was not working. At each point when it appeared that I was at the end of a road, I would discover that God had been preparing a new road for me to follow, and I just hadn't seen it yet. But I kept trusting and it always opened.

During my time at Point Loma, about three years after the automobile accident, one of my other sons contracted a rare blood disease that was leading to certain liver failure. The doctors told my wife and me that he would probably die. I felt as if I had been cast out to sea. I couldn't think straight. Nothing made sense. I couldn't grasp onto anything solid. As members of the campus community gathered in the hospital room, I remember the prayer that Jim Bond prayed. We gathered in a circle, held hands, and Jim said, "In whose hands would we rather be than in the hands of a loving, heavenly Father?"

When he said that, my feet hit bedrock.

I still have many theological questions. Why did those girls die in that accident with my son? Why is it so hard to trust God when we are inclined to trust ourselves? Why do we tend to associate our circumstances with whether God loves us or not? Someday the blinders on our minds will be off. That's something to look forward to!

Both sons survived their traumas. But even when it looked like they would not, even when my security network failed, even when it looked like I was a business failure or would never be financially solvent, I knew at least this: God is good regardless of my circumstances! For my life, that's enough.

Forty-two years ago, Dave walked into our office and wanted the opportunity to tell us about the advantages of leasing equipment rather than buying outright. It was a fascinating discussion, and I was overwhelmed with his knowledge of the equipment leasing business. We did start leasing equipment from his company, which was the largest equipment leasing company in the world.

Three years later, we had the biggest catastrophe we had ever experienced. It was the Platte River flood of June 16, 1965. Forty-eight hours after the flood, Dave's boss flew in from Minneapolis and he and Dave came over to observe the damage, which was devastating. Dave's boss said, "You do anything and everything you can to help the Johnsons get back in business, whatever the cost."

From that day forward, Dave and I grew to not only be very close friends, but also business partners on several occasions. It doesn't make any difference how much a person knows until you know how much he cares, and that is the greatest attribute that has continued to make Dave Kerr the largest and most successful equipment leasing man in the United States. The banks that Dave has dealt with, the business friends and customers that Dave has had, the community and his family feel the same way about him.

He sponsored me into the Young Presidents Organization in 1970, and I sponsored him into Rotary. He continues to be a loving, caring husband and father of three boys, who are in business with him and his daughter. Dave and his wife of 60 years live in Denver as do all four of their children and nine grandchildren.

14 Trusting God at Every Stage of Life

David R. Kerr

"Hear my prayer, O Lord,
give ear to my supplications:
In thy faithfulness answer me,
and in thy righteousness...
Cause me to hear thy lovingkindness
in the morning;
For in thee do I trust:
Cause me to know the way
wherein I should walk;
for I lift up my soul to thee."
Psalm of David 143

I CAME TO FAITH IN JESUS AS A CHILD AND NEVER substantially rebelled or strayed too far from that belief. No matter when a person comes to the truth of Jesus Christ, His love and forgiveness pour out abundantly onto us, and we are changed forever. But what believing from my earliest days has meant for me is that from my youth I have been aware of His presence and have been able to turn to Him throughout my life, and have experienced His help and blessing at every turn.

I was raised in a strong Christian home. My grandfather, David R. Kerr was a Presbyterian Minister, and my mother and father were faithful churchgoers. I was baptized by my grandfather, Dr. Kerr, shortly after my birth in 1922, and have always felt over the years that the good Lord heard and honored the prayers of him, and my family for me. Many of my young memories are of church, Sunday school, our pastor, Vacation Bible School, and mission trips. I mention my family's faith here because this environment of Christian belief surrounded me as a child, and there was very little doubt to me in their words or behavior that it was true. The Christian faith was part and parcel of my family life and who I was as a young man growing up. I have never seriously doubted the truth of it.

It wasn't until World War II, however, that my faith became practical reality. In 1943, after slightly more than two years as an engineering major at The University of Denver with a military deferment, the War Department ended all draft deferments due to the large losses in Europe and the Pacific. I was then 1A in the draft, and decided to see if I could qualify for the Navy V5 program. It was for college men who would be cadets in the Navy flight Program. If a man qualified, the Navy would pay their college education until graduation, when the flight training started, and hoped he would be a Navy Pilot.

After four days of extensive tests in San Francisco, and a wait of a week, the Navy Department called and said I had passed. I was sworn in for an agreed 10 years in the U.S. Naval Reserves. I returned to D.U. as a Navy Cadet, very pleased with my choice. However, within a few months, the War Department told the Navy that if they didn't need the 50,000 highly qualified men they had in the colleges of America, they would immediately be classified 1A and drafted into the Army.

Within two weeks we all were called to active duty in the Navy. I was sent to the Naval Air Station at Livermore, California in the East Bay Area and given a sailor suit and "boot" camp by tough marines. I was assigned to work on airplanes, go to school half day to learn about the Navy and to be put through extremely tough physical training by marines and physical training instructors, all of whom were tough, if not diabolical. This is where the rubber meets the road, and my prayer life began in earnest.

Livermore was a primary flight Naval Air Station. They had some Stearman N2S planes, for training, and another primary trainer, a Timm, which had a wooden fuselage and wings. There were many fatal accidents with the Timm and all were eventually grounded and destroyed by the Navy. I was sent to some of the fatal crash sites and was face to face with grim reality as we picked up the wreckage. The gravity of the situation I was in became increasingly more real to me.

After three months we were assigned to the College of Wooster in Ohio. It was now, as my life was caught up in the extreme challenges of being a military man, that my faith in God went from a more simple belief into an actual realization of the power of God personally in my life.

It was late November and bitter cold in Ohio, south of Cleveland, not far from the Great Lakes. Mornings were spent in class after a 6:30 A.M. wake up and a 7 A.M. muster and march to the chow hall. The PT "jocks" (commanding officers) thought in order to make men out of us they should remove all hall doors and require all windows to be left open all night to the Ohio winter. The afternoons were spent after lunch with a swimming lesson after which we were given 3 ½ minutes to put on our sweat suits and stocking caps and report to the grinder track where we ran, jumped, crawled for a ¾ hour run. The stocking cap froze to my head. In a few days the College of Wooster's infirmary was full of cadets with severe colds and pneumonia. The local hospital was also full.

At this point I also was seriously ill, but they sent me back to my bunk in the freezing cold room. In desperation I went to the balcony of the small college chapel and said "God, you just have to help me. I am sick, sick and only you can cure me." By the next morning I felt much improved and was able to attend class where there were very few other cadets, and in fact was able to assist some others who were very sick. I knew that the Lord had healed me that night.

By February the three months Flight Preparation School was over at Wooster. I was in the upper 10% of the class, and so I was able to pick the University of Wyoming for my War Training School, which was where I did my first flying. Between snowstorms we flew Luscomb Silvairs at General Breese Field. We were told if you could fly these planes in the constant Wyoming wind you could probably fly anything. It was a challenge but great training. I was eventually made company commander over the entire cadet company in Laramie, and was able to graduate at the top of the class with a 4.0 in everything including flying, ground school and officer aptitude. I had never been a great student before, but I realized how high the stakes were here, and felt God's help all around me.

I next was sent to St. Mary's College at Moraga, California in the East Bay. This was "pre-flight" which was tough, tough physical training including two or three day survival hikes, crawling under barbed wire, climbing high walls and running until you could run no more. There was extensive ground school on all phases of Navy flying, navigation and aeronautical engineering. I spent a lot of time in the beautiful chapel there praying to the Lord for survival in the program.

Shortly before graduation the entire cadet wing was called into the main auditorium and the commander started reading names. He read all but the top 10% of the total in the room. All of us had been in the program for nearly one year. The Captain said the Navy Department had announced that the pilot losses in the war had been smaller than anticipated and the entire V5 cadet program had been cut 90%. All of the cadets whose names had been read should return to their barracks, pack their sea bags and prepare to be transported to San Diego as seamen. He asked them to leave the auditorium immediately. Many were so shocked that they could not even get up.

After they left he said, "You who are remaining are the upper 10% of the class and you will be given a two week leave to go home before reporting to NAS Norman, Oklahoma for Primary Flight Training." I was number three in the class by the composite grades over the one year in the Navy. I knew that the Lord had been with me all during those difficult days, and had helped me in more ways than I could even count. I was so grateful to be part of the handful who would still be able to be Navy Pilots.

Then it was on to Norman, Oklahoma. The introduction was quick and complete: half school, half flying the Stearman N2S made by Boeing. It was called the yellow peril and is a 2-place open cockpit tandem biplane with the student in the front and the instructor in the rear. The communication between the two is by a "gosport" helmet. The helmet is cloth in the summer or leather in the winter and the instructor has a cloth mouthpiece that he can talk into. This is hooked to a long rubber tube, which goes to the student's earpiece of the helmet. The student hears the instructor but cannot talk back. There is no radio.

The primary flight training includes all basic flying and every aerobatic maneuver including spins, inverted spins, inverted flight, loops etc. Precise formation flying was also learned.

Spot landings were required to land in a 100-foot circle after a short final leg in slow flight. For some reason I had trouble with this and nothing else, since all of my other flying and grades were 4.0. It seemed impossible to land in that circle four out of four times. This was necessary to train for carrier landings. The only down checks I ever received were given here and I had to report to the Captain who said "Kerr, you are so good in everything I will give you Captain's time (meaning two extra hours of instruction) and a top officer flight test. Normally this is not given and this extra training is due to your nearly perfect record." Two extra hours of instruction were given and then I had the critical one and only chance to hit the spot and stay in the program.

I was scared. I went to the chapel and prayed, "God, please help me in this critical fight test." This was it after 15 months in this program. If I failed this test I was out. I arrived at the flight line, did the preflight check in the Stearman and awaited the senior instructor. A marine instructor arrived, a Lieutenant, who I had never seen before, nor ever saw again. He said, "You fly the plane and do three spot landings." As we approached the field each time a prayer was said and I will always feel that someone was making the landing for me, as all three were perfect. The marine was either an angel, or the Lord himself landed that plane. I know it wasn't me.

Now the final tests were behind me and I graduated there in Norman, Oklahoma. After a one week leave I went on to Pensacola, Florida, where I learned to fly large sea-planes, and many types of land planes. I received my Navy wings of gold and eventually became an instructor there and at NAS Atlanta, flying many types of Navy fighter planes.

There are so many stories that I could tell of the Lord's hand of protection, his direction, and his blessings during the remainder of the war, my college years, and my years in business. Many times in business the extreme financial duress, the stress, the betrayal, and the testing of ethics made me so thankful for those days in the Navy when I learned to lean heavily on the Lord. In my years of being trained, and then of training others during World War II, we had a very real enemy to defeat. As life went on I realized that there is still a very real enemy who seeks our defeat, and though working often through people, that enemy wages war on the spiritual level. The tools that I've used in that war are not really much different: prayer, obedience to the commanding officer (the Lord), a deep commitment to high standards and ethics, hanging in there in trust and hope, and more prayer.

After college, a fraternity brother and I formed an equipment company to handle school buses, funeral coaches and ambulances. We were soon offered, and accepted, many other franchise opportunities, including dump truck bodies, lift gates and hoists, farm bodies, aerial towers and many others. We expanded quickly in those years moving shortly to a large shop, formerly the State Patrol building. Our success was rapid and we became the largest provider of truck bodies and equipment in the Rocky Mountain area.

By 1962 my fraternity brother and I had a substantial disagreement on company ethical policies and other matters. He would try to cheat manufacturers by falsifying bid prices for extra concessions. Ten percent of the company had been sold to each of two sales managers. It was obvious that there was no room for compromise in our positions on ethics. Either you operate ethically and completely above board, or you don't. He talked the other two into voting me out with his 40% and their 20%. In some ways it was a devastating moment of betrayal. I prayed many prayers. Fairly quickly thereafter many of the top manufacturers came to me, and simultaneously a dear friend provided office and shop space. A new company quickly overtook the old company.

In due time a new company, Kerr Equipment Company, was formed as a subsidiary of General Leasing Corporation of Minneapolis Minnesota. The relationship with General Leasing Company was preceded by the fact that two of my clients asked if I would "lease" equipment to them. Rental was well known, but not long term leasing. I had heard of a man in Minneapolis whose family owned auto dealerships, real estate and a leasing company. I called him and he said the call was timely since he would be at the Brown Palace the next Tuesday and we could have breakfast. We met and that started a fine and mutually profitable business relationship. I was a one third owner with him and his brother. I became Vice President of General Leasing Company, renamed GELCO, and was also named President of the Rocky Mountain Division, and President of the Western and Pacific divisions in 1962. They had vast interests including auto dealerships. I had numerous contacts in the Rocky Mountain West. I was taught the long term vehicle leasing and fleet management business and we prospered together. By 1964 we were the largest privately held fleet leasing company, and in 1968 the company was taken public.

My partner was of a different faith from mine, and his heritage gave him brilliance in business. He was a man of straight and fair business ethics so we agreed on every matter of business. During all of this time I prayed each day for success, and my prayers were answered many times over.

It was also at this time that I was asked to join the Young Presidents Organization (YPO), an international association of top executives who had reached substantial measure of success before their 40th birthday. This great blessing would benefit me in a major way all of my life. During the years as an officer of YPO I had the opportunity to meet with a number of world leaders: three United States Presidents, the Premier of Italy, King Constantine of Greece. We had a private audience with the Pope, dinner with Henry Ford II and met personally with many top corporate executives.

Through YPO I met an entrepreneur who had moved from the East and quickly built a huge resource business in oil partnerships. Late one New Year's Eve at his huge ranch I was asked many questions about leasing and he asked me to join him by putting together leasing partnerships. When asked how much I was making and what my ownership was he said he would double that. The decision to leave GELCO took much prayer. The parting with my partner was friendly and he said if it didn't work out we would again get together.

The new association was vast and intriguing with trips to many foreign capitals and U.S. cities. We always traveled in a fleet of planes that I leased to the principal company, financed by many partners in our leasing companies. We knew all of the original astronauts and I hired Capt. Walter Schirra to run one of our leasing companies. He was the only astronaut to fly all 3 U.S. spacecrafts: Mercury, Gemini and Apollo. We became life long close friends. Three other astronauts were on my board.

Many transactions with top banks were completed in the U.S., England, France, Portugal and Italy. In the first year, $80 million in corporate leases of planes, cars, trucks and oil field equipment were written.

I purchased a Lockheed Electra Turbo Prop 102 passenger airplane from Pacific Southwest Airlines. It was a fine plane with relatively low hours on airframe but many landings, since PSA flew short routes. I financed the lease with friends at United Banks of Colorado. The plane was converted from 102 passengers to a 40 passenger executive plane with three staterooms. The plane was used to fly to board meetings and other flights to Europe. I leased other planes to the companies with partnership money including four Learjets and a Lockheed Jet Star.

Once, a number of us were headed to London for a board meeting in the four engine Lockheed Electra. A fuel stop was made in Reykjavik, Iceland. While refueling, the weather lowered to zero ceiling and zero visibility. The corporate president ordered the pilots to take off. The nearest alternate airport was over 600 nautical miles away and I said no, we should wait. He was adamant about continuing. Fortunately, both Captain Schirra, and General Joe Foss (the outstanding Marine Ace in W.W.II) were with us on the flight. Together they escorted the president back to his stateroom and told him that we would take off when the weather cleared, as all of us knew that if we lost an engine on take off we could not get back into Reykjavik, or to anywhere else. We all began to wonder if perhaps the president was no longer making good decisions.

Within a few years the principal company's owner became carried away with his wealth and power, and overextended in every way. His vast empire was beginning to fail which quickly impacted my company because of his ownership. I was saved by good business ethics, constant prayer and by the fact that he never understood my leasing company. I found the answer by quickly securing all of my senior money sources with assets of the leasing partnership. As a consequence, when the major company went down, all of my banks were secured.

As the parent company began to fail there was a huge shortfall at the bank on several of the airplanes. They had lost substantial value and there was a large amount due at the bank over the value the planes would bring when sold. I secured the shortfall at the bank with a first mortgage we had on a fine motel in Indio, California. The parent company principal was very angry at this, saying that he was not paying any banks. It was a clear conflict of ethics at this point, but there was no doubt in my mind that if money was owed to lenders, they would certainly be paid.

I also had purchased two long range Boeing 707s from Qantas Airlines, which had been used in the Los Angeles/Australia route. I leased them to Braniff International Airlines and the deal was made with Harding

Lawrence, the then president, and Ed Acker, the chief operations officer who soon went to Pan American World Airways as President. Lawrence's wife was Mary Wells, the well-known head of Wells-Rich, a major New York advertising agency. We met with her several times as well. I financed the lease with money I obtained from Ford Motor Credit through my long relationship with Ford. I soon leased Braniff their only 747, which was used on the Dallas/Hawaii route. All of these leases were paid in full in due course.

In the course of finding money for the partnership equipment leases, we borrowed $2.5 million from the Ohio Public Employees Retirement Fund. I only needed about $.5 million at the time so I loaned $2 million to a good friend's company. The resource company was beginning to show signs of failing. My friend and I were at the Young President's Organization University for Presidents in Monaco and we determined to pay the loan back, with interest, as soon as we returned, which we immediately did. The Securities and Exchange Commission in due course went after anyone who was associated in any way with the resource company president, so they sued my friend and I, claiming that the money we had borrowed was a "security," not a "loan."

I took many trips to Columbus, Ohio, and New York City to the SEC Southern district office. It was an intense and harrowing time, as my friend's stock began to suffer, and the legal bills mounted.

I prayed hard and long. Then, quite suddenly, the SEC said, "You are right. It was a loan, and you paid it before term with interest. We are dropping all charges, but you are never to borrow any more money from the Ohio State Public Employees Retirement Fund." They can rest assured that I never will. Once again, served by common sense integrity, and reliance on the Lord, I was able to emerge relatively unscathed from a complicated and difficult business collapse.

Sometime later, I was told by a good friend, who was a large-scale contractor, that the principal had told him that I had stolen $1 million from him by paying banks the money they were due. I was able to tell him that he also had been accused by the same person of stealing $1 million for repossessing an expensive guesthouse in Palm Springs. All banks had in due course shut off the president of that parent company. My credibility on the other hand, with all the lenders with whom I had dealt, remained untarnished.

In 1972 I reentered the vehicle fleet management business. We had emerged from the previous enterprise with fine credit, and we bought a large Ford dealership, which was run by my oldest son, then a Chrysler Plymouth dealership, and we also advanced rapidly in the vehicle fleet business. By 1984 we had become the dominant fleet management company in the Rocky Mountain West. Concurrently we built a new Buick dealership, and it was run by my second son.

In late 1983 my oldest son, who was the President of Kerr Leasing and Fleet Services, was called by the General Electric Capital representative who stated that their top management wanted to meet us. We were asked to come to Stamford, Connecticut and New York City to meet with Gary Wendt who was the head of G.E. Credit (later G.E. Capital). They said he was the toughest executive in the world. I said we love tough executives, but we asked, "Is he fair, and is he smart?" If he wasn't fair we would not do business with him, and if he wasn't smart we could not do business with him. He was tough, and fair and smart. After due diligence we signed an agency agreement using their money and our knowledge. The first eight deals were won, six of them on the West Coast. Gary Wendt and Bob Wright (who later headed NBC and still does) called and said,

"You were not even the low bidder and you got them all? How?" We said we do just three things: client service, client service, client service. They said, "We are going to buy your company", and they did. My third and youngest son was also working with us at this time, and my sons and I give all the credit to the Lord as we put the world's largest corporation into the fleet management business and ran it for them.

As my close family knows, through all of the life experiences, my wife and I attended church, tithed, and prayed through seemingly impossible situations and the Lord always came through. It was not always as fast as I would have hoped for, but the help has always come to me. The Lord's timing is perfect, and he waits so that there can be no doubt that it is Him. The Lord has never failed me.

In retrospect, I would always advise others to cautiously and prayerfully seek the Lord's will before entering into endeavors both personal and business, and a great deal of struggle can be avoided. However, in a fallen world there will always be struggle. I am by nature decisive and prone to action, and have, I'm sure at times, stepped out in front of the Lord's plans. He has, however, always been faithful to see me through, and to work His good purposes and His provision through it all in ways that can only be Him, and to declare His Glory in ways I might not have seen if it hadn't been for all the struggle.

A more recent story perhaps illustrates best the truly miraculous provision and deliverance of the Lord through very difficult business deals and financial circumstances.

In 1982 I was awarded the 4th Denver Area Buick Dealership, and we designed and built a building to house it. By 1989 Buick had added two more dealerships in the metropolitan Denver area and we began to lose money, a lot of money. The small Buicks at that time were identical to Chevy, but $100 more, and the fine large Buicks were sold

167

with intense competition. We had asked General Motors to give us the GMC Truck franchise; however, it was given to the Oldsmobile dealer next door. My company, Kerr Leasing and Fleet Services, was the largest purchaser of GMC light trucks in the United States. We were buying over 4,500 pickups per year for one cable client alone.

We asked for the Pontiac franchise, but were turned down since they had enough other dealers in our metropolitan area. We had no choice but to notify the local Buick representative that we were canceling Buick. He did not believe us, and did not send the notice to senior management. He said, "Nobody cancels Buick." We called the local GMAC representative on Thursday and told him we were closing the store on Monday and would return all cars to his facility. Within hours we had a call from the General Manager of Buick who scheduled an immediate meeting. He said to us, "Please don't close the store. We (Buick Motor Division) will buy out the franchise." And they did just that, in a very fair manner.

The GM Realty representative said they didn't want to lose the facility, but the GM board wouldn't approve the purchase of any dealer property at that time. They did, however, want a four year option to buy the property. Our family had prayed that we would have a satisfactory recovery from our large losses. They felt that the property was worth $3.5 million. We thought it was worth nearer to $4 million. All my sons and I met with GM and $3.7 million was agreed upon with a $1 million payment for the option. We came out of that meeting with some awe at what had transpired, and a check for $1,000,000 in our hands.

Four years later, actually four days under four years, I got a call from the head of GM Real Estate. "We've got some bad news for you. We're not going to exercise our option." The good news was that they had essentially given us the $1,000,000, which had long since been invested and/or spent. But the bad news was that I then had a huge tax liability, since the option payment had just become income. With some quick tax advice, we had GM transfer the option to my son, which gave us an additional year to shelter the income. Their rent was reduced from $35,000 to $25,000, and at the end of the lease they moved the Buick franchise to another location.

Now I had empty property. We had a short-term used car dealer in there who quickly went broke. Then there were a series of unsuccessful tenants. The realtors said I could get $2.5 million. I owed $2.7 million. I knew the property was a great location, and worth far more than that, but there were no takers.

Simultaneously, our leasing company had collapsed, primarily due to a major bank backing out of a $50 million credit line eight months into a non-cancelable contract, due to their huge losses on an unrelated acquisition. Their problem cost us huge amounts in lost business and prestige.

Financially we were in very troubling times with little income and major outflow of capital. Things seemed pretty desperate. I also was the co-signer on a note with my daughter and her husband for a property in Tennessee that was in imminent foreclosure and in serious arrears on its property taxes. A foreclosure there would take us all into bankruptcy. I was in my seventies, and began also to experience heart trouble from the stress, ultimately resulting in having a pacemaker installed. I found myself at one of those places where I was completely beyond my own resources to fix the problems.

My daughter was visiting at this time and as we frequently do, she and my wife and I were sitting at the breakfast table in the morning and praying with some fervency for God's help and intervention, for wisdom, and for provision to get through the next few months financially.

Later that same morning, my wife and daughter were at

the store when my wife pulled out of her purse an envelope that her dear aunt had given her at a reunion several weeks before. She had put it in her purse and forgotten about it. As she fumbled with the envelope, two checks fell to the floor, each for $10,000. One was for her, and one for me. There was a moment of confusion followed by sheer joy and hilarity as we witnessed our prayer answered through the kindness and generosity of a relative. The timing of that precious gift was so clearly beyond coincidence in all of our minds.

Soon after that on another morning the phone rang in the middle of our prayer. It was the owner of a large Lexus dealership. "Dave," he said from out of the blue, "would you lease us the Arapahoe Road property for the next five or six months while we're rebuilding our existing facility?" We were dumbfounded. We were able to negotiate a mutually favorable lease, and ultimately, due to delays, they were in our building over sixteen months, and sold more cars at that location than they had at their other one.

Due to their prestige and success and tenant improvements to the property, we priced the corner property at $5 million. We eventually had an offer from another auto group in town to buy the building for $3.3 million and a ten year $1.7 million note guaranteed by Ford Motor Credit. At the same time a large jeweler in the neighborhood offered us nearly that much for the property and his property (an entire block) in trade. A large realtor and friend said, "Dave, that's your best deal. Just take it." But I knew I didn't want more real estate, and I believed that the property was worth more.

At that moment another large automotive group called and needed to move a Lincoln Mercury dealership out of a poor location. After some negotiation, $4.8 million was offered, and was finally accepted with two premium cars of our choice each year for the next five years with license and insurance. The deal was closed in August of 2001, exactly thirty days before September 11.

Through another amazing series of events, after much prayer and negotiation, in early October of 2002 the bank in Tennessee called and offered to cancel the note we owed them for $1.55 million if we paid them $900,000 by November 1st. Because of the deal we had made on the above property, we had the $900,000 and we were able to buy out the note in a foreclosure sale on the courthouse steps two days before Christmas. We paid the back taxes and installed proper management. The property began to generate adequate cash flow, and it was eventually sold at substantial profit in 2005.

We could not have dreamed of, nor orchestrated, those events. We had to hang in there, we had to work the deals, had to always make decisions from the highest ethical standards, but ultimately we could see clearly that it was the hand of the Lord that delivered us from the financial catastrophes that any one of those situations could have brought. And I want to thank Him here publicly, and give Him all the Glory for his personal and tender care through all these 83 years. All of business and life is just the stage set for the God of Glory to reveal Himself to us, to reveal Himself through us to others, and to bring us into a relationship with Him that will last forever. I am so grateful.

A friend from Kansas City, John Shore, called me many years ago and asked me to take time from my schedule and meet a friend of his, Rosey Grier. He said Rosey had just been hired by San Diego County to spend ten days a month helping reach out to a certain segment of the community on a regular basis.

I committed to spending a few days a month with Rosey as he made his way around the county, interacting with people in a way I had never seen. Everyone, young or old, loved Rosey. Wherever we went, people wanted his autograph, wanted to visit with him about situations they were facing, and he never failed to make them smile from ear to ear.

I had gotten to know a young, enthusiastic African-American, Estean Lenyoun, who wanted to meet Rosey and share a business idea with him. I put a meeting together and the two of them related so well that they went on to form Impact Urban America. Their company trains Hispanics and African-Americans in Southeast San Diego to be available and skilled for almost any kind of employment opportunity that the business community needs.

Rosey's heart for God and his desire to make a difference for the Kingdom of God with his gifts, talents and experiences has changed many people. He and his wife Margie have a son, Rosey Jr., and they live in the Los Angeles area. As a singer, actor, bodyguard, football player and celebrity, this gentle giant is constantly being used by God.

15 Turning From Darkness to Light

Rosey Grier

FOR A LONG TIME, MY LIFE WAS AN EXCITING mix of pro football and Hollywood celebrity status. Pro football was a great adventure. Working on presidential campaigns was exhilarating. But after Bobby Kennedy was assassinated I felt like I was being washed ashore on a desert island. All of my idealism for the future – all of my hope for a change for the better – became part of a foggy sadness that came over me. I couldn't put my heart into anything.

Even when I got a major television role, the producer said, "Aren't you happy about it?" I said I was. "You don't act like it," he said.

What complicated things was that my personal life was out of control. Even though I was trying to help kids stay out of gangs and get their lives in order, I wasn't doing anything to help my own life. I wasn't able to keep my commitments in my first marriage, and my second marriage was deteriorating fast. I wanted a woman to love and care about me, to work with me – but not someone to whom I had to remain committed and for whom I had to be responsible.

Finally, I told our little son that I was going to get a divorce.

"Dad, you shouldn't get no divorce," he said.

"You don't understand, and I can't explain it to you."

"Tell me, dad, tell me."

I tried, but I couldn't tell him because I was crying. I don't know if I was crying for him or for me. Probably both. Eventually I looked at little Rosey and said, "I want to teach you something before I go. I want to teach you to pray."

I taught him the only prayer I knew, the Lord's Prayer. "He's your Father in Heaven, but He's always close. He'll be with you even though I'm not. He's always taken good care of me, and He'll take care of you, too."

The Carter campaign took a great deal of my time, and the rest of me went to talking with kids in trouble, lawyers and business people. In addition, I earned my living as an actor, singer and writer.

But none of it eased my loneliness. The joy and satisfaction I derived from my work with the nonprofit groups began to disappear. Helping kids find a life when they thought there was nothing for them made me feel great. But I saw that as fast as I could pull twenty out of the soup, twenty more jumped in. I hired lawyers with my own money for some who had gotten into trouble, doing everything I could to help them get going. I worked myself into a frazzle getting all the people I knew to come and talk to the kids, to share with them, give to them and love them. I was visiting schools and speaking, but it was not enough. In fact, sometimes it even seemed hopeless. We helped many young people, but we lost some to violence. We lost a lot.

I remember one time lecturing kids from the street about doing right.

"Rosey," one kid asked, "what is right?"

I opened my mouth, but before I spoke I realized I had nothing to say. So I said, "I don't know. I'm going to find out and let you know."

Before I could come up with an answer for him, he went out with a group of kids. They all got high on something and, for no reason, they beat him to death. I went to his funeral and wept with regret. If only I'd had an answer.

Realizing that it was not possible to save all the kids we worked with was a tremendous blow. All I wanted was to stop the violence and get people to care for one another. That sad knowledge made my personal prison of loneliness and unhappiness close more tightly around me. I was missing something in my life. I had fame as a football player, a singer and an actor. And I was doing my best to help kids in trouble. But I was not happy, joyful, peaceful or content. The more I thought about it, the sorrier I felt for myself.

After several nights of melancholy and depression, one of the men in my nonprofit group pounded on my door to check on me.

"Do you ever read the Bible?" he asked.

"I don't understand the Bible," I said. I picked up one that someone had given me and looked at the pages, but nothing caught my eye. It seemed worlds apart from what I was going through. Whoever heard of the Bible solving any problems? So I closed it and went back to feeling sorry for myself.

I had to fly to Chicago not long after that, and the flight attendant said to me, "You're Rosey Grier, aren't you?"

I was really depressed and didn't want to talk to anyone, but I said, "Yes I am."

She said, "I've been watching a man on television, and I think you ought to watch him."

"What does he do?" I asked.

"He teaches."

"What does he teach?"

"The Bible."

She was the second person in the last four days to bring up this subject with me, and I didn't know what to make of it. The Bible hadn't entered my mind for years. We talked for a while and she asked for my phone number.

When I got back to Los Angeles, I shut myself in my room. I understood what bitter loneliness was all about. I dropped into a pit.

Then it seemed I heard an answer. "Why don't you kill yourself?"

At that moment, I understood why people kill themselves, even when they are afraid of death. Depression's iron grip thrusts them to the bottom of the pit of despair and tells them they have nowhere to turn, no one to trust, no peace. Suicide seems the only alternative.

But moments after my thoughts of suicide struck me, I thought of the time I taught little Rosey the Lord's Prayer. Then I heard myself repeating, "Our Father, who art in heaven…" I said the Lord's Prayer over and over, crying all the time. I held onto it like a pole stretched out to a drowning man.

The next morning was Sunday, and the phone woke me up. A strange voice said, "Rosey Grier?"

"Yeah?"

"My name is Ken Ludic."

I didn't know any Ken Ludic.

"My wife told me to call you. She's an airline stewardess. She asked me to call and wake you.

I remembered her from the Chicago flight.

"Get up and turn your television on," Ken said. "The man whose program she wants you to watch is coming on."

So I got up and turned on the television.

"God bless you," he said, and hung up.

"This is dumb," I thought. "A guy calls me up, I don't know who he is, and he tells me to watch a program. I don't know what it is, and I'm sitting here like a dummy gonna watch it."

A choir came on and sang a verse, "If they were going to convict you of being a Christian, would they have enough evidence? What does your life show?"

What did my life show? I was a desperate, lonely, middle-aged man with hundreds of friends and acquaintances – none of whom could help me now.

Then the camera picked up this black man with a Bible in his hand, and he began talking about a verse, and said God loved the world so much that He gave His only Son… that whosoever believeth in Him should not perish, but have everlasting life. I picked up the Bible I hadn't read in years and tried to find the verse he'd named – John 3:16. I had no clue as to where to find the book of John. I flipped from back to front and from front to back without any luck. Finally I figured there must be a table of contents, and I found the page reference for the Gospel According to St. John. I turned to it and found John 3:16 and it said exactly what the man had read

It said "everlasting life." I decided to call little Rosey. I thought he would like to hear this man, also.

I called my ex-wife, Margie. Our divorce had been stormy and the subject of a lot of publicity, so she was never pleased to hear from me. "What do you want," she asked icily.

"I really want you to let little Rosey watch this preacher on television. You can listen, too."

She resisted at first, but I pleaded with her. "He's really going to want to hear this." They watched it that morning.

In spite of my Baptist pedigree, I knew nothing about God and Jesus and the Holy Spirit. I had been baptized when I was seven, and I knew some gospel songs and hymns. But, as good as those things were, I had not made Jesus my friend. I had no relationship with God. What I did know about Him was religious and not personal. Suddenly I saw how badly I needed that personal dimension – a relationship.

As I listened to the preacher teach the Bible, a thread of hope began to grow in my heart. His sermon was not a commentary on current events and the ills of society – I knew enough about those. Instead, he commented only on the text of the Bible – with abundant applications to my daily life. I made it from week to week by watching that program.

Margie and little Rosey continued to watch every week, as I did, and when little Rosey was with me, we watched it together. One Saturday night Rosey said to me, "Dad, can we go over there?"

"Over where?"

"You know, that man we've been watching on television. Can we go over there?"

"Oh, Rosey, I don't want to go over there."

"Why not, Dad?"

I didn't have a good answer, so I said, "Well, sometime we'll go over there.

"Tomorrow, Dad! Let's go tomorrow!"

At 5:30 the next morning little Rosey woke me up. When we got out to the car, a heavy fog blanketed the area, and I was about to say, "It's too foggy to go to church." But it was as if he were reading my mind. Pretty perceptive for a seven-year-old.

"Dad, when we start somewhere, we don't turn back, do we?"

We finally made it and the place was packed. I hadn't been to church in more than twenty years, and I noticed that everyone except us was carrying a Bible. When the pastor, Fred Price, began to speak, it was as if he were addressing me in counseling chambers after listening to me spill all my troubles. Many questions I had been asking for years began to be answered that Sunday morning. I saw that it is possible to be involved in religion but not have a genuine relationship with God. I wanted to know this Jesus Dr. Price was talking about.

I became convinced that this was the missing element in

my life. Through all my years I had tried to fill a hole in my life that God had put there, and which only He could fill. But I had tried to fill it with people, fun and pleasure, with good works, with money and power – all things that decay or get stolen or die. I learned that John 3:16 means what it says – God gave His Son to get us back. But He never forces our love in return. No matter what our response or lack of it, His love is steady.

At the end of the service, Dr. Price asked anyone who wanted to accept Jesus and become a new person to raise his hand. A lot of thoughts came to my mind. "You're not going to raise your hand. All these people are going to be looking at you. You're a football player, a movie actor, a singer. You're somebody. By raising your hand, they're going to think you don't know anything. Don't raise your hand. You can do it later. This is your first time in this church, and you're going to raise your hand? Why don't you wait? You can do it later."

Up went my hand. Tears began to flow down my face. They were tears of relief because I had at last found a hand to hold, the hand of God which would meet my need – the hand of a friend. Then I saw that little Rosey had his hand up, too, and tears were running down his face. Afterwards we talked with a counselor from the church who led us in accepting Jesus as our savior.

The two of us walked out of that church that morning as new creatures in Christ.

That was the beginning of a changed lifestyle for me. Little Rosey and I got Bibles and began going to church. Soon we could find verses without looking in the table of contents.

After we had attended that church for several months, Little Rosey said, "Dad, could we take mom to church with us tomorrow?"

"Oh no," I thought. I didn't want anything to do with

Margie. She had cost me plenty.

"I don't think so, Rosey," I said.

"But Dad, why not?"

No matter what my feelings about Margie might be, she was his mother. If I said anything against her, little Rosey would be hurt, and rightfully so. "Well, sometime," I said. "We'll take her sometime."

"Tomorrow, Dad. Tomorrow, huh?"

I called her, figuring she would decline my invitation anyway. After all, my distaste for her company was more than matched by hers for mine.

"Little Rosey and I were thinking, would you like to go to church with us?"

"Yes," she said. "I'd love to go."

"You would? Well… we have to leave early."

"I don't mind," she replied sweetly. "What time do you want me to be ready?"

"Six," I said.

"I'll be ready."

I didn't know what to make of it. She was being so nice.

We found seats near the front and little Rosey sat between us. At the end of the service Margie shocked me again. She raised her hand and went up for counseling. She accepted Jesus also, and began going to church with us every Sunday.

Several months later I began to date my ex-wife. For the first time, I was dating a woman just for the pleasure of her company – without designs or ulterior motives. We had fun and enjoyed going places together. We laughed and had things to talk about. We had been together five years when we were married, but it had never been like this.

After a while I asked her why she so readily accepted my invitation to church, when I was so sure she would turn me down.

"I never saw anyone change the way you did in the

months after you started watching Fred Price on television," she said. "And you only got better when you started going down there in person. I wanted to know more about anything that made such a dramatic and wonderful change in you. It had to be real. And I had been watching Fred on television for a while before you extended the invitation. By the time you called, I was eager to go."

For the first time I knew how it felt to be in love because I was falling in love with Margie.

After we dated for about two years, Margie and I decided that we were ready to give marriage a serious try. This time, each of us had a foundation in our lives, Jesus Christ, Who gave us assurance that we could succeed in Him in spite of our former failure.

Most of my motivational speaking engagements were cancelled after I began talking about my new life in Christ, but I was able to speak to many Christian groups, and begin a new organization in Los Angeles where young people were able to learn the Bible and a trade. I also lost my relationship with the Kennedy family because of my support for Jimmy Carter, and that hurt me deeply. I asked the Lord to show me if I had treated my old friends unfairly or had done something to earn their wrath. It upset me so much at a political convention, that I had trouble sleeping.

One morning, though, I woke with these words on my heart: "I have allowed this to happen to free you from your idolatry. You must have no other gods before Me. I alone am the Lord."

Idolatry is a subtle thing. I had never seen mine before that moment. God had sent each of the Kennedys as gifts into my life. But I had focused my sight on the gift to the exclusion of the giver. And that, I found out, is something that God will not tolerate. Jesus said, "You shall know the truth, and the truth will set you free." I was set free that morning.

My life, with its history of broken marriages and failed commitments, is a parable of the kingdom. When I finally called on God to help me – beginning with my desperate recitations of the Lord's Prayer – He took the broken pieces of my life and made me whole. Then He took the broken pieces of my family and made it whole. Those are miracles of restoration and reconciliation that point us to God as the authentic source of supply for all our needs.

Centuries ago, Paul, the apostle of Christ, was arraigned before a king named Agrippa. As he addressed the charges that had been brought against him, he described the work God had given him to do: "… to open their eyes and turn them from the darkness to the light and from the power of Satan to God, so that through their faith in Me they will have their sins forgiven and receive their place among God's chosen people" (Acts 26:18).

My eyes were opened. I turned from darkness to light and from Satan's power to God's. And through faith, my sins were forgiven and I received my place among God's chosen people. And now I serve God by helping others to experience the same. That is what the Church is supposed to be doing on earth, not forcing everybody to think alike, but showing God's love to everyone.

The answer to wickedness lies not in the halls of Congress, nor in the corridors of the White House. It sits, instead, atop a hill called Golgotha, and it stands at the entrance of an empty tomb.

About fifteen years ago Tim LaHaye asked me to do him a personal favor and spend about an hour with a friend of his from Colorado who had moved to San Diego. That time with Bill Kennedy started one of the most incredible relationships I've ever had.

Bill is a fascinating guy with a quick mind and a lot of creative marketing skills. We continued to meet and developed a great friendship. One day Bill and I were having lunch, and his fifteen-year-old son was with us. Bill told me that a lawsuit had been filed against him for something he had not been involved in. The longer he talked, the more unbelievable the story sounded. His son cried and cried, and I realized that this was real and that it wasn't just a story.

Many months later Bill was sentenced to a twenty year term and was sent to a federal penitentiary. During the trial I learned to appreciate Bill's heart and his resolve to not admit to committing a crime that he did not commit. I made a promise to write to Bill every week while he was in prison, thinking that he would probably be out in a year or two. That was thirteen years, and more than 650 letters ago. Bill remains a man committed to the truth.

Bill's wife, Debbie, has been so faithful to him over the years, especially these last thirteen. She has championed his cause in trying to get the truth out, and has visited him faithfully as much as financially possible. Debbie has reached out to their two sons and daughter as few other mothers could, and has continued to love and pray for Bill every day with support and wisdom. I thank God for wives like Debbie and how she has been there for Bill.

The Truth Will Set You Free

16

Bill Kennedy

I AM WRITING THIS FROM PRISON. NOT AN emotional prison or a spiritual prison or any other kind of metaphorical prison. I am in prison. Literally.

In the 42nd chapter of Job, he says he has finally come to know God. Before Job's difficulties, he had heard *about* God. But after his trials, Job said he came to *know* God. I feel that I finally understand what Job was talking about. My children weren't killed as they were in the book of Job, but it seems like a huge meteorite hit all of us. I was taken away from them and their lives were changed as a result of my imprisonment.

This was not what I thought my life would be like as a new Christian. When I first accepted Christ I was under the impression that if I just behaved and didn't step out of line, then everything would come up roses. But for more than a decade in prison, God has allowed me to see Him in ways I never imagined possible.

Since we can't understand God, we create a god that we can understand. I created one out of silver and gold, and carried it around with me everywhere I went. In my god's eyes, I was doing very well with my life. At that point I did not understand Jeremiah 17:9 which says, "The heart is the most deceitful of all things, desperately sick. Who can fathom it?"

Even though my parents divorced when I was one, my father was the most influential person in my life. He was an honorable man with a Ph.D. in physics, and he instilled in me important values about money, politics, economics, and conservative values.

By the time I was thirty I had graduated from college with a degree in geology, was married with three children, and was active in my church and in local politics. The value of precious metals began to rise during that time, and I was fairly successful in buying and selling them. Friends started asking for my help in buying them, so pretty soon I had a company that was selling millions of dollars in precious metals.

As I look back, it seems that I had more courage than brains. My marketing powers were greater than my business sense, and I didn't have the wisdom to hire people with the business sense. I didn't really intend for the business to grow as fast as it did. In one year it grew by more than $40 million. An accountant looked at my company and said that our marketing was blue chip, but our back office was in the Stone Age.

One of my mentors at the time told me that, as I was becoming a millionaire, if I didn't keep God first, I would not have any peace. That was a warning I did not heed. Successful businesses are stressful. As things got busier and more stressful, I stopped spending time with other men and leading them to Christ. It used to be one of my priorities, but I became too busy being successful. Oswald Chambers said, "Whenever we put other things first, there is confusion."

Within the next four years our sales grew to $167 million, and my company was selling 25 percent of the world's investment supply of platinum. My interest in politics was also great, so I bought the magazine *The Conservative Digest*. I interviewed Ronald Reagan in the Roosevelt Room of the

White House and talked with him about standing up to the Soviet Union.

As the metals business boomed, I finally hired a manager who pointed out several flaws in our practices. His plan prompted some cutbacks, which led to some employees stealing our company's mailing list. Anyone in a sales company knows that the mailing list is one of the chief assets. They started competing companies, and our business went into a panic. Eventually the company went into Chapter 11 bankruptcy protection so that we could reorganize.

During my ownership of *The Conservative Digest*, I met a man who ultimately saved me from myself. During my company's reorganization, my stress levels were off the chart. It was so bad that my wife finally confronted me about my temper. A hot-tempered man is an offense to God. He is selfish and angry because his pride gets stepped on. He is out of control and is really angry at God because only God can be at the center of the universe. Proverbs 15:18 warns about people like me: "Bad temper provokes a quarrel, but patience heals discords." A bad temper leads to sin. That was me. And my wife had had enough. I couldn't understand her problem – I tried to defend my attributes, which only led to more anger.

My wife insisted on my getting counseling, and I finally agreed to it because I thought it would save my marriage. I called Tim LaHaye, and he agreed to counsel us. Tim introduced me to the Holy Spirit. Tim showed me in his own book about anger that he had had similar issues, and that God delivered him from his spirit of anger. God delivered me that day. I learned to go to the Holy Spirit when I began to boil. This was the single most important thing that helped me get my company out of bankruptcy. My wife is convinced that one of the things that led to the bankruptcy in the first place was my inability to manage my anger.

I learned to commit myself to Ephesians 4:29, which

says, "Do not let any unwholesome word come from your mouth except that which is helpful to others that it benefits all who listen." Tim helped restore our marriage, and quickly became one of the most influential men in my life. All of us need people in our lives who model Biblical principles. They put flesh on the Word. Unless we see Biblical truths applied to practical living, they are just sayings. Tim continued to live out those principles, and was a key to my other crises later in life. My company's bankruptcy became a minor problem compared to the future.

Chapter 11 seemed like the best option for my company, because I was determined to fully pay back all of our creditors. I worked out a plan and went to court to show I could pay out $18 million over ten years. The creditors and the court approved the plan, and I was relieved. I was being investigated during this time to see if I had done anything illegal, but my lawyers assured me that I would not be indicted for anything as long as I kept paying back the creditors.

As a way to start paying back my creditors, I signed a contract with the government of Kuwait just after they were invaded by Iraq. I was a registered foreign agent for them. I wanted to make sure I wasn't doing anything illegal, so I hired a lawyer with a business background, whom I had met when he was a clerk during my company's bankruptcy proceedings. I was too naïve to see his ulterior motives, and to miss the political undercurrents going on in the U.S. about the first Iraq war.

The Wall Street Journal did a story on my lobbying efforts on behalf of Kuwait, saying that I was trying to get votes in the Senate to authorize going to war. Federal prosecutors began investigating me again, without my knowledge.

During this time God began bringing some very strong believers into my life to disciple me. Through prayer and Bible study, I began to develop a heart for those who are lost. Driving home from a study in the book of John, I prayed that God would use me to reach those who did not know Him.

Two months later there was a banging on my front door so loud that I thought someone was trying to break in. Federal agents had surrounded the house and had an arrest warrant for me, charging me with fraud. They handcuffed me and took me to a detention center for the night. One of my cell mates was a Hispanic man who did not speak English. But he was weeping to the point of being torment- ed, trying to read his Spanish-language Bible. I don't know Spanish, but I was able to find the Psalms for him, and he calmed down immediately.

Twenty-three of my former employees were also arrest- ed that day and charged with fraud. I couldn't believe the indictment, because none of it was true. During my initial hearing the prosecutor claimed I was an escape risk and that I had started the Persian Gulf war. The magistrate laughed and let me out on bail – Tim LaHaye and two oth- ers put their property up for collateral.

Having put most of my earnings back into the company so I could pay back creditors, I could not afford another attorney, so the court appointed one. It seemed that the prosecutors' case was flimsy, and I was assured by my attorney that I would be found innocent. But in the trial it seemed as if the prosecutors had inside information on how my lawyer was trying to defend me. All of the others were acquitted or their cases were dismissed. But I was found guilty of money laundering, and sentenced to twenty years in prison though I never did anything of the sort.

The first thing I did in prison was begin to memorize the first eleven chapters of the book of James. I was determined not to let my feelings get the best of me. My wife was 1,200 miles away, and had to go back to work after 23 years of being home raising our kids.

Tim insisted that I call him regularly, and he put me on a Scripture reading regimen. Through that, God began revealing sin to me. Each day I became convicted about something in my own heart. At the same time, inmates began approaching me because they wanted to talk about God. I never imagined that God could use me in these men's lives. He taught me that my helping them would relieve me of my own pain. One inmate, 32, had killed his childhood friend when he was thirteen. He had spent all but eighteen months since then in prison. He was also a heroin addict. He came to my cell every night, and finally told me that I was the first "free world Christian" he had ever met, meaning I was a Christian before coming to prison. Apparently that was a rarity.

God transformed this inmate's life because he began reading the same Bible chapters I read.

From the very beginning of my time in prison I tried to stay busy, trying to be a witness for Christ. An elderly man came into jail one day and no one wanted him as their cellmate, so I asked to take him in. It turned out he was a former member of the church I belonged to. He had lost his ranch to the federal government and had been filing illegal liens. He was obsessed with rebuilding his empire – it was all he could talk about. During my time with him I sensed God saying to me, "Thirty years from now, what will matter is not what you achieve, but who you touched for My sake." God used that time to show me in His Word, in I John 2:15-17: "Do not love the world or anything in the world. If anyone loves the world, the love of the Father is not in Him. For everything in the world – the craving of sinful man, lust of his eyes and the boasting of what he has and does – comes not from the Father, but the world. The world and its desires pass away, but the man who does the will of God lives forever."

It dawned on me that previously I had been a nominal

Christian at best. I attended church three times a week, gave more than our tithe, and helped people financially. But my real love was not God; it was trying to influence the direction of this country toward more conservative ideals. I loved my goals more than I loved God. Psalm 37:4 says, "Delight in the Lord and I will give you the desires of your heart." I had not been delighting in God. My projects were my delight.

C.S. Lewis described me when he wrote, "The prostitutes are in no danger of finding their life so satisfactory that they cannot turn to God. The proud, avarice, the self-righteous are in that danger." I was certainly proud and self righteous. But God, I asked, why twenty years?

This is when God brought me to the book of Job. In chapter 38 I began to see God for who He is and who I wasn't. I was the lord of my life. He taught me to watch out for my grumbling through Philippians 2:14. He showed me that I needed to give thanks in all things in I Thessalonians 5:18. One day, after listening to me gripe on the phone for fifteen minutes, Tim LaHaye told me to read five Psalms to count off ten things I'm grateful for. I hated that advice, but I knew he was right. The scripture showed me that a lack of gratitude is sin. Giving thanks relieved my depression. All my crutches were gone. And it seemed that God had me right where he wanted me. But occasionally it seemed that God had gone to sleep and simply forgotten me.

In his book on Moses, Chuck Swindoll said there were three truths God told Moses during the forty years in the wilderness: 1) circumstances that turn against us make us dependent on God; 2) circumstances that force dependence teach us patience; and 3) circumstances that teach us patience make us wise. I read this section over and over.

But he also points out our common responses to His direction: 1) we are afraid; 2) we run away; 3) we fight; 4) we tell everyone.

There were many days when I didn't know how I would make it one more day. Prison is so full of hate, expletives and anger, and no encouraging word is ever spoken. Friendships are difficult to develop, especially for Christians. The first two years I was housed with many violent men who mocked me and threatened me. After a year or so, though, several told me that they had given their lives to Christ. They were afraid to tell anyone for fear of intimidation by those who were big tough guys on the outside, but little boys on the inside.

After I had been in jail for a month, the prosecutors in my case offered to substantially reduce my sentence. I appeared in the prosecutor's office in leg irons and handcuffs, and the prosecutor told me that I could get out of prison much sooner if I would tell a lie about my lawyer. It's strange how our justice system works – they sentence you to so much time in prison that you'll say virtually anything to get out. But the prosecutor was shocked when I told him I declined his offer.

I was soon transferred to the Federal Corrections facility in Lompoc, California. This was where I had my experience that Job had in chapter 40. This was where God brought me down to my very core, showing me who I really was. I asked Him to reveal my sinful heart. I asked him to show me who He really was. It seemed that God had only been a concept until then. I told God that I wanted to be done with hanging onto my self or my sin. I told God that all I wanted in return was to wake up in the morning with joy. Waking up in prison is like waking up in hell. It is eternal torment.

The Bible told me that God loved me, but I wanted to *experience* that love. I wanted more than words on a page, even though they were His words! So every morning I walked around the prison track praying over scriptures and memorizing them. It still seemed that something was missing, something that kept me from intimacy with God. The only love I had really experienced was from my wife. I wanted the love that I read about in scripture. In the middle of one day, God broke through to my heart and I sensed Him saying, "Bill, I love you so very much – never doubt it for a moment." I wept with joy all afternoon. God loved me! I could live intimately with Him! I have never doubted God's love again.

For many mornings after, I studied God's word. He peeled off one layer at a time, revealing the deepest parts of my soul. He was gentle, and I wanted to please Him. He wanted me broken and to give Him unconditional surrender in order to rebuild me. A lifetime of bad habits and just plain sin had to go. My new level of relationship started looking outward. Soon I was discipling as many as seven men a day.

Since my conviction I had been trying to find out whether my trial had been properly conducted. After this experience with God, though, I stopped all my efforts and decided to see whether God wanted me to follow my suspicions. Blackabee's book, *Experiencing God*, helped me with this decision. Before I could pursue my own case any further, I felt that God showed me I needed to get past my bitterness and anger over my injustice. Eventually I repented and forgave my prosecutor and others.

Then God showed me my self-centeredness in my marriage. Debbie never complained. Some of our old friends assumed she would divorce me. I was so focused on myself that I didn't see her pain. In my obsessing about my own case I put a lot of pressure on her, lecturing her on what she should be doing to help me. I was not ministering to her. But on that track in Lompoc I changed. During the next visit I told our children that their mother was a much better Christian than me because she exemplified the life of Christ.

Prison is harder on families than it is on the prisoners. The prisons are usually hundreds of miles away from the loved ones, and phone rates are much higher than they are outside the prison. It was expensive for Debbie to visit. Plus her standard of living had collapsed. She had to move to an apartment in a bad part of town because that's all we could afford. We had a daughter in college who was barely making it financially, a teenaged son who was devastated by my absence, and a mentally handicapped boy who was also hurting.

Tim LaHaye and others sent me enough phone money so I could call Debbie every night. I also tried to prepare a devotional for our teenaged son. One night my wife was crying when I called her. It was just before Christmas and she had needed emergency dental surgery, which wiped out our bank account.

We prayed on the phone and within two days Dwight Johnson and members of our church brought over a check that more than covered the bill. This happened several times when we were at the very last dollar. Our Sunday School class at church supported us. Even my old 8th grade science teacher, Dr. James Dobson, sent my wife a check during an emergency. We never told anyone about our emergencies. These provisions came without any solicitation on our part, but from the prompting of the Holy Spirit on their hearts.

These experiences taught me that God was more interested in our character than in our comfort. When we were totally dependent on Him, he provided more than we needed. During one conversation with our Sunday School teacher, I began complaining about the unfairness of our plight.

"Bill, who are you ministering to?" he asked

No one, I thought. It was all about me. But it's not about us, is it? It's about God, and letting Him use us in the lives of others. That is what God means by living the abundant life in Luke 9:24.

As I continued to walk the Lompoc track, God began to show me how to relate to the men in that prison. The characters in prison are like the characters in the bar scene in *Star Wars*. It was like they were all from a primitive tribe, and they frequently upset me. But I sensed God saying to me, "Bill, I love these men. I don't love what they do, but I love them. Try to look at them through My eyes, not yours."

God gave me the worst bunkmate in all of Lompoc. But God used him to lead another to Christ. My bunkmate, Salazar, refused to speak to me as we lived in this six foot-by-nine foot cube. He was rude to me and I responded in kind. This went on for months. I sensed God telling me to love him, and for every mean thing he did, I gave him kindness. Eight men in nearby cells watched this. Eventually one of the men, from Colombia, who hadn't spoken to me in two years, asked me if I had a Bible he could read. He accepted Christ soon after. I believe it was because he saw love in action regarding my bunkmate.

After several years of not pursuing anything regarding the fairness of my trial, Tim LaHaye told me that he was taking some of the royalties from his *Left Behind* book series to find me a Christian lawyer to get to the bottom of my case. I rejoiced in this, and remembered Swindoll's line from one of his books, "I try, I fail, I trust, He succeeds."

My new attorney, Craig Parshall, read more than 100,000 pages on my case and interviewed many people. Six months later he told Tim that, not only was I innocent, but that I was also an honorable man. My excitement began to wane, though, when three more years passed and nothing changed. I wrote Psalm 119:82 in my journal: "My eyes fail, looking for your promise; when will you comfort me?" I asked this many times, not to complain, but just wonder-

195

ing. An interesting wrinkle developed in the case during this time of extreme discouragement. The law clerk I had hired years before confessed to my attorney that he had been working secretly with the prosecutor during my trial. He said he had been threatened with prosecution if he didn't help get me convicted. This was like having an NFL spy tap into the play-calling communication system to steal the opponent's plays.

Of course this is unethical and illegal, and it made my trial a farce, so we took this information to the appeals court. They said it was too late.

A disappointment of this magnitude can be devastating. It is so easy to get angry with God and lose faith. I was depressed for months.

Little things helped keep me focused, though. The Sunday School class back home paid for my wife to visit my daughter when she gave birth to our first grandchild. Tim LaHaye kept in touch and stood by me. James Dobson put my story on his radio program. I tried to give thanks to God every time my heart wanted to give up. That helped put in perspective that twenty years is nothing compared to eternity. God continued to use me to help others read the Bible and learn to pray and to become followers of Christ. One inmate was the biggest drug dealer in the entire prison. He finally got caught and spent a year in solitary confinement. But he read the Bible the entire time as a result of a study Bible I had given him. This former gang member gave his life to Christ and continued to be one of the most respected men in the compound. He was one of the few who did not care what his peers would say about his new life in Christ.

Every morning when I get out of my bunk I have a choice to focus on either God or prison. So I start each day with Galatians 5:22-23: "But the fruit of the Spirit is love, joy, peace, longsuffering, gentleness, goodness, faith, meekness, temperance, against which there is no law." Then I thank God for what I have. One of my daughters married a Godly man and they have three wonderful children. She is teaching new converts. Her husband is a professor of psychology and has a grant to study the children of inmates. Another son is the vice president of a technology company and he and his wife, an emergency room doctor, have one child. Our last child lives on a ranch for the mentally handicapped in Arizona – his tuition is paid for by friends.

I am often tempted to ask what might have been, but that's a trap. All of us have regrets. We live in a fallen world. Heaven will complete us – and I don't think of it as the "after" life. I think of this as the "before" life. I know God is good and I am privileged to witness His redemptive work in me and others. To think He would use me sends shivers through my spine. The reason I don't have regrets is that I have come to know God the way Job knew Him. I am thankful for Job and for Paul, because their stories encourage me. Maybe my story will help someone else who is going through troubling times.

We're all in some kind of prison – figurative or literal. My prayer is that God will use that prison as he did for Job, Paul, and me, to show us His true nature, so that we might do more than know *about* Him. He wants us to *know* Him!

Jim and Dottie came to Denver in the early 1960s and we had the pleasure of meeting them and getting to know them very well. His objective was to give Denver a youth program that would change lives. It was fascinating to see how he made the Youth For Christ program one of the top programs in the country. After his Denver success he was made part of the International YFC program and started training YFC directors all over the world. When I joined the international board, the world headquarters was in Switzerland, and Jim was very concerned about the high price of doing anything there. So he made a fabulous deal with some businessmen in Singapore and moved the international offices there. He also kept an office in Denver.

Jim had an incredible ability to focus on his office responsibility, the people on his team, his leadership, and the 110 countries YFC participates in. It was amazing to watch him raise more than half of the international budget, in addition to handling his other responsibilities.

We got together every week he was in town to play tennis, and I marveled at the number of projects he could have going at the same time. He has the right balance of physical, mental and spiritual activity. Betsy and I had the privilege of visiting much of the world with Jim and Dottie, and in all of these years and those trips, I never saw him waver from his objective of making a difference for the Kingdom of God. He has a true servant's heart. Thank God for men like Jim Groen.

A Hand on My Shoulder

Jim Groen

IT SEEMS FUNNY NOW, BUT I WAS VOTED BY my high school senior class as "The Person Most Likely to NOT Succeed!" I knew why my classmates voted that way – I was small for my age, slow to mature, afraid of life, and a failure as a teenaged Christian.

But something happened when I was sixteen that stirred my imagination about my future and slowly started some self-confidence. It was a simple thing, but often in life it is those small things that make such a big difference. I had a job at the J.C. Penney store in my home-town of Parsons, Kansas, and one day, before the store opened, I was arranging clothes in the men's department. A man with white bushy hair came down the aisle and put a hand on my shoulder. I had not seen him before.

"Son, I need young people like you in my company," he said, as he looked me straight in the eyes. "If you work hard, you can go right to the top."

It was James Cash Penney himself. That hand on my shoulder made me think that I was capable of something great.

A similar experience happened when a missionary to Cuba spoke at our church. He gave me a hand-painted gourd with a map of Cuba on it and challenged me to pray for this small island so close to our own southern border.

That personal attention from the missionary was like another hand on my shoulder, and made me think that I might be interested in missions.

I worked my way through college by playing in a trumpet trio and singing in a men's quartet recruiting for our college, and we appeared at many Youth for Christ Rallies. I ended up working in youth ministry and then with Youth for Christ in Denver, and spent the next 33 years at every level of the Youth for Christ mission. Those years taught me valuable lessons about serving Christ, and I think they apply to everyone in all walks of life and in all stages of life.

1) Sometimes, the opposite of what we're told is true! In the 1960s I was asked to lead an evangelism team of young people to India. Missions experts of that era said that teenagers were not qualified for ministry overseas, and that they might damage the work of the gospel. For three and one-half months our team crossed the nation and thousands of young people were exposed to the message of Christ. Everywhere we traveled doors opened for the gospel. My vision for youth ministry grew, and the building blocks for a half-century of ministry in India began to emerge.

2) Young people have the power to change the world. After I was elected president of Youth for Christ International, I discovered that there were more than one billion young people in the world. So we launched a "One Young Billion" program in more than 100 countries because we knew that in that group were the future leaders of the world. Our mission was to go where the people were, and present the gospel in a language they would understand.

Today the number is about two billion, and in many countries more than half of their population is under the age of twenty.

Several years ago I was taking the Denver Youth for Christ chapter to Washington, D.C. for a national convention. Just before leaving, a business man called me and said he wanted to sponsor a teenager named Paul Phillips to attend the convention. "Paul really needs your help," the man said. Well, Paul was nothing but trouble the entire trip. Halfway to Washington we found out that he was the leader of a gang and had been suspended from school. His father died an alcoholic. His mother, while drunk, fell off of their front porch and died of a broken neck. Paul found his security in this well-known group of criminals.

When the convention was over, and we were trying to head back to Denver, we couldn't find Paul. We waited and waited and finally were about to leave without him, when he showed up with one of the convention's counselors. Paul had stayed behind after the last meeting to give his life to Christ.

After we got back home I visited Paul's high school and asked them to give him a second chance. The change in Paul was dramatic. By the end of the year Paul was elected president of the Youth for Christ club, and attendance grew so much that we had to meet in the school auditorium. Many of the new members had been with Paul's gang.

Several years later we located Paul. He had a doctorate and was a professor of educational psychology. We asked him to participate in a telethon for YFC, and that night viewers donated more than $700,000 to help reach others like Paul.

3) Music opens doors to the gospel. Music is the international language of the soul. It has the power to touch hearts and minds in ways that are undeniable. I have seen music open doors to countries such as North Korea, Cambodia, Cuba, Israel, Estonia, Russia and many others.

I was in Russia with a team of YFC musicians two years before the collapse of the Soviet Union, during a time when the country was still hostile to Christianity. One night, after we conducted worship services, a group of young leaders asked if we would put on a Gospel Music Festival at the Lenin Cultural Palace. My initial human response was that it would be impossible. But six months later, our Russian contacts were granted a permit for the first gospel concert to be held in the Soviet Union. We put on the concert, and when the invitation was given to accept Christ, people ran forward to respond. I had never seen anything like it in my life.

We went back the next year for another concert, where 10,000 people stood in lines to receive a New Testament. When we ran out, people tore theirs in half to share with those who didn't receive one. More than 17,000 others left their names with us for a Bible to be mailed to them.

For 70 years these people had lived and suffered under the reign of the USSR, and for 50 years lived in fear of a fatal confrontation with the United States. They were starving for God's word, which had been denied them for so long.

Two years later we went back and, with the help of the International Bible Society, had four million New Testaments to give away. We happened to be there during a major confrontation between the Russian military and the newly elected party led by Boris Yeltsin. Citizens stood shoulder to shoulder facing down tanks. Along with religious leaders in the area, we began handing Bibles to everyone in the tanks and on the street. The tanks did not attack. The KGB approached us and asked for Bibles. A black limousine pulled up and the tinted window rolled down – a diplomat requested two Bibles. We were mobbed for God's Word!

We also put on one of the most memorable concerts I have ever witnessed. On Sept. 7, 1991, 48 hours after the Soviet Supreme Council convened and voted to eliminate Communism from their constitution and consign it to the pages of history, 300 gospel singers were on the stage in the Kremlin's Palace of Congress. The Korean evangelist Billy

Kim was the speaker. When he asked those who wanted to accept Christ, nearly everyone in the 6,500-seat auditorium stood. Billy said, "Please sit down. Perhaps you did not understand me." He then asked them again to stand if they wanted to follow Christ. They stood again. The sound of this great audience praying the sinner's prayer will be treasured in my heart forever. We gave Bibles to everyone there, including the Kremlin guards who stood in line, waiting for their copies.

It was the power of music that opened this and many other doors. This day a page in Christian music history was written.

4). Local leaders are the key to spreading the gospel. My early concept of missions revolved around Europeans and North Americans taking the gospel to the world – indeed, history shows the heroic efforts of missionaries and generous Christians in the West who have built and financed schools, hospitals, churches, evangelistic efforts, and translated the Bible into the languages of the world. But when I traveled with groups of young people around the world I became very impressed with the leaders who were already there – who needed someone to put a hand on their shoulder the way J.C. Penney did to me. These leaders needed encouragement, empowerment and practical training.

I calculated the salary of a foreign missionary for one year and realized that the same amount of money would fund 60 full-time Indian leaders for a year. They would understand the culture, not have a language barrier, and could not be asked to leave the country. This discovery ultimately led me to developing lifetime career training for emerging leaders – to plant the vision in their hearts and provide tools to help them become more effective in taking Christ to their nation.

One such leader was a young pastor who had survived

the killing fields of Pol Pot in Cambodia. During Pol Pot's brutal rampage, 90 percent of all leaders were eliminated. Most pastors were killed or fled the country. In 1998, as Cambodia was nearing the end of three decades of horror and civil war, I visited this young pastor in Phnom Penh. He and I planned for the first spiritual leadership conference ever held in that country. Our goal was to invite a representative group from each church denomination to participate. A year later we sponsored that conference. Approximately 500 leaders attended. Every province of the country was represented, and God performed a miracle.

I invited Billy Kim to tell the dramatic story of revival in his Buddhist nation, and how the same thing could take place in Cambodia. We closed the conference with the Lord's Supper. As I stood at the communion table with my Cambodian brothers, I looked across the audience. Everyone was weeping. A powerful spirit of unity was sweeping through their hearts.

When I participated in the Billy Graham Amsterdam Conference in 2000, I watched 12,000 indigenous pastors and evangelists from every corner of the earth, and I felt God's hand on their shoulders. The future belongs to them! This is their century! How beautiful on the mountains are the feet of those who bring good tidings of peace! The feet of white, black, yellow and brown have joined to bring the light of Christ to dark places. It is an exciting and undeniable force!

5) A door isn't closed just because someone says it is. Before I went to India, I read the autobiographies of the prime minister Jawaharlal Nehru, and of the famed missionary E. Stanley Jones. While in New Delhi I suggested to our hosts that we set up a meeting with the prime minister. Everyone told me that it was impossible. He's a Hindu, you're a Christian, he's too busy anyway, they said. But Nehru was a fascinating man – highly educated, one of the world's most distinguished leaders – and I wanted to meet him. Eventually I was able to procure the phone number of his appointment secretary. I explained who I was and asked for a meeting. He said no. But then he added, "I like American music and have an idea. Every Thursday the Prime Minister allows anyone to sit on his great lawn. He receives questions and answers complaints. Why don't you come and maybe you can meet him there?" So not only did I get to meet him, but our group got to sing for him!

Years later, through Billy Kim, our musical group was the first American music group to visit North Korea. We were invited by their government to participate in their Festival of Music and Arts to honor their "great leader," Kim Il Sung. Few Americans had visited this country of 22 million people. It was a nation shrouded in mystery.

Thirty days before our departure, North Korea pulled out of the anti-nuclear non-proliferation treaty. All visas were cancelled and all foreigners were asked to leave the country. People on our team cancelled their plans to go. I met with the North Korean Ambassador to the United Nations and informed him that we would not be able to make the trip to his country – our national leaders told us we would not be safe there.

Personally, I was relieved that we weren't going. Raising funds for the trip had been difficult. Many people warned me not to go. I couldn't find anyone to tell me what to expect there. I was concerned.

After telling the ambassador we would not be attending the Festival he said, "Mr. Groen, are you a man of your word? It would greatly disappoint our leaders if you did not fulfill your promise." I told him to look at the newspaper headlines. "All visas have been cancelled," I said.

"Don't worry," he replied. "Our government's invitation is a guarantee of your safety. Visas will be waiting for you at our embassy in Beijing."

So we flew to Beijing, and I was very restless. I could not sleep. We were going to visit one of the most repressive nations in the world. I signaled for our music leader to meet with me in the back of the plane, where we talked and prayed.

We were drawn to the Old Testament story of King Jehosaphat, who learned that a vast army was marching toward his country. He called upon his people to fast and pray. Then the Lord said, "Don't be afraid or paralyzed by this mighty army, for the battle is not yours, but God's" After Jeshosaphat conferred with the leaders, he determined that a choir should lead them into battle. The king selected the best singers in the country. They were to be clothed in sanctified garments. When the time came, they began to march ahead of the soldiers to battle. They sang, "His loving kindness is with you forever."

When the enemy heard the choir singing they were so confused that they began fighting with each other. That day, God gave King Jehosaphat a great victory.

I looked forward into the plane's cabin and saw our choir asleep in their seats. For the first time I knew that God was with us and that He would give us a great victory. Peace came to my troubled soul.

In Beijing our visas were waiting for us. But the representative there told us that, while he thought we should make the journey because we might be able to learn something useful for their government, he added that if something were to happen to us in North Korea, there was nothing anyone would do to help us.

The flight to Pyongyang was just under two hours. When we arrived and rolled to a stop, I looked out my window. Hundreds of Koreans cheered and sang as we came down the steps of the plane. A red carpet led us to a VIP room where we were received and held a press conference. The battle was the Lord's and this became the first of several visits to North Korea to distribute Bibles and preach the gospel.

6) Sometimes a broken heart is a good thing. I remember hearing Bob Pierce, the founder of World Vision, pray, "Lord, break my heart by the things that break yours." That prayer was on my heart as I took a team of young people to Calcutta, India, one of the most congested cities in the world. We visited the Kalighat Temple, the most famous of the Hindu temples. The name Calcutta is derived from the word Kalighat.

When we entered the temple we were shocked to witness the sacrifice of a black goat. An aid to the priest washed the goat in holy water, locked its head between two pieces of wood, and beheaded the goat with a machete. A Hindu family had brought their sacrifice to the temple, giving thanks for the successful sale of a piece of property.

I asked the priest if he would take our group through the temple, and he said, "I will take you on tour if you give me five minutes to explain what I believe as a Hindu." I said, "Fine, if you allow us five minutes to explain what we believe as Christians." He explained that Kalhi was a goddess with three arms, three legs and a third eye in her forehead. She is one of the principal deities of Hinduism. She demands various kinds of sacrifices. A century ago, infant children were offered as sacrifices at this temple.

When it was our turn to explain what we believe, our group sang a powerful arrangement of the song "God so Loved the World." As they sang, a crowd gathered to listen. When the song concluded, tears streamed down the cheeks of the priest. "No one has ever told me about Jesus before," he said. I gave him a New Testament and asked him to read everything I had underlined. "This will help you learn about Jesus," I said.

Just outside that temple is a large block building divided into two sections – one for women and one for men. On the door is written, "The Home for the Dying Destitute." Before she was world renowned, Mother Teresa and the Sisters of Charity built this home of compassion. It was established to care for those who had been abandoned or for whom no one cared. Next to the door was a hand-written note, signed by Mother Teresa: "Dear Ambulance Drivers – if you see someone dying or lying in the gutter, or if you find someone with an incurable disease, please bring them to me."

We stepped inside and saw dozens of people lying on cots. Small bowls for rice and water were nearby. On the walls were handmade signs that read, "God loves you," "God is here in this place," "We love you," "We will take care of you, and "You are in the arms of Jesus now." One of the sisters, knowing that I was president of Youth for Christ, came to me and said that there was a teenager near death in the women's section. "Please come and pray for her," the sister asked. The girl was sixteen, and weighed only 75 pounds. She was dying of malnutrition.

When I took her hand in mine she was too weak to speak. She opened her eyes when I put a damp cloth on her forehead. Through an interpreter I told her stories from the Bible. I asked her to squeeze my hand if she understood what I was saying. She often did. I told her that God loved her and had a wonderful home for her in heaven, and that God would give her a new body. She opened her eyes and looked at me for a long time, and squeezed my hand very tightly. I felt the language of God's love flowing between us. I lifted that little body into my arms. She was breathing very slowly. Then I felt her slip into the arms of Jesus.

It was a moment forever burned into my heart.

I visited Mother Teresa a few years later and asked how the funds were coming in for her many projects. Without hesitation she raised her hand to heaven and said, "We pray and God provides." Then she told me about a German

man who came to her compound with a television camera crew. "If you allow us to follow you around today, I will return to my country and raise $1 million for your work" Mother Teresa turned him down. She said, "I have met many like him who make movies of our work and we receive very little in return." After he left, a Hindu woman arrived and gave her 10,001 rupees. She said to Mother Teresa, "This is my life savings. It is all I have." Mother Teresa accepted her gift and said, "Christ wants our all. God will take care of that lady."

One of my close friends in Denver was Dr. Rick Ferguson, senior pastor of Riverside Baptist Church. Before he was tragically killed in an automobile accident he recorded these words about Mother Teresa:

"Only seven days separated the deaths of two women known best by their first names. When each died, the world wept. Though grief, shock and tears were common commodities shared by the entire world, the lives of Princess Diana and Mother Teresa were in stark contrast. Their lives represent both ends of many spectrums.

"One had an empire's wealth at her disposal. The other had no position of her own. One traveled daily among the world's sick, hurting and poor. The other was the headliner at the affairs of the rich and famous. One had the life of inner turmoil; the other possessed pease passing all understanding. One continually sought purpose and meaning; one spent her life being served. The other spent her life serving others. One was a princess in a worldly kingdom; the other was a servant in the Kingdom of God.

"Many women envied Diana's lifestyle, the opulence, power, comfort and opportunities she enjoyed. We couldn't make sense of the news that she never found joy, satisfaction, peace or purpose in that lifestyle. She had the world in her palm, yet happiness and meaning slipped through her fingers.

"At the same time, few of us would have chosen the life of Mother Teresa, the sacrifice, intense labor, thankless reward, hardship and loneliness. But few would argue that this woman's life contained more purpose and meaning, more personal peace and satisfaction than did Diana's. Mother Teresa was a servant to the forgotten people of the world. She demonstrated that servanthood is more than a lifestyle. It is a simple life dedicated to God."

When Mother Teresa was buried, she was given a state funeral. Leaders from more than fifty nations attended. She will be remembered as a friend of the destitute. The words dying and destitute have never left my mind after my visits there. They show a microcosm of the world: Many are dying without Christ in their hearts, and are destitute of spirit.

7) Sometimes the highest levels of government are open to the Gospel. After our encounter with India's Prime Minister Nehru, I established an important principle to never use subversive tactics to enter a difficult nation. I determined that it was important to introduce our ministry with dignity and make it known we were a Christian organization.

When I read the story of E. Stanley Jones, I was impressed that he moved among statesmen and leaders. He was a confidant to Franklin D. Roosevelt and a friend of Mahatma Gandhi's. So when I traveled to Cambodia, I arranged to visit the Kingdom of Cambodia's embassy and met with the Charge d'Affairs, Mr. Tan Vunyaung. I explained that my organization wanted to help his country and asked if he would help me arrange to take a delegation of businessmen for an official visit. I asked if he could set up meetings with government ministries. I told him that one of our government leaders would be with us and asked if we could sponsor a dinner for Cambodian government leaders. I asked if we could have a meeting with Prime Minister Hun Sen, and whether Mr. Tan could accompany us on our trip.

I had no idea what answer to expect from a country where Buddhism is the state religion. The Ministry of Religion building has a sign that reads, The Ministry of Religion and Cults.

"You would do this for my country?" Mr. Tan replied. "We are trying to get your government to help our people, but so far, the response has not been good."

When our delegation arrived at the airport in Phnom Penh, Mr. Tan and a delegation of government leaders met us as we stepped off of the plane. Every day we visited a different government ministry for a briefing on the challenges of rebuilding the country, which for the past three decades had lived with the horror of Pol Pot's killing fields and through a civil war.

Colorado State Senator John Andrews Jr. addressed more than 150 government leaders about the principles of leadership that were important in his life. He said that the principles of the life of Jesus had made more impact on him than anything else. Each guest received a gift of *The Jesus Film* in the Khmer language.

Our final meeting was with the Prime Minister. It became the first of many meetings together.

Now when our teams go to Cambodia, we often go to a poor village to distribute rice. We ask the Prime Minister or the King to select the village. When we arrive, the village chief receives our team. We are allowed to explain that Christians in America are praying for the Cambodian people, and that the rice is a gift from them. We give each person there a fifty-pound bag of rice, which will feed a family of six for a month. We also give each person there a Gospel of John. The people have such joy on their faces when they receive these gifts! And on most occasions a gov-

211

ernment television crew is with us and puts our story on the news.

We were also able to meet with King Sihanouk and deliver thirty tons of rice to be given to the poorest of the poor in his country. He invited us to his palace for a ceremony, and I invited several pastors representing all the protestant churches in Cambodia to accompany us. When I introduced the pastors I said, "Your majesty, the rice we give you is from the Christians in your country. We want to thank you for the freedom you have given them to build churches throughout your land. They pray for you. They are building strong character into the lives of the people that will help your country become strong."

When we left, the king's servants came on their knees, bearing a gift for each of us.

Mr. Tan now has a new assignment in Phnom Penh. He and his wife have prayed to receive Christ.

E. Stanley Jones said, "If you want an effective, godly ministry, you will need Wet Eyes, Bent Knees and a Broken Heart." Forty years since that first visit to India, the building blocks for ministry are still relevant in a changing world. The same principles guide us today – to train and support national leaders; to put vision in their hearts and tools in their hands; and to use creative ways to take the light of Christ to the difficult places of the world.

My wife Dottie has been my partner in ministry and my life's companion. Except for Christ, she has been the most influential person in my life. Nothing of value could have happened without her partnership. She has supported and influenced every quest and dream. She has stood strong during some of life's experiences that we still do not fully understand. She is her own person, is a constructive critic, is widely read and is a great mother and marvelous grandmother. I can say, with the writer of Proverbs 31:11-12, "Her husband can trust her, and she will richly satisfy his needs. She will not hinder him, but help him all her life."

Through the example of my parents I came to recognize a final life principle: The power of a seed when planted. In 1935-1936, Willis Clay was a missionary to India and had just one convert, named P.K. Paul. When Willis Clay came back to the U.S. he spoke at the Open Bible Institute where my parents were students. They were so moved by his testimony that they contributed money to buy property for a church to be built in India by this convert. It became the mother church to hundreds of other churches in India years later. As Bible School students they had little to give, but the seed they planted has brought forth great fruit.

Through these experiences and observations on effective communication of the gospel, I am so grateful to God for being the true Hand on the Shoulder to each of us. May we extend that hand to those around us and throughout the world. As Torrey Johnson, the founder of Youth for Christ used to say, "The past is great, the present is better, but the best is yet to come!"

Thirty-two years ago a good friend of my brother's, Frank Kocur, asked if my wife and I would host a party for a friend of his who was running for Colorado State Senate. We agreed, as long as we would be able to meet the person first and get to know him. When we met Tim Philibosian and Lyn we were very attracted to them as a couple who loved the Lord, loved life and loved each other very much. The commitment they had for each other was so warming and apparent – it was evident that these were people of sincerity and compassion.

Tim has more gifts and talents than most men I have met. He had the largest Christian law practice in Colorado, and was licensed in Colorado, California and Washington, D.C. He went back to school to get his divinity degree, and for many years was recognized by many as the premier authority on the New Age Movement. He is also a member of the Mensa organization.

After Tim sold his law practice he joined me in my company, Sturgeon Systems, as our in-house legal counsel. He helped me evaluate many investment opportunities and business relationships as well.

Tim was asked to become senior pastor at Trinity Church in Santa Barbara, where he served for nine years. Tim and his family of two boys and a girl have suffered more medical hardships and setbacks than any family I have known. Despite these circumstances, Tim and Lyn have remained strong in the faith, resolved to live like Christ.

Be That Man

Tim Philibosian

W<small>ASHINGTON</small>, DC, <small>IS A CITY CHARGED WITH</small> electricity. Energy pulses, radiating from every building surrounding the Mall. Nighttime intensifies the sensation as the monuments and government structures, bathed in dramatic lighting that enhances each angle, magnify the sense of drama and excitement that makes Washington the most powerful city on earth.

I lived there.

My office was on Pennsylvania Avenue, between the White House and the Capitol—across the street from the National Gallery of Art, next to the National Archives, home of the U.S. Constitution and the Declaration of Independence. A short time later, I moved further down Pennsylvania Avenue to an office overlooking the city's most famous street and with a view of the Washington Monument.

Not bad for a 25-year old from California.

As a recent law school graduate, I had accepted a job as trial attorney with the Federal Trade Commission. It was our task to investigate and litigate violations of unfair business practices perpetrated by some of the largest companies in the world. The dollar amounts ran into the billions. When news of an investigation was published by the press, a company's stock could fall precipitously. The prestige

18

and potential of such a position were enormous. Extensive travel, courtroom drama, immediate access to powerful executives, and frequent battle with some of the nation's most influential and highly compensated lawyers were constants in my life.

As far as a legal career goes, I had it made. Yet my entire life was about to change in an instant, by a means that I never anticipated.

The image of the Lincoln Memorial illuminated at night will be forever implanted in my memory. It was not the first time I had captured this view, but this particular evening it touched me as never before.

While driving my car, I was listening to a message by Dr. Walter Martin, the founder of the Christian Research Institute and author of the influential book, *Kingdom of the Cults.* My heart was pounding, I could feel my blood racing as I heard him quote from and expound upon Paul's words—to *Timothy*—in 2 Timothy 4:

> "I give you this charge: Preach the Word; be prepared in season and out of season . . . For the time will come when men will not put up with sound doctrine. Instead, to suit their own desires, they will gather around them a great number of teachers to say what their itching ears want to hear. They will turn their ears away from the truth and turn aside to myths. But you, keep your head in all situations, endure hardship, do the work of an evangelist, discharge all the duties of your ministry."

"That time has come," thundered Dr. Martin. "Men are not seeking truth. They are turning to myths, to ear-tickling teachers who tell them only what they want to hear. We need men today who are willing to take a stand, who are willing to refute false teachers, men who are willing to endure hardship, to pay the price." Then, he shouted,

"WHO WILL BE THAT MAN?" [Dr. Martin's words have been paraphrased.]

I practically jumped out of the car, thrusting my fist through the roof of that 1971 Mercury Capri (fortunately, the sunroof was open) as I shouted back, "I WILL BE THAT MAN!" Little did I realize the significant price that would be extracted from me for the words I spoke that night.

As long as I could remember, I had been a follower of Jesus Christ. Through high school, my parents took me to church every week. It was seldom a burden for them, for I delighted in seeing my friends and learning more about God and the Bible.

When I enrolled at the University of California at Santa Barbara, I was confronted with challenges far beyond anything I had faced until then. UCSB is one of America's top public universities. Nobel laureates and world-class programs attract some of the nation's top scholars and researchers. However, UCSB is also known for its party school atmosphere. With its Southern California beach location, year-around balmy weather, and 10,000 students living off-campus in one square mile, every possible personal indulgence is readily available. Drug and alcohol abuse and sexual "liberation" were the majors of many who attended UCSB.

Standing firm as a follower of Jesus Christ was a challenge. During my first year, it was not uncommon to step across bodies passed out in front of the door in order to get to church on Sunday mornings. As a participant in theater and drama, I was invited to closing night parties that featured recreational drugs and rooms where the new frontiers of sexuality, marijuana, binge drinking and LSD were being explored.

Due to God's grace, my parents' encouragement, and friends who shared my beliefs, I not only continued attending church weekly, but also participated in campus evangelical groups, taught a class of junior high students in a local church, and participated in a Bible study with my peers in my junior and senior years.

During my studies at Santa Clara University School of Law, I was extremely active in a local church. During my third year at law school, I participated in a musical group comprised of young adults, sang in a quartet, and assisted in the direction of a musical. At the same time, I was working for a private law firm, assisting in the office of the public defender, serving as notes and comments editor of the law review, and carrying a full course load. No wonder I contracted mononucleosis while studying for the bar exam.

When I arrived in Washington, I found my colleagues at the Federal Trade Commission were among the best and the brightest from the nation's law schools. The enormous complexity of the litigation, the extremely high dollar amounts involved, and the skill of the opposition's attorneys dictated high commitment and competence from our staff. Therefore, when my peers discovered I was a Christian, they were capable of asking probing questions that challenged my knowledge.

While my faith was never shaken, my ability to defend my beliefs definitely was. That is when it hit me: I had spent four years studying economics and three years studying law. It was now time for me to spend time studying that which I considered the most important aspect of my life— my belief in God.

The passion to devote myself for a period to the study of Bible background, preaching, teaching, Greek, and Hebrew nearly consumed me. The challenges from the lawyers at the FTC and from Dr. Martin ("they will not believe in truth but will turn to myths") energized me to study apologetics (the art of defending the faith) and aberrant religions.

This desire came almost simultaneously with the commitment to "be that man" that I had uttered in my car. Fellow attorneys were stunned when I announced my intention to leave the FTC without a job offer, without even knowing for certain what I was going to do. They could not understand that an individual on the fast track to fortune, as most government anti-trust lawyers were (by taking a job in business or with a private firm after a few years with the government), would voluntarily leave his position in order to pursue his beliefs in God.

Big cities not only provide big challenges, but they also offer big opportunities. In Washington, one of these opportunities is the Prayer Breakfast Movement. For many years, numerous individuals have met one-on-one and in small groups, crossing party lines to love one another, share their struggles and joys, study the Bible, and pray together. For a few moments, rivalries are set aside, political differences are overlooked, and agendas are ignored as powerful officials, lobbyists, judges, White House and Hill staff, internationals, lawyers and businesspeople meet to share their lives with one another. The National Prayer Breakfast annually brings together the President of the United States with thousands of people and leaders from throughout the world who hear words of encouragement from the Bible and pray together.

For the next few months after leaving my position with the FTC, I worked with the Prayer Breakfast Movement, meeting with individuals, attending prison Bible studies, and exploring ministry and educational alternatives. Deciding that it was time to commit myself fully to the task, I made two significant decisions: first, to get married; and second, to attend seminary.

For the past year and half, I had been dating Lyn Kirby, a woman who shared my interest in Christian service. She and her roommates lived in a former embassy which was renamed Trinity House, located only a few blocks from

Fellowship House, the nerve center of those associated with the Prayer Breakfast Movement. The women at Trinity House were committed to sharing the principles of Christ with those in Washington, no matter what their income, status, or affiliation. The dedication of these women attracted and influenced me, and I found myself drawn particularly to Lyn.

Realizing I did not want to face life without her, I proposed to Lyn and two weeks later we were married—in Fellowship House on the day of the National Prayer Breakfast. That was a miracle in itself!

Two days after our marriage, Lyn and I boarded a plane for Vancouver, British Columbia. After one semester at Regent College, we moved to Colorado where I completed my Master of Divinity at Denver Seminary.

It had always been my intention to resume my legal career, so I accepted an offer from a Christian lawyer to unite with him in the practice he had started some years earlier. Our firm quickly grew, and we eventually added four other attorneys and staff to handle our increased workload. I continued teaching in a local church, and soon had a large class of adults that satisfied my desire to teach.

Seeking to serve the Lord however I could, in 1980 I ran for the State House of Representatives. Although I was a complete unknown to the politically involved, I was able to gather significant assistance and encouragement from contacts with numerous churches.

The election was so close we did not know the results until the next day. Although I had prevailed in 21 of the 27 precincts, I lost the closest election in the state. One of the great ironies that struck me is that it rained the entire day of the election. Such a rain is uncommon in the Denver area in September, and that weather kept back many who were fearful of leaving their homes to vote in the rain. Since I prevailed among the elderly, and their turnout was particularly low, it is likely I would have prevailed had it not rained. "Who's in charge?" my campaign manager bellowed when I expressed my frustration. "Who controls the rain?" God does. I ached for a long time when I entered Denver and viewed the golden dome of the Capitol. "God, don't you want your people in office? Don't you want those who will defend biblical values, support the right to life, stand against pornography, and deal with those issues that are undermining our communities and schools?" But God, in his sovereignty, decided I had another path to walk.

One day at my law office, I received a call from a woman who gave me news that would forever change my life. "The New Age is moving into your school district." New Age? I did not know what it was. "You'd better look into it," she said. "You'll be shocked."

Although I had studied the cults and the occult in seminary, the term "New Age" was not part of my studies. Its influence was just beginning. After some quick study, I learned that the New Age Movement is basically Hinduism in the dress of Western culture—Maharishi Mahesh Yogi meets Madison Avenue.

Since I had just run for public office, I was known to the school board and the superintendent. When I showed up at a monthly school board meeting with numerous supporters, the board was obviously curious to know why we were there. At the conclusion of the meeting, I approached the superintendent and two of the board members and asked, "I'm just curious to know how you intend to justify to the press that you've dropped music, art and PE, but you're able to introduce soul travel, incest and becoming one with a tree?" "What?" exclaimed the superintendent. "What are you talking about." I presented him with the book list and excerpts from several of the books.

The next day I received a call from the superintendent. He told me I was right, the books were part of a new supplemental curriculum, but that he was withdrawing all of them immediately. That evening, I received a call from Dr. Gordon Lewis, professor of theology at Denver Seminary. "Tim, you accomplished in one night what 100 years of missions work in India cannot do. Once Hinduism gets in, it cannot be removed."

Naturally, I felt great for what we were able to accomplish and what Dr. Lewis had said. Confirmation came in a challenge I heard: "Don't do what others can and will do; do what others can't or won't do." There were plenty of lawyers to handle divorces, wills, or property line disputes, but how many of them were keeping New Age curriculum out of the public schools?

Compelled by these circumstances, I approached my senior partner to tell him I was going to take a six month leave of absence. That was in April of 1983. I never returned to the full-time practice of law.

A local businessman offered to give me an office, secretarial assistance, and a small salary in return for my part-time services as corporate counsel. This gave me the freedom to explore additional alternatives in the "can't or won't do" world that now fascinated me.

In 1985, at the invitation of Dr. Lewis, I became the first Executive Director of Evangelical Ministries to New Religions, an organization that sought to unite the counter-cult ministries throughout North America. It was during this time I met, as a board member, Dr. Walter Martin, the one who had challenged me, "Who will be that man!" Dr. Martin and I formed a close relationship that was to build over the next few years.

Recognizing the limitations of representing so many diverse groups, I left EMNR and formed my own non-profit organization in 1987, Rivendell. Our desire was to stand against those people, ideas, institutions and elements of society that sought to promote religious beliefs in conflict with Christianity, whether they be aberrant religious beliefs or cultural practices that conflicted with biblical teachings. Our activities were diverse. We conducted seminars throughout the nation on topics such as Islam, Satanism, witchcraft, the New Age Movement, and Mormonism. We provided workshops and training sessions on the right to life, creation/evolution, reincarnation, psychics, apologetics, education, and persuasion skills. We sponsored debates surrounding the visit of the Pope to Colorado and with professors at universities. I debated the ACLU at the annual convention of the Colorado Bar Association, and the topic of pornography at the annual convention of cable TV owners and operators. We published a newsletter, responded to individual issues, and consulted with people throughout the nation.

A few years later, a local church called me as its Teaching Pastor. The church provided office space, phone answering, and, more importantly, a home base that offered accountability and opportunity to grow spiritually. The consistent group of supporting and encouraging people gave me the courage to confront the challenges that were part of my everyday life.

The church ordained me, and helped me to establish myself more fully as a pastor in a local church. One-fourth of my time was committed to the local church, three-fourths to Rivendell.

I believed that I was following God's leading and building my ministry just as he desired. I was teaching a large adult class in a significant church on a weekly basis, and developing a ministry that had taken me not only to much of the United States, but also to India and the Philippines. Desiring to be confident of God's guidance, I decided to commit the last few months of 1991 and January of 1992 to understanding fully the direction that I should take. I spent much time in prayer, consulting with others, and seeking a plan and direction for Rivendell and the teaching ministry at the church.

In late February 1992, I was scheduled to speak at the opening session for a men's conference in the upscale ski resort, Beaver Creek, Colorado. A few years earlier, a group of men from a church in Dallas visited Beaver Creek and determined to make their journey an annual ski retreat/Bible conference. I had spoken at the conference in 1991, and was privileged to receive an invitation to return as the opening night speaker.

I prepared diligently for the trip, and drove eagerly toward the mountains. Even though snow started to fall, I was not deterred. I had driven these mountains many times, and knew I could navigate the roads without difficulty.

The driver ahead of me apparently was focused on something else. His car spun out of control, slid across the highway, and came to a thudding stop against a guardrail. From my vantage point, I could see the driver's head smash against the steering wheel, then lay still. Virtually without thinking, I drove past the wrecked vehicle, stopped alongside the highway, and ran back to render assistance. By the time I reached the car, the driver was cognizant, although dazed. I helped him out of the car, and we started to assess the damage to the front end.

That's all I remember.

I was told a driver in a pickup truck was accelerating too quickly for the conditions, spun out of control, and hit the wrecked car which then hit me. Later, a neurologist told me I was hit by a force equal to that of Reggie Jackson taking a homerun cut at a fastball. I was flung about thirty feet, and lay motionless on the snow. Those who came to render assistance thought I was dead.

It took 45 minutes for an ambulance to reach me. All I remember of the ride to the hospital was a few simple questions ("What is your name?" "What is your phone number?" "In what state do you live?") and reaching my hand to my thigh to discover my jeans had been ripped.

I was in a coma for several days, attached to machines for which I was very grateful when I regained consciousness. My vision was seriously impacted, the most obvious manifestation of which was double vision, which required that I wear an eye patch. The severe blow to my forehead damaged the olfactory nerves so that I lost my sense of smell, and therefore had a difficult time distinguishing any taste. My ability to walk was seriously affected. I had terrible headaches and required enormous periods of sleep. My memory was sketchy, my ability to speak impaired.

Once released to my home, I realized that I could not do those things necessary to continue my ministry. I had an extremely hard time standing, walking, reading and speaking. My memory lapse prevented me from recalling past talks, memory verses, names, phone numbers, dates, and outlines. How could I prepare my talks? How could I plan any more seminars? How could I study and prepare for future engagements? Would I be able to write or speak effectively again?

Naturally, pressures began to rise at home. No longer could I play with the children or assist them with their homework. I could not help with yard work. Speaking on the phone was painful and laborious. Reading was out of the question. When would this end?

My mind was plagued by new doubts. "God, why would you allow this? All I was trying to do was serve you. I gave you my legal career. I gave you my commitment, my life. I took three months to plan, to organize, to design a schedule that would enable me to speak to as many as possible and build the ministry. I sought you all along. Why would you allow this to happen?"

My questions were from the depths of my heart. The

case was articulated as well as any lawyer could do. It reminded me of Jeremiah's pleading with God in Jeremiah 12: "God, I have a case against you. You've asked me to represent you, to speak. I've done that, and all I've received in return is sarcasm, taunts, threats, prison, the stocks, even death threats from my own family. God, is this what you want? Why do you allow wickedness to prosper? Why do you do things this way?" God's response to Jeremiah is classic: "Jeremiah, what are you whining about? I haven't asked you to do any more than I've asked of so many others. I'm training you for the battles that lie ahead. If you can't walk with the footmen, how will you ever learn to run with the horses? And that's where I want you, Jeremiah, running with the horses. Taking on the biggest, boldest, fiercest challenges ever, and conquering because you and I are working together. Don't quit, don't be content simply to get by. Run with the horses."

That was God's message to me as well. "Tim, if I wanted your life to be easy, I would have made it so. But I don't want you to be content with the small battles. No, Tim, I want you to learn to run with the horses. So get tough—because you have no idea what I have in store for you."

"Be that man!"

"Run with the horses!"

I did not quit, I did not give up. As I look back, I realize that I was standing there at that time because of a commitment I had made years earlier: "Lord, I will be that man!" This was my chance to prove my earlier statement. In retrospect, however, I admit that if I had any knowledge of what was to transpire over the next few years, I may not have been willing to persevere.

After being confined to the house for months, I became eager to celebrate my gradual yet incomplete improvement. My first significant venture was a camping vacation 75 miles away to Lake Dillon with my family and some close friends. We set up the tent and camp site, and settled in for our first night away since the accident. Around 3:00 a.m., I cried out in pain to my wife, "Take me to a hospital." "What's wrong?" "I don't know. I hurt so much. Get help." We left our three young children in the tent, waking and informing our friends of our plight, and set out in search of a medical facility in this mountainous part of Colorado.

Amazingly, we were able to find an emergency medical facility. My pain was so great I had to be assisted from the car. Some hours later, I discovered I was suffering from the agonizing pain of a kidney stone.

The next day, back at the camp site, armed with pain killers should there be a recurrence of my problem, I again cried out, "Why, Lord? I've never experienced such pain in my life. Why now? Why during my first time away with my family since the accident? I almost died five months ago, my family has been shattered by all that has occurred, my career has been devastated, my wife has had her world turned upside down, and this was our first attempt at some escape. Why such agony?"

God's answer? Silence.

Splitting headaches. Vision challenges. The inability to smell. Self-doubts about my career. Fears about my health. Financial questions. And still—silence.

Almost exactly one year after the car accident, I was again preparing for the Beaver Creek speaking engagement. Despite my anxieties, the men had asked me to come back, to report on the accident and share what God had been doing in my life. A few days before I was to leave for the mountains, I developed pink eye. The doctor prescribed medication which caused excruciating pain when I put it in my eyes.

My wife called the nurse who said, "Yes, it can be painful. Just tell him to tolerate it." Refusing to believe it should hurt like this, I read the label carefully and found that the medication I had been given was mistakenly dispensed—it was not meant to be put in the eyes.

The nurse on the phone (it was almost midnight) told us to go immediately to the emergency room. An ophthalmologist was brought in who spent the next several hours rinsing and observing my eyes. When he released me, he said I should be OK, but that my eyes would be extremely sensitive for the next week or so and that I could not drive. Two men from the Beaver Creek conference picked me up so that I could tell the next part of my amazing saga.

The car accident had almost killed me. My vision was significantly impacted. I could not smell, so my taste was affected. The kidney stone taught me pain as I had never known. The medication mistake nearly cost me my sight. When would this end?

Still, I wanted to "be that man" and "run with the horses." What strategy would Satan try next to destroy me? Silly question: He assaulted my family.

Over the next few months, the following occurred: My older son, JT, was on roller blades when he was pushed by a friend. JT fell, breaking his arm. An general anesthesia operation was required to set it, and that operation had to be repeated six months later because it was not done properly the first time.

My younger son, Mark, ran into a basketball pole which cut his face seriously. Numerous stitches were required.

My daughter, Joylyn, had to be taken to the emergency room (as had the other two) when she began choking on a fish bone that required professional expertise to remove.

JT was at a youth camp when he was misdiagnosed as having the flu. It turned out he had appendicitis. Several days later, when he finally was taken to a hospital for an emergency operation, the surgeon told us he had been within hours of dying.

Mark was at the church when one of the youth staff took

a swing with a broom stick at a piñata. He missed the stick and crushed Mark's cheekbone, nearly putting out his eye. Another emergency room visit and more stitches.

JT had not recovered fully from the appendectomy. I was speaking in North Carolina when Lyn called: His temperature would not go down. He had to have another operation. His fourth in less than two years.

Even Lyn was not exempt. Of all things, she cut her *tongue* on a the crust of French bread. We were on the way to the emergency room when the bleeding finally stopped.

Over a year after my accident, nerves in my spinal column were so impacted that I could not hold a book. Bev, the world's greatest physical therapist, relieved the pain by providing therapy for six months in exchange for theology lessons.

I used to say that there were two reserved parking zones at the emergency room: ambulance parking and "The Philibosian Zone." It seemed the staff knew us all by name. "Ah, Mr. Philibosian. Your regular room?"

Physical challenges never seemed to relent. The worst— at least since the car accident—occurred in July 1995 when we were staying near Lake Dillon, Colorado, for a family vacation. Immediately before our return to Denver, we took a family photo of all of us on our mountain bikes. From our condo to the photo spot was only a block or two, but we decided to take the long way back.

For me, it turned out to be a *very* long way back. I missed a turn and fell off a cliff, hurtling over huge boulders and experiencing a sensation I had never before felt. Lying on my side in the dirt, I was aware of Lyn and Mark's presence. "Tim, Tim! Are you OK?" shouted Lyn. Crying, screaming, again and again, "Tim! Tim! Are you OK?" I could hear, but I didn't respond. I wasn't sure if I was OK. Something was not right.

JT flagged down a fireman who called paramedics. Just

like *Rescue 911*, I was taken up the cliff on a backboard with cables. After a short stay in a medical center, a helicopter flew me to the emergency room at Denver General Hospital. Diagnosis: a broken back. Fractured vertebrae. The doctor told me I had just lost one-half inch, something one of my stature can ill afford.

My hospital room became a gathering place for friends to reconnect. "Why, I haven't seen you since Tim's last accident!" The hospital receptionist literally told visitors, "Tim's room? Just follow the crowd." Another one heard, "Just go toward the noise." I think my bed was used to hold the salsa and chips as much as to support me.

After my release, I had to stay in a hospital bed for five months. The bed would not fit in our bedroom, so I was confined to our living room. Since my back was broken, I had to wear an uncomfortable brace or lie flat in the bed that entire time. In order to turn, which I had to do every few hours, I had a bell which I rang, waking Lyn so that she could assist.

"God, why are you doing this? Why are you allowing this to happen? All I've wanted to do is serve you. I've given you everything. What more do you want from me?"

His answer: Silence.

Once again I was reminded: "Be that man! Run with the horses!"

It was during my recuperation that a church in Santa Barbara, California, called asking me to be its Senior Pastor. I had spoken at the church and knew a number of its people. Events worked together to the point where I agreed to accept the position.

When I spoke at Beaver Creek and told the men I would be moving to Santa Barbara, one of the men rushed up after my talk and said, "Thanks, Tim, for building my retirement portfolio. I just called my broker and told him to invest everything in Santa Barbara hospital stocks." It turns out that might have been a pretty good idea.

We were in Santa Barbara for a few weeks when Joylyn was running our dog, Charlie, on the beach. Joylyn stopped. Charlie didn't. Joylyn was tossed in the air like a rag doll, breaking her collarbone.

JT was playing soccer when he twisted and broke his leg. It required his *fifth surgery* to set it properly.

Mark started playing tennis at a high level, but his freshman year in college was virtually taken away when he suffered an extremely painful bone bruise that prevented him from playing most of the year.

Despite these setbacks, many wonderful opportunities came along.

Leading a local church in adapting to new circumstances, forming cutting-edge ministries, renovating old facilities, and securing funds and plans to construct a new building.

Participating in additional speaking opportunities in Colorado, Arizona, Washington, DC, and various California locations.

Serving the body of Christ internationally in Israel, Russia, India and Cambodia.

Living in a beautiful resort community.

My determination was to "be that man" despite Satan's many attempts to sidetrack me. There were times of disappointment, heartache, and frustration, but I never gave up, I never went back. I never doubted God, although I sure thought at times he could have worked out things a little differently.

For decades I had made myself a willing target, representing Christ in secular places. I had spoken out at the university, during law school, and while serving as a government attorney, asserting the weaknesses of religious fallacies and debating those who attacked traditional values. I had taught large classes, and I had spoken before significant conferences. I debated on college campuses, before secular forums, and on hostile radio programs. But none of that prepared me for the most painful and harsh disparagement I would soon have to face.

Satan's new strategy was to attack me personally, emotionally, and spiritually, challenging my self-confidence, leadership and abilities—from critics within my own church.

This was the most devastating attack of all.

When I planned the first church-wide fundraising effort to modernize our facilities and construct a new building, a surreptitious counter-effort was planned. Rather than support our drive to upgrade our deteriorating facility, some spread the word, "Let's meet at the cross on the lawn and pray against this effort." While our campaign was successful, the seeds for future provocation were sown.

Some in the church began to question my decisions, undermine my authority, challenge my leadership, and belittle my messages. Rumor, innuendo and accusations began to spread throughout the church. Divisions were formed, disunity became common. Gossip became acceptable behavior.

In the past, I had always built consensus, unified groups, and brought peace. Suddenly, cracks and fissures were developing around me, even among my staff. Seemingly petty issues became matters so serious that people were leaving the church, and doing so bitterly, scarring the reputation of the church and, far worse, Christ himself.

Some left the church as we moved toward contemporary music, some because we went to more casual dress. An usher erupted because a woman assisted in passing out bulletins. At least one left because the American flag was not on prominent display. Most hurtful was the accusation that I did not preach the Word of God. After sacrificing my legal career, attending seminary, and devoting my life to teaching the Bible, I was being accused of not teaching God's Word. This was almost more than I could bear.

The confidence I had in my teaching was eroded. The trust I had placed in some of my closest friends was betrayed. The hope I had for the growth of the church, its influence on the community and the maturity of its people was quickly fading. The joy I had previously experienced in ministry had vanished.

It was painful to realize this was happening to me. Satan could not get to me by attacking my status, money, health, or health of my family, so now he was attacking my self-confidence, reputation, friendships and faith.

One night, while working in my office after dark, an explosion shattered the window a few feet from my head. I fell to the floor, reached up, grabbed the phone, dialed 911 and cried out, "Someone just tried to shoot me!" I began shaking convulsively, sobbing, afraid. "God, I can't take this anymore. I can't go on like this." When the sheriff came, he discovered it was not a bullet, but a fist-sized rock that had been thrown at me. While we do not know who threw it, we can only assume it was meant to inflict serious injury.

Finally, I was at the breaking point. I asked myself, "Will you continue to live the faith you have been speaking of all these years?" While I refused to back down from my commitment to "be that man," I realized that God was leading me to a new battlefield. On July 31, 2005, after 9-½ years of serving the church in Santa Barbara, I resigned.

The conclusion to this chapter remains unfinished. I love the local church. People in Santa Barbara have come to know the Lord and follow him more closely. The church touched people throughout the world. My family and I built intimate relationships that will last a lifetime. But the cost has been very high.

God has something else in mind for me. Perhaps he had

to present me with a very challenging situation to get me to the next level. Each step has prepared me to climb higher, to reach further. Like a miner's lantern, God has illuminated my path only a few feet at a time. I cannot see far, so I take only one small step until the light shines a little further ahead.

I wish I could see more. I wish I could know more. I would like to think that the future will be less painful, less stressful, less costly than has been the past. But I think Jeremiah would have said the same, let alone Job who sacrificed everything for God.

At the time of the writing of these words, I am still wounded, still recovering. But I am confident of my desire. It is the same desire I expressed when I thrust my fist through a car roof thirty years ago. I still want to "be that man."

It has been my privilege to speak before hundreds of thousands of people. While I will not know this side of heaven what impact I have had, I am confident God is not finished with me yet. New opportunities lie ahead.

Concerning my status, finances, accidents, family injuries, personal attacks, losses, struggles, and abandonment—I admit that I have been hurt. The negatives have had a significant impact on me and my family. I cannot deny I would have preferred an easier road, especially for my family. But I have to rest in the God in whom I have placed my faith and my trust.

Dawson Trotman was the founder of the Navigators, one of Christianity's most successful ministries. He was a mentor to many, challenging them to memorize Scripture, pass on the faith, and disciple one another. He lost his life while saving a young girl from drowning. Someone ran up to his wife to tell her of the unfortunate accident. Her spontaneous response was to quote Psalm 115:3—"Our God is in the heavens. He does whatever he pleases."

That is our call as well—to trust God, even when the circumstances seem to be more than we can handle. Our God is in the heavens. He is in charge. He knows what is happening. He controls circumstances. He desires our best.

To think anything less would be a disgrace. It would be to doubt God and His majesty. To give up, to doubt, to quit when circumstances seem to be going against us would deprive us of our opportunity to let God use us for His glory, to work through us in a way that can be clearly seen as God's accomplishment and not ours. Moses did not quit when the people rebelled—and God led them to the Promised Land. Elijah did not quit when the prophets turned against him—and God brought fire down that consumed the altar. Daniel did not quit when the king's edict prohibited him from praying—and God led him out of the den of lions. Paul did not quit when he was beaten and jailed—and God used him to plant churches throughout Asia.

Winston Churchill wrote,

"To every man there comes in his lifetime that special moment when he is figuratively tapped on the shoulder and offered a chance to do a very special thing, unique to him, and fitted to his talents. What a tragedy if that moment finds him unprepared or unqualified for that which would be his finest hour."

All of life is preparation for the next finest hour. Who knows what God will do in and through a man devoted to him? All I know is that I want to be ready.

I want to be used by you, Lord, in any way you choose. I want to be ready to serve you no matter the cost.

"Tim," asks the Lord, "Are you ready to run with the horses? Are you willing to be that man?"

"Oh, Lord—May I be that man!"

When I first met Larry Poland more than twenty years ago, he was headed for Hollywood, recognizing that somehow, some way, there had to be a way to reach the super stars for Christ. I have known many men with a strong resolve to make a difference in the Kingdom of God, but none any stronger than Larry's.

He knew that the media industry has the strongest influence in the world, and prayed that God would use him in a special way to positively impact it. Every quarter, Master Media, the non-profit organization that Larry started, sends out a prayer calendar with names and companies of media leaders with a request that every person listed on a different day would receive prayers from God's people. We all know that God can change hearts if enough of us will pray for them on a regular basis.

The way God has used Larry and Master Media is truly a miracle. What a blessing it is for us to witness how God's love and direction has so positively affected the media industry for Christ! We're seeing more quality movies and movie stars with the courage of their convictions to be counted for Christ. TV sitcoms are beginning to have more quality shows with care and concern about what they say and how they say it. The family unit is being more properly postured as the caring, loving American family that has been the strength of this great country for more than 200 years.

It is amazing what God has done and continues to do through Dr. Larry Poland and his miracle workers at Master Media.

Finding God in Hollywood

Larry Poland

WHEN I WAS A KID GROWING UP IN A SMALL town in the Midwest, I didn't know anything about Hollywood or the entertainment industry. But a friend challenged me to consider ministering to media people in Hollywood. I said I wasn't interested, but made the "mistake" of saying that I would pray about it! I decided to do some research before I made my decision. For six months I interviewed people in management positions on the topic of how their personal faith affects their lives and decisions in the entertainment industry.

I think deep down I expected that there was a conspiracy, that there was a smoke-filled room on Sunset Boulevard with people in black capes dancing around boiling pots, wringing their hands, chanting and trying to figure out how they could systematically steal the souls of America. In my research I found that this was not the case. I found that the people inside Hollywood were bright, creative and fun people. I loved them. They were wild and crazy.

There was only one problem: They were lost.

My definition of "lost" is living by a set of standards that dismantles and destroys your life. What I discovered was that the women, by the time they reached thirty, and the men, by the time they reached forty, were pretty well dismantled. It was frightening to see people when they got to

19.

that level. They typically fell into two categories: The hard, scarred and cynical bunch, or the searching-or-found-something bunch.

The hard, scarred and cynical bunch had many hardcore, kick-'em-in-the-groin feminists. Those women were angry, rightfully so, at what men had done to them. If men lived according to God's principles and expressed God's character, I believe there wouldn't be very many of these angry people. The men in this group were tough, in-your-face business people who would rather cuss you out than look at you, which only confirmed and consolidated how lost they were.

The searching-or-found-something bunch is made up of those who reached a threshold of success and asked, "Is this all there is?" They explored everywhere for something that would provide some meaning to their lives. They tried substance abuse to find some peace and escape – which, of course, only led to bondage.

I'm telling you, the hunger and thirst for something meaningful in Hollywood is epidemic.

The apostle Paul told his young disciple, Timothy, "Mark this, my friend Timothy, there will be terrible horrific times in the last days. People will be lovers of themselves, lovers of money, boastful, proud, abusive, disobedient to their parents, ungrateful, unholy, without love, unforgiving, slanderous, without self control, brutal, not lovers of the good, treacherous, rash, conceited, lovers of pleasure rather than lovers of God, having a form of godliness but denying its power, and there is nothing you can do with that." That paragraph describes Hollywood.

People always ask me, "Why does Hollywood hate religion?" I say, "Hollywood loves religion! Hollywood has all sorts of religions!" The comedian Johnny Carson said, "Hollywood is the only place where you can raise a finger to hail a cab and start a religion." In Hollywood we have the Shirley MacLaine School of Theology, we have Scientology, all kinds of New Age stuff, and Deepak Chopra. Hollywood loves religion. It just can't stand any religion that has an objective definition of sin. So it has contempt for Orthodox Jewish beliefs and for Bible-believing Christian beliefs.

The American entertainment media are the most influential industries on the planet. Entertainment is one of this country's chief exports. I have been in about ninety countries, and in very country I see the obvious influence of American media. In a public restroom in Siberia, the community towel was hung on a Mickey Mouse hook. In Zagreb, Croatia, a banner across the city's central plaza promoted a Leslie Nielson film.

Despite its influence, anywhere from seventy to ninety percent of Americans are angry at Hollywood. They say it is destructive to the family, and that it erodes values.

So how have Christians approached Hollywood and its influence?

For about fifty years we took what I call the "Isolate and Condemn" strategy. Where I grew up it was a mortal sin to go into a movie theater, even if you went to a decent movie, because we wouldn't have anything to do with that industry. We'd rather have our kids grow up playing piano in a house of ill repute than have them go into Hollywood. So we let the industry go its own way, and we isolated it and condemned it from a distance.

Then we established a "Separate but Equal" strategy, where we had Christian television and Christian film. Billy Graham poured money into World Wide Pictures, and he made some wonderful movies with redemptive messages. Then came Christian radio, Christian books and Christian music. It's a multi-billion dollar industry. Has it had an influence on Hollywood? Unfortunately, not very much. I guess this approach was originally designed to be a change agent for Hollywood, but best estimates have the Christian media holding about four to ten percent of the market.

Meanwhile, Hollywood, television and music have saturated the world with their products.

About twenty years ago, Christians got really ticked. The first two strategies didn't work, and stuff was getting worse and worse. We got more and more angry and said, "We've got to shut these boys down." We sent out letters saying that we needed to "Hit them in the pocketbook – that's the only language they understand." So we developed the "anger" strategy. We said, "Put the screws to them. Start a boycott. Protest."

It eventually dawned on me that the Great Commission didn't say, "Go into all the world and protest all the bad stuff people do." Suppose you discovered a tribe of cannibals, and you said, "We've got to stop cannibalism. Nuke the cannibals. Nuke the tribe. Protest and boycott cannibalism. Picket those cannibals." It would never work. You wouldn't even be able to get your church missions committee to buy into it.

But many church groups buy into the mentality of "Nuke Hollywood." They generate anger strategies, and I believe they missed something. John 3:17 says, in my translation, "God sent not his Son into the world to condemn Hollywood, but that Hollywood through Him might be saved."

So after doing months of research on Hollywood, I fell in love with the people there. There's still a lot of nonsense, and a lot of things that come out of there offends me, but I discovered that these are *people*.

Think about it – if you were going to influence the widget industry, wouldn't it make sense to find out who runs the widget industry, build a relationship with those men and women, share the wonderful Good News of Christ's redemption with them, and then watch them change and spread their influence over the widget industry? We would witness the quality of widgets rising and the destructive influence of widgets falling, and the widget industry transformed!

That's what I thought we needed to do. We needed a strategy, not some haphazard plan like the televangelist who claimed he would slip into Hollywood and reach everyone for Jesus within thirty days. It doesn't happen that way. You can't out-hype Hollywood.

What was needed to reach Hollywood was a strategy for developing relationships. Hollywood is an old-boy system, made up of mostly old and mostly boys.

My grandmother used to say, "You catch more flies with honey than with vinegar." That works with executives, too. Remember, these are all *businesses*. We don't work with celebrities. They are treated like baseball cards, hired and fired at will. We work with those who run the businesses – the board chairmen, the producers and directors. And all of American media is run by about 500 people.

To build these relationships I figured that the most scarce commodities in Hollywood were unconditional love and trust. See the irony? Isn't that what Christians are supposed to know intimately? Isn't that what Christ showed us? Because of Christ we can meet a person whose lifestyle and values we despise, but we can say with all honesty, "I love you, my friend, and I accept you where you are." That's what Jesus did to us at some point in our lives.

The Church's three strategies failed. Why? Because they weren't spiritual strategies. There is no power on the planet that really works if it isn't based on spiritual power. An aerospace scientist told me once that "All of life is essentially a matter of power." You have to have the power to get up in the morning, to turn the alarm off, to get to your job. You have to have spiritual power and emotional power. All of life is a matter of power. The strategies the Church used to try to reach Hollywood failed because they relied on human power.

A few years after our ministry got started, a staff person said, "You know, nothing is going to happen until we start mobilizing specific, extraordinary prayer for people in Hollywood." It seemed so obvious, but we had never done it.

Since we knew that there were only about 500 people really running things, we were able to focus on specific people. Many Christians have never thought to pray for the people who run Hollywood – they are too angry to pray for them. We put together a daily prayer calendar with the names of the 365 most powerful people in film and television, and suggested that, on a very specific day, everyone pray for that influential person. One woman wrote to me and said, "Thank you for changing my attitude toward Hollywood. I was praying through this Media Leader Prayer Calendar and came across Madonna. I started praying for her, and my whole attitude changed about her. It has also changed about all of the people on this list, because I realized I was wrong. I shouldn't hate these people. They just need Jesus."

Those other strategies failed because they weren't spiritual. It's not by might. It's not by power. It's not by boycott. It's not by protest. It's not by lobbying. It's not by pressuring. It's by my Spirit, says the Lord. By my Spirit. We have the God of the universe in our bodies, and the Spirit of God wants to do the same kind of revolutionary resurrection He did when He spoke the world into existence, and when He raised Jesus from the tomb and set Him into full life and vitality again.

If we follow the principles of the Bible, even if they seem dumb, they work. It's amazing, that stuff written five thousand years ago works today, but it works in your financial life, in your relational life, in your emotional life, in your personal health and spiritual strength. It works because it's God's Word. It works in Hollywood, too.

I have to confess that I began to wonder if God's principles could work in Hollywood. Absolutely nothing happened for the first two years I was there. But one morning I was driving and I sensed God saying to me, "You haven't seen much happen, have you?" I don't hear audible voices, but this came screaming through my mind, and I know I didn't generate it. Then the message said, "Well, today you're going to see my Mighty Hand."

That day a vice president at NBC received Jesus with me over lunch at a Japanese restaurant across the street from the studios in Burbank. Ninety days later he showed me a script where he had crossed out four-letter words and skin scenes and said, "I don't know what's happened to me! I've become a lot more conservative since I became a reborn Christian." He hadn't been given a clinic in fundamentalist propaganda. He just had the Holy Spirit. When the Holy Spirit begins to take over your life, He changes the way you think. He changes the product you put out.

Hollywood was a vast wasteland in the 80s. It took me three years to find 300 professing Christians, and we knew some of those were flakes. They would go on a Christian program and give a glowing testimony, but they were still sleeping around or doing cocaine.

Before long, though, there were more than 2,200 committed Christians in the business. The number keeps going up at a rapid pace. Now there are more than 4,000.

We worked out an arrangement with the American Bible Society where they custom-designed Bibles for media professionals. The Bibles weren't black, they didn't say "Holy Bible" on the cover, they didn't have gold edges and they weren't the King James Version. They were attractive, hardbound volumes that said, *The Master Plan: God's Word For Media Professionals*. It's in very readable English. It is organized so that it tells a passage for every one of life's experiences: joy, sorrow, acquiring wealth, you name it. But it clearly presents the Gospel. It clearly explains what sin is – that's important, especially in Hollywood, because people there don't believe there is such a thing. This is a user-friendly Bible, and it is creating a spiritual revolution.

We measure the success of our ministry by the GAFF method: growth, access, favor and fruit. Growth in the ministry, access to people of influence, favor with the people that we meet and spiritual fruit. The Lord has given us a trust relationship at the executive level of more than 400 media companies. It's all private and confidential. It's not the kind of relationships where you can drop names, solicit funds from people you're ministering to, get them to read your brother-in-law's script or get your niece an acting job. That's the only way we could maintain credibility and trust with people. It can't happen when somebody is hitting on them all the time.

I met with a senior executive at one of the studios who told me he was a believer, but didn't know why he was still at the studio. "I can't let my own kids see the trash that this company puts out," he said. "I am embarrassed to be associated with this company, and I don't know why I'm here."

"I know why you're here," I said. For more than fifteen years, I've been praying that God would raise up at least one totally committed, holy living executive in every major company in film and television and New York, and you're the first guy we have found at this company. So you're the designated hitter."

He smiled and said, "That'll work. But I feel so alone."

I invited him to the discipleship meetings we were holding with executives from other companies. His first day there, he nearly wept. He discovered brothers and sisters in Christ, right in the same business that he thought was Godforsaken. But is anything really Godforsaken? The others embraced him literally and figuratively, and prayed for him. They prayed over him.

About a month later he called.

"Hey Larry, I found another one!"

"Another what?" I said.

"Another Christian."

The man he discovered was the studio's senior vice president of finance. He had never told anyone he was a Christian because he felt that the price would be too high for someone to know. So this guy came to the discipleship meetings, and the two went back to their company like Jesus' disciples – two by two. They prayed together privately and asked God to use them at the studio. They started discovering other believers at the studio – one group of women had been meeting secretly, like in the catacombs, for months, praying that God would do a work at their studio. They decided to meet together for prayer, in the board room.

"In the board room?" some asked. It was right across from the chairman's office. "What if people find out?"

"Of course they're going to find out," our friend said. "But if they start firing people, they'll have to start with two senior vice presidents."

So every week the group meets in the board room. Then it expanded into a Bible study on Tuesday and a prayer meeting on Wednesday.

It was like, "Can anything good come out of Nazareth?" Could there be any redemption? Could anything save the film and television industry? Yes, yes, yes. It can happen as long as Jesus is alive and well, because His name means salvation.

The reason we have trouble finding the answer to the problem in our homes, our businesses, our communities, is that we have deployed all the wrong strategies for trying to deal with evil. Any strategy that isn't spiritual doesn't work. Any strategy that isn't biblical doesn't work. Any strategy that isn't fired and fueled by the Spirit of Christ and the spirit of unconditional accepting love, doesn't work. We don't have to approve of the nonsense they do, but then God puts up with our nonsense on a daily basis. So we can't get self-righteous. Their sins are different from our sins, but Jesus had much more to say about self righteousness than he ever did about homosexuality. Sin is sin to God. We are called to show people that the ground is level at the foot of the cross. We need to say, "I've got my problems, and you've got your problems, but Jesus can solve them if we just turn to Him."

I spoke recently to a Jewish man who produced 120 television shows in a recent year, and his work is in seventy countries around the world.

"Before I came to know Jesus as my Messiah," he said, "I had only three categories for Christians: Nazis, Catholics and fund raisers. I didn't know there were people in America who loved God, loved Jews liked me, until I walked into a party in Malibu."

He had been experimenting in the occult, consulting a psychic and a palm reader. But at this party he was drawn to a couple and couldn't get away from them. They were Spirit-filled believers. In the middle of the night the man experienced what he thought was a heart attack, but it was Christ speaking to him. The next morning he called the man he had been drawn to the night before, told him what happened and said, "I wonder if that could have been Jesus Christ talking to me?"

The man from the party said, "It sure sounds like it to me."

The producer immediately accepted Christ. He began restoring his relationship with his wife and daughter. He was radically transformed with his own Damascus Road experience, and the messages in the shows he produces have also changed for the better.

About ten years after arriving in Hollywood I sensed a spiritual thaw, and then, a few years later, began to see the harvest. It was like working in a closed country where there was a public stance against bringing in the Gospel. But what is a closed country to an omnipotent God? Hard ministries may be slow, may take more prayer and more time, but what's hard for God? Is anything too hard for Him? I don't think the word "impossible" is supposed to be in our vocabulary.

On days when I get discouraged, or think that I can't see God's activity anywhere, I remember Moses talking to God, where Moses was very frustrated because things weren't going right. Then God said, "Moses, when did My arm become short that I cannot save?" That's a good word for us in Hollywood, too.

Whenever there is a person who is an absolute standout in his profession, it's a good idea to get to know that person and find out what makes him tick. So it was for me with Bill White. He has been involved in the financial services industry for half of his adult life, and he has such a resolve for the Lord, that he made a huge impact for the Kingdom of God through his Five Star Financial Services Company.

Bill started studying an opportunity which involved people between the ages of 75 and 85 who wanted to make a contribution to the work of God's Kingdom. He hired attorneys and accountants to make sure the concept was legally, morally and ethically correct. He has focused on this service for several years and is taking the concept all over the country.

I have tremendous respect for professionals who take the time to not only study scripture, but who also become very knowledgeable from those studies. Bill developed such a love for prophecy that he developed a college-level course on it, which he teaches at several New England universities, including Yale. The classes are full every semester he teaches them.

Working in marketing and sales for several public companies, Bill discovered a lot about business, which helped him formulate the plans for developing his own business.

Bill and his wife have two college-age children and live in Connecticut. Their son recently received a leave from West Point to pursue a two-year study in a school of theology, after which he will return to complete his college degree and his time in military service.

20 Drugs, Death, and a Love Letter From God

Bill White

THERE'S THE QUICK VERSION OF WHAT GOD has done in my life, and there is the extended version. Here is the quick version: I have been through significant trials, family tragedies, business failures, and two near death experiences, and have endured indescribable physical pain, spiritual awakening, failure and revitalization, have raised many millions of dollars for charities, and come through it all only by experiencing how real and merciful and gracious our God is.

That's it. That's the quick version. If you don't want the details, stop reading.

The extended version goes like this:

When I was 3½ years old my parents divorced. I was one of five children ranging from nine months to eleven years old. Both my parents re-married within three years. Each step-parent had a child from their previous marriage and each new marriage had one new child. So we were 5 + 2 + 2 = 9. The two households were forty minutes apart – Old Greenwich, Connecticut and New Canaan, Conncecticut. Whoever you didn't live with during the week, you traveled to be with on the weekends. So growing up I felt, at times, pretty much like a human ping-pong ball.

I lived with my mother and step-father my first year of first grade, then my father and step-mother for my second year of first grade through third grade, then with my mother and step-father fourth grade through eighth grade. I went to three more schools after that.

My older brother began doing drugs in seventh grade and I started smoking marijuana occasionally in fourth grade with one of my best friends Steve who used to steal or buy pot from his older brother. By seventh grade, I was starting to smoke marijuana and hash more frequently and by eighth and ninth grade I did LSD occasionally. In tenth grade I overdosed on LSD and almost died, ending up in the hospital.

By that time, I felt I did not have much of a relationship with my dad even though, as much as he was a workaholic, we always had fun with weekend and vacation skiing or sailing trips.

In between my Junior and Senior High School years, one of my friends, Steve Miserocchi, who had stopped doing drugs, became a Christian, asking Jesus to come into his life and be his personal Savior. At first, as he began sharing with me, my reaction was: after all we had been through together, he had now become a "Jesus Freak." But every time I saw him, he seemed happier than I had ever seen him before. Occasionally, he shared bits of the Bible with me. This was really strange because I had grown up with exposure to four religions: Catholicism, Congregationalism, Christian Science and a little exposure to Judaism through classmates. By the time Steve began sharing with me about being born again, I had kind of made up my own religion: Do more good than bad, and when you die you go up instead of down!

Steve, on the other hand, had grown up with almost no religion, and suddenly he was reading the Bible, which I never did, and quoting verses, none of which I had ever heard before. I remember at one point he was sharing with me about his experience of becoming a Christian, and said that a Christian is simply a person who has invited Jesus Christ to come into his life to be his Lord and Savior. I had never heard that before. Steve shared with me that the moment I asked Jesus to come into my life, all my sins (and he knew a lot of mine) would be forgiven by God. That sounded too good to be true.

So I went off to college with really no idea what the purpose of my life was. I remember in astronomy class, my first semester, being overwhelmed with the incredible vastness of the universe. The professor put up slide after slide on the screen showing us the earth as it looks from the moon, then of our solar system, then our galaxy and then myriads of galaxies and then a final shot showing the depths of space with billions of stars and then he said "all the light from these stars that you are seeing left before the earth was, and is just now visible to us!"

A few months later I was up late watching TV and the movie *It's A Wonderful Life*, starring Jimmy Stewart, came on. The point of the movie was that Jimmy Stewart's character had a chance to see what the world would be like if he never lived. He found out that he had a profound, positive, impact on hundreds, if not thousands, of lives. For me, at the end of the movie, I began to think about my life. Through my drug days I had lied, stolen, and done a lot of things I wished I had never done. Then the words from my friend Steve came back to me and, with tears, I prayed a very confused prayer: "God, Lord, Jesus, if You are really there, I want to be forgiven of my sins and I want to live the life that I was meant to live."

In that moment, something happened. For the first time, I felt something of the presence of God and I felt something of His love and forgiveness. I went to bed laughing and giggling, "Steve was right! I can't believe it. He was actually right. God really does love me and He has forgiven me!!!"

During the next couple of months, I had a lot of strange

experiences, where I felt like God was following me wherever I went. I began to read the Bible, and the words, which once were confusing and kind of boring, came alive, and I began to understand what I was reading. Eventually I came to realize that the Bible is two things. First, it is a love letter from God to us. Second, it is a divine refrigerator. Whenever I would read it and pray, I felt inwardly supplied and strengthened. I also experienced more joy, rest and peace.

I met some Christians who were visiting my college campus. They introduced me to the wonderful ministry of Watchman Nee and Witness Lee. Through these two brothers' writings I was introduced to God's eternal purpose (Ephesians 1:1-14), how to enjoy Christ in my daily life (Romans 10:12-13; 1 Thessalonians 5:23; 1 Corinthians 12:3; 1 Peter 2:2-3), and how to have a wonderful, supplying, daily church life (Acts 2:42-47). I also read several spiritual biographies by Chuck Colson, Hudson Taylor, George Mueller, Joni Erikson Tada and Watchman Nee that really inspired me.

Reading *The Late Great Planet Earth* by Hal Lindsay sparked a 29-year passion, love and study of biblical prophecy and fulfillment.

At college, though, I quickly learned how difficult it is to live the Christian life alone. I had not found much fellowship there, and some Christian friends from Chicago called me every couple of weeks to see how I was doing. With each phone call I was spiritually lower. One day I received a package in the mail from them: a round trip airline ticket to come out to Wisconsin for a Thanksgiving Christian Conference. The love in that letter and the airline ticket melted me and gave me hope. At that conference, I reconsecrated my life to Christ and the Church and was able to find a Christian family to live with.

I also attended a ten day Bible training seminar on the

book of Ephesians. In that seminar, Witness Lee spoke on God's eternal purpose, life practices like reading the Bible (he encouraged us to read through the Bible every year by reading three chapters in the Old Testament and one chapter in the New Testament every day), calling on the precious life-giving name of Jesus (Romans 10:12-13; Genesis 4:26; 2 Samuel 22:4; Isaiah 12:4, 55:6; Jeremiah 29:12; Acts 2:21; 1 Corinthians 1:2; Acts 9:14,21; 2 Timothy 2:22; Acts 7:59), praying every morning, reading and memorizing the Word (Ephesians 6:17-18, Colossians 3:16-17) and fellowshipping as much as possible (Acts 2:46-47; Romans 16:5; 1 Corinthians 16:9; Colossians 4:15; Philemon 2). During the next three years I read through the entire Bible three times. This period was a tremendous blessing and foundation to my Christian life and Church life. I felt that God went to a lot of trouble through 1,100 years and 41 writers to write man a love letter, and very few people really read it, including Christians.

One morning, during my sophomore summer in college, I was up early praying and reading the Bible and came to 1 Corinthians 7:8 where Paul talks about remaining single and not marrying so as to serve the Lord more without "distraction." I began to cry uncontrollably. Since childhood I had this dream of getting married and not getting divorced. Those who have lived through broken homes know that even in the best cases, there is something wrong. The Lord Jesus says in Matthew 19:8, "He said to them, Moses, because of your hardness of heart, allowed you to divorce your wives, but from the beginning it was not so." For me, I just wanted to find that special someone, settle down and get married, have children and provide for them all the things I felt I had missed as a child. With tears I confessed this to God and then consecrated my life to Him to live a single life and never get married. I don't remember telling anyone about this but I do remember a precious period of loving the Lord supremely and His doing many marvelous things in my life.

About a year later, I was listening to an awesome message on cassette by a dear brother name Eugene Gruhler about *God's Eternal Purpose and Satan's Strategy Against It*. In this message he laid out plainly the wonderful eternal purpose of God and then he began to delineate all the tools that Satan uses to frustrate us: drugs, alcohol, pre-marital relations, the world, etc. Then he began to talk about marriage. He referenced 1 Corinthians 7:7 "Yet I wish all men to be even as I am myself; **but each has his own gift from God,** one in this way (to marry), the other in that (not to marry)." He shared that you should use your college years to be constituted with God and God's Word and give yourself to serve Him. Then when you had completed all the training that God had ordained for you (i.e. technical training, or Bachelor's or Master's or Ph.D.) and were in a position to think about marriage, find an older brother who has been married at least twenty years because all the other brothers do not know what they are talking about. Ask the brother to pray with you on a regular basis for a wife, and instead of just window shopping for a wife, let God work one of His greatest practical blessings to our Christian life and church life by blessing us with the counterpart, helpmate, of His choosing.

It was an amazing message and I saw marriage in a way I had never seen before. I had never comprehended that there was a "gift to marry" and a "gift not to marry." Concerning this point, he said, "Some indeed do have the gift not to marry as our brother, Paul, but most have the gift to marry." God spoke to me in the most precious, tender way: "I give you the gift to marry." Oh the tears of joy as God spoke to me. He had to take me through this period to gain my heart absolutely for Him and also to see what the purpose of marriage really was – not just the fantasy I had dreamed up. Well, I began praying for a wife right away! I was faithful to the brother's word and I did not date all through college and when I graduated and began my one year training program I sought out a dear older brother, Elton Carr, who prayed with me from time to time.

One day at work, after I had graduated, I was having lunch with about ten of my fellow "trainees" and in walked this unbelievably beautiful girl. I bowed my head in front of everyone and prayed out loud, "Lord, if you are ever thinking about a wife, she looks great!" My friends laughed at me and we finished lunch and went back to our training session. We spent six weeks at the General Electric International Training Center in Rockville, Maryland, and then six weeks back in our home office (Boston for me). Six months later, I was in Rockville for a three-week session that was particularly intense.

One night I worked really late, woke up late the next morning, missed breakfast and had to wait till the morning break around 10 a.m. to dash over to the headquarters cafeteria to wolf down a donut and milk out of the vending machine. I sat down and there she was again. Wow, was she beautiful. I thought, "Gee, I wonder whether she is a Christian?" I swallowed hard, said a little prayer, and walked over to her.

"Oh hello," I fumbled. "My name is Bill White and I am from Boston. Would you like to go out tonight?"

"No, thank you" she said.

"Oh, how about tomorrow night?" I said.

"No, I am busy." I was really getting nervous and thinking I was doing a terrible job, but I persisted.

"Well, how about Friday night? I just would like to get to know you a little. We could go out for a quick dinner and I will get you home early."

She looked me over and said, "Well, all right."

We were married five months later. This year we will

celebrate 25 years together and we have two wonderful children, a son, 21 and a daughter, 19. What a God!

After four years and some success at General Electric Information Services Company, my father, who owned a small automation, machinery and development company, put me through a rigorous interviewing process to see if I was ready to join the family business, which it turns out I was. My grandfather was a brilliant inventor who founded the Tork Clock Company and later sold it to his brother, whose son helped it grow and advance to the company it is today – Tork Controls, a multinational company. My dad had a tremendous stretch of success in the 1960s with a company he had founded called Automation Engineering Laboratories, Inc. AEL invented the automated stitching of pockets on pants for Levi Strauss and some other great technology. At one time it blossomed to 300 employees and was ranked as one of the fasted growing companies in New England. Unfortunately, that success was short lived and in the 1970s AEL went under and my dad had to start all over from scratch.

By the time I joined the company, it was hovering around $1 million dollars in revenue per year with a lot of ups and downs. One of the things we began to do is target industries that might have significant numbers of companies with the same automation needs. We began to have some success with some automated robotic palletizing systems for the printing industry and we hired my older brother, Rick, to help with the finances and overall management of our growing company. We went from around $1 million in revenue to $10 million in revenue in two years and did a private placement with Rosancrantz, Lyons and Ross in New York in preparation for our dream to go public.

During this time, Rick and my two younger brothers, Bob and Roger, began doing cocaine a lot. Rick began to frequently miss work, and his relationship with my dad deteriorated.

Drugs, Death, and a Love Letter From God

We made some mistakes, putting too many eggs in one basket and perhaps missing one or two offers that, in hindsight, might have saved the company during the 1989 collapse in the capital markets. With seven bank failures in the state of Connecticut alone, and venture capital drying up, we began a two year nose dive, going out of business in 1991.

By then I had organized several interventions for all three of my brothers, including searching for them in the drug zones of Bridgeport and New Haven, as well as in Philadelphia. All three had received Christ as their Savior, but the insidious drug addiction kept creeping in and ruining their lives.

Finally, my youngest brother, Roger, had the "click" in his 4th rehab. Approximately a week after I had brought him a Bible, he told me "Bill, I finally got it! If I don't have sobriety, I have nothing and will lose everything." That began an awesome positive two year climb for my brother that culminated in his going back to college, working full time and getting engaged to a beautiful Christian girl he had met at a church fellowship. My other two brothers continued their struggle.

Meanwhile, I was devastated by the business failure and the feeling that I had let my dad down. I put my resume together, highlighted all my accomplishments, my last being President of Printing Technologies, Inc. and contacted some corporate head hunters and waited for the interviews and offers to come in. Nothing happened. I had a good resume, some great accomplishments, was in the prime of my life, was serving the church and I just assumed God would immediately take care of a new job and career. I was even praying with several brothers I served with twice a week.

But it seemed the more we commanded the Lord, the farther away He was. Finally, after a year of being out of work, on a Saturday morning, I was sitting on my living room couch with my wife, crying and trying to pray, ready to file for personal bankruptcy and feeling pretty much like the biggest failure on the planet and all of a sudden the Lord said, "Why haven't you told the brothers and sisters at church about your financial struggles?" The truth was, although I was praying with two of the elders I served with twice a week, I did not want all the brothers and sisters at church to know that I was a complete failure. I had been the president of my own company! And now I could not financially provide for my family and was on the brink of personal bankruptcy? I couldn't say all of that. The Lord's loving light shone on me and the sin of my pride was thoroughly exposed. I repented with tears to my wife and then the next day at church, with many more tears, to the whole congregation.

After the service, brother and sister after brother and sister came up and said, "brother Bill, we had no idea." I was so ashamed at my further sin of not opening to the Body but was immediately comforted by the outpouring of love and prayers on our behalf. That night, the brothers who take care of the church finances knocked on the door with a stack of anonymous envelopes filled with enough cash for our mortgage payment, food and immediate bills. Now the tears of joy just flowed. What a God! What a precious Body!

Two days later, I received a phone call from a recruiter who said, "Bill, I know you are not open to moving out of Connecticut because of your service to the church but I have just told Eastman Kodak not to hire a guy they want to extend an offer to for a newly created position and has been open for exactly a year." I about fell off my chair. "Could this be the Lord?" But what about all my service to the church in Hartford? What about the prayers for more pay, less hours, less travel, office closer to home (I had commuted one hour each way for seven years). What would the brothers think?

He faxed me a job description, and it read like my resume, literally drawing on everything I had done up to that point in my career. I would be sales manager for all new products and services, interfacing with all of top management for Eastman Kodak's Diconix Division in Dayton, Ohio. "Lord, what is in Dayton, Ohio?" I looked in my church directory to see if there were any brothers I knew from church conferences out there. Al Fletcher was there. Now there is a brother you can't miss, with his fiery red head of hair! I called Al and he said, "Bill, we have been praying for a year for the Lord to send us a couple to help the embryonic church life here in Dayton solidify." That was it. I knew we were going to Dayton. The brothers in Hartford agreed it was the Lord and, with quite a a few tears, we moved to Dayton, Ohio. What a God!

Life was good. I loved my new job. My children loved their new school. My wife and I were growing together with the other brothers and sisters there in Dayton and we loved our new home, a five bedroom red brick colonial with two car attached garage and ¾ acre of beautiful land in a three year old development.

To add to the joy, my youngest brother, Roger, was about to get married and I was going to be his best man. I was so proud of him. I had literally picked him off the streets of Bridgeport, retching and half dead more than once, and taken him to inpatient rehabs. He had gotten sober, was living a wonderful life, was on fire for the Lord. He had one of the best phone messages I ever heard "Hello, this is Roger White and have I got a verse for you, 'For whosoever shall call upon the name of the Lord shall be saved!' Leave your message and I will get back to you just as soon as I can. Have a great day!"

One Monday morning, around 6 a.m., I was just coming downstairs for prayer and the phone rang. It was Roger. "Roger, how are you? Why are you calling so early?" "Well,

I thought you might be up and I wanted to talk a bit and have some prayer together for my upcoming wedding." "Sure" I said. We talked about his job and his studies and his beautiful fiancée and her two children from a previous marriage and then had some wonderful prayer together.

Six days later, around 3 a.m. Sunday, the phone rang and it was my dad crying his eyes out.

"Bill, we have lost him, we've lost Roger".

"What? No! What happened?"

My brother Roger that Saturday night had just finished a home Bible study with his fiancée and her two children, and they invited her nephew to come over and play Monopoly. He was overjoyed. Roger got in his car to drive the ten minutes to pick him up. He drove around a corner and the left tie rod snapped, sending Roger directly into a telephone pole which killed him instantly.

At the funeral service, I shared with everyone his salvation experience, his conquering drugs through God's mercy and strength. I shared with everyone his love of God's Word and many favorite verses we had read together and were going to use in his upcoming wedding. There were many AA people there who had grown to love this dear addict who had such a big heart and was so faithful after two years of sobriety to keep going to meetings and helping out. Quite a few people got saved that day and that was a comfort, but deep inside I was in a crisis of my faith.

"Why… why… why… Lord… I don't understand… You used me to save his life how many times and now this... Lord please I don't understand… help me… please… I need to understand…" I prayed this prayer every day for weeks. Eventually, after several years my prayer changed. "Lord, I know you don't have to tell me…but it would help so much in my walk with You…I am stumbling and I just don't know how to break through… Please have mercy on me and forgive my lack of faith… strengthen me to believe

Your Word that all things work together for good... I am grateful people got saved through his death but, Lord, I miss him... Why did You take him?"

Then one morning, I was praying such a prayer and all of a sudden it was just like a divine video of thoughts streaming through my brain. The Lord reminded me of that last phone call, of Roger's extra need of prayer because he was working full time, going to college, about to get married and about to be a father of two children. The Lord showed me how it was starting to overwhelm him and the old thoughts were starting to come back and he was considering using drugs again. But the Lord just said, "No, my precious child, you have accomplished what I have ordained for you. It's time to come home." The Lord just took him at the prime of his life, 27 years old, with the most shining, wonderful testimony of God's love and operation in his life. God spoke to me, "just think if he had died while on the streets doing drugs?" Actually once he did die, was taken to the hospital, was revived and he went right back on the street doing drugs the next day. God saved him from a death of misery and great shame to a death of glory.

No one could deny God had done a miracle in Roger Sherman White. He was at one time the worst of street addicts, pawned my parent's car, broke into their home and stole their TV and VCR and pawned them for drug money while they were away. Yet, for his last two years on this earth, no one lived a more victorious, Christ-filled life. He humbled himself every day, every week to go to AA meetings to stay sober. And he brought so much joy to my parents and the family those last two years to see God working in his life so powerfully. When God was through mercifully sharing all this with me, I just wept with the deepest appreciation for a loving God whose heart is so good toward us.

Around this time, toward the end of 1991, there was a

call for brothers and sisters all over the earth to pray and consider going to Russia as missionaries. I knew according to Biblical prophecy and fulfillment that it was likely that the door would only be open in Russia for a certain period of time. I knew that if we went it would not be easy for the kids or my wife; but the more I considered literally selling everything and going over to the most atheistic society perhaps in history, with 88,000 professors of atheism, I just felt compelled. So with much prayer and fellowship with my wife, and with concern from our parents, we put in our application.

When our application was rejected, I was devastated. "Listen, Lord, it took a lot for me to literally give up everything to serve you full time, perhaps for the rest of my life. I know I am not particularly gifted like many brothers but I do love You, I have Your Word in my heart and I want to minister to others." The more you talk to God, the more He talks back. I sensed Him saying, "Live your life at work as if you were ministering full time in Russia." I was not entirely sure I knew what the Lord meant, but I gave myself to learn how to live an overcoming life in my humdrum, sometimes hard charging, full of temptations, corporate work life.

The first thing I did was park every day in one of the last rows of the parking lot for our 500,000 square foot building so it would take me longer to walk all the way to my office. I used this time every day to pray, sing, call upon the precious name of Jesus and pray for my co-workers. Before long, dramatic things began to happen. People got saved, I was in two Bible studies at work and I was splashing Christ on a lot of people according to John 15. If you are filled in the Spirit, abiding in Christ, the gospel is effortless. You become the gospel. Pretty soon I was dubbed with a new nickname that spread like wildfire and I kind of liked it because it always reminded me to exercise my spirit and be alive with Christ, which is not always so easy. My nick-name – "Mr. Happy!"

After four years in Dayton, we felt the Lord was really moving in the church there and we began to look to move to the University of Dayton to begin a campus ministry. We found this perfect old house with nine bedrooms and were just looking into the finances when I got a call to go to Denver.

While I was in my hotel room there, Bill Lawson, from our former church in Hartford, called. Bill explained that the church was growing quite rapidly and had some very critical needs and the brothers had been praying and con-sidering before the Lord for the last year how to meet these needs, and I kept coming up in their prayer and fellowship. So he was calling to ask me to pray and consider coming back to Hartford. I began telling Bill all the exciting things the Lord was doing in Dayton, and how Beth and I were going to be buying a house right next to the campus and as I was going on and on, Bill finally said: "Are you not even going to pray?" I assured him I would and we had some prayer together on the phone.

As I knelt to pray in my hotel room, the verses from Romans Chapter 1 came to me: "Paul, a slave of Christ Jesus…" (Romans 1:1a). I prayed: "Lord Jesus, here I am. I bring this matter to You concerning the need for the Church in Hartford. I am just Your slave." Then the Lord began to shine His light: "Yes, you are My slave, but you are a run-away slave, a disobedient slave, a slothful slave, an unfaith-ful slave, an unprofitable slave…" As the Lord's light shone into my inner being I could only confess, calling upon His precious name, asking for fresh forgiveness and cleansing in His precious blood. As the tears stopped, I just prayed: "Lord, as Your slave, I just ask You what do you want me to do?" As perhaps clear as I have ever heard or sensed the Lord, He said, "I want you to go." Whew…! It was all at once the most liberating and yet somewhat terrifying experience. What was my wife going to say? The brothers wanted me to come and serve full time. Were we ready for this? Was she ready?

As I called my wife from that hotel room I prayed, "Lord, You have to speak to her and make her clear." The initial response from my dear wife was not exactly what I was expecting: "What are you, nuts? Here you go again. Bill, what about the kids? They love their Christian school. I love their school. I love our house. I love the church life here. We are finally just getting on our feet financially after the devastation of the two years of going out of business and then being out of work for a year. Are you sure?" I could tell my wife was not happy so I prayed for instant wisdom and then said: "Honey, I won't do anything until the Lord speaks to you. Let's just take the first step and pray."

The brothers and I continued to pray and a couple of weeks later, as I was praying one morning in my study, she came in, tears streaming down her cheeks: "The Lord wants us to go," she said, and she gave me a big hug. Whew. "Thank You Lord. Thank You for Your faithfulness."

In addition to my work at the church, I taught a four-week series on Biblical prophecy and fulfillment at Central Connecticut State University, Trinity and Yale. It was inspiring and also very rewarding reaching out to college students who where all around the same age I was when I got saved. I loved helping them see that only God could have possibly written the Bible with prophecies spanning hundreds and thousands of years fulfilled to the day, week, month and year with such exactness, and then helping them to see the Bible for what it really is – God's love letter to man (John 3:16; 20:31) and a divine refrigerator (John 6:57, 6:63; Jeremiah 15:16).

Then the Lord saw fit to put me through one of the most

severe trials of my life – physical pain and suffering. I was always athletic, loved working out and, while I had had my share of injuries, was not particularly compassionate and sympathetic to those truly suffering. I remember my mom suffered from a lot of back pain while I was in high school, and I often thought to myself, "If mom would just lose some weight and work out a little, she would be fine."

God knows our heart, and in 2000 His sovereignty allowed me to blow out a third disc in my lower back. I had blown out two other discs over the previous fifteen year period, ending up in the hospital each time and then enduring months of physical therapy. The first disc I blew out was in a decathlon. Years later, while playing basketball, I blew out the second disc. Then came Mother's Day 2000, and after being back in Connecticut for five years I still had not yet dug my wife a garden. Well, she got a garden and I ended up in the hospital with a third blown disc, except this time it was really serious. There was so much nerve damage that I kept going into terrible spasms that felt like 10,000 volts hitting me. Eventually, only through heavy medication and a half-body cast which I ended up wearing for over a year, were the doctors able to keep me stable. I spent a year going from specialist to specialist trying to find a doctor to do a triple disc fusion surgery. I traveled to Johns Hopkins Lahey Clinic and tried some alternative medical approaches along the way. Finally, in December of 2001 I was introduced to some doctors who felt they could help me.

There was one major problem, however. Through over one year of being on heavy medications, my body kept getting used to the drugs and the doctors had to keep increasing the dosage to keep me stable. At the time of the surgery I was up to 240mg of OxyContin a day (half that dose would kill the average person), plus Valium and an anti-inflammatory. The anesthesiologist said there was nowhere to go for pain management after surgery, and this was one of the most painful, invasive surgeries possible. The first surgery opened nine inches down the front, took out all the organs, removed the three discs and inserted three cadaver spacers. The second operation cut open nine inches down the back and installed two nine inch titanium rods, a titanium plate and six titanium screws to hold it all together.

After the two surgeries, I did not really sleep for seven days, but just went in and out of consciousness. The pain was horrific and they could not give me any more pain medication or they said it would kill me. At that point, physically and somewhat psychologically, I was ready to die. Anything to get out of the pain. Then, after being discharged home a week later, I had emergency surgery because all the medication had disrupted my digestion. Then, just in case I had a shred of natural strength left, I fell and tore ligaments in my foot, ankle and knee and ended up with an ankle brace, knee brace and still had nine inches of staples up my front and down my back. I just wanted someone to shoot me and get it over with when the final blow came.

Moving at all, even in bed, was only accomplished with great difficulty. I tried to pull myself to a semi-sitting position when the main muscle in my neck popped and my head was practically like a rag doll's with little support, and very painful. At that point, while I am ashamed to admit it, if there had been a firearm in my house, and I could have gotten to it, I would not be here today

I had gone from bad to bad to worse to I don't know what. At this point, I was nothing, I had nothing and I could do nothing and it seemed impossible to believe that I was ever going to get better. I felt I would never be a real husband to my wife again, I wouldn't be able to work, I couldn't be there for my two precious children who every day asked: "How are you daddy?" and I could not lie and would have to say: "Not so good but thank you for your prayers." And they faithfully prayed day after day, week after week, month after month, at home and in their Christian school, as did so many dear brothers and sisters. I felt like I could never be a good, functioning brother in the church and yet I was supposed to be an elder. I felt like I was just one big failure holding on by the slimmest line of faith possible.

Our finances quickly became a mess. Two years before, I had left the comfort and security of corporate America and short and long term care insurance for the waters of entrepreneurship, where if you don't work, you don't eat. We went through all our savings and except for anonymous gifts from dear brothers and sisters, we would have gone bankrupt or worse.

One day, my wife was at the store and I became thirsty for some juice. Using my walker, I struggled to the kitchen. As I entered the kitchen, the pain was overwhelming and I just cried out with tears, "God, you have to help me. I can't take this anymore..." Just then the telephone rang. It was a dear sister who, though I knew her, had never called me before and never since. She said "Brother Bill, the Lord gave me this verse for you. I am late for work so I just have time to read it to you. It is Isaiah 41:13 "For I am Jehovah your God, Who takes hold of your right hand, Who says to you, do not be afraid; I will help you."

After thanking her and hanging up, I just cried and cried. Somehow, as unworthy as I am, God had called me in such a special way and reminded me of His tremendous love for me and that it was He Who would bring me through. It was a tremendously encouraging and strengthening experience. But my trial was far from over.

One week after this, I developed an ulcer from the stress my body was enduring. There was nothing the doctors could do because of the closeness to such major surgery.

267

They said I would have to wait till I gained more strength before they could do diagnostic testing. I was intermittently in great pain from the ulcer on top of everything else.

The brothers faithfully visited me and the church prayed relentlessly for me but I was now entering the darkest period of my entire life.

As I began to not be able to sleep, I became the weakest I have ever been in all three parts of my being. Physically, I was a wreck to say the least. Psychologically, I was between deep depression and just trying to deal with the pain while somehow keeping enough of a façade up so my whole family didn't implode. Then began the most relentless, merciless onslaught from Satan I have ever experienced. Every night, after my wife drifted off to sleep, he came to play, like a satanic video, every bad thing I have ever done in my life and every failure since I became a Christian. I wept night after night, confessed my sins repeatedly and claimed the precious cleansing blood of Jesus. I tried rebuking him, but in my weakened state, I mostly agreed with his lies. I deserved this and worse.

The lie was simple and straightforward. "God does not love you. You are uniquely evil and bad. God has shown you so much and you have been so unfaithful to all God has shown you. Now, God is going to kill you slowly and painfully because you deserve it, you miserable excuse for a human being."

After a few weeks of this torture, I had it. I began to dream how best to take my life with the least shame to my family. Since I did not own a firearm (thankfully), the options were all a little scary but it seemed the only way to end all this pain and all the guilt I was feeling from the nightly onslaught. Then, in a mercifully isolated moment of clarity one morning, I thought: "What are you thinking?! Now, you are really sick. Call the brothers! Now!"

I knew I had to call one of the most faithful men of God

I know, Bill Lawson. When I called, his wife Beth answered and said he was traveling, but would return the next evening. We arranged a time to talk and as always, Bill faithfully called me at the appointed hour. He asked me to go to my bookshelf and look for a little booklet by Witness Lee called *God of Resurrection*, a book that God used to save my life. As we began to read page one, we came to a sentence: "The objective of all personal suffering is the accomplishment of God's eternal purpose." What? "Bill, this is not helping!" Bill responded, "Hang in there, we are going to read this booklet through." So we continued and, page by page, I began to see God's incredible working through our environment, sovereignly arranged by God so that He could gain in us the real gold, silver and precious stones. Oh how costly but oh how precious.

First, through the life of Job, and then through the Apostle Paul, Brother Lee shared God's good heart to each of us, but with His eternal purpose in view. With Job, at the end of all his trials and then God's revelation, Job says, "I had heard of You by the hearing of the ear, but now my eye has seen You; therefore I abhor myself, and I repent In dust and ashes" (Job 42:5-6).

With the Apostle Paul it is even more dramatic. Just after Paul (then named Saul) saw the light from heaven, fell to the ground and heard the voice saying "Saul, Saul, why are you persecuting Me?" he responds, "Who are You, Lord?" And Jesus responds: "I am Jesus, whom you persecute. But rise up and enter into the city, and it will be told to you what you must do" (Acts 9:4-6).

Then, in one of the most amazing conversations recorded in the Bible, God speaks to a disciple name Ananias who is praying and decides to question the God of the universe, Who just happens to be speaking to him!

"And the Lord said to him, rise up and go to the lane called Straight, and seek in the house of Judas a man from

Tarsus named Saul; for behold, he is praying; and he has seen in a vision a man named Ananias coming in and laying his hands on him so that he may receive his sight. But Ananias answered, Lord, I have heard from many concerning this man, how many evil things he has done to Your saints in Jerusalem; and here he has authority from the chief priests to bind all who call upon Your name. But the Lord said to him, Go, for this man is a chosen vessel to Me, to bear My name before both Gentiles and kings and the sons of Israel; **for I will show him how many things he must suffer on behalf of My name**" (Acts 9:11-16).

As I read this, I said to myself, "Give me a break! Saul/Paul just gets saved and the Lord says He is going to show him how much he is going to suffer? On behalf of the Lord's name? What is this?" Then the booklet covered the transcendence of the revelations given to Paul to the point that eventually he says that **to him it was given to complete the word of God!** Imagine. Having the boldness and the realization to say that it had been given to you to complete the word of God! And with over half the New Testament written by such a one as Paul, look at his life after he got saved which he recounts toward the end of his life, approximately seven years before his martyrdom: "Ministers of Christ are they? I speak as being beside myself, I more so! In labors more abundantly, in imprisonments more abundantly, in stripes excessively, in deaths often. Under the hands of the Jews five times I received forty stripes less one; (Note: a leather belt with large metal hooks that ripped the flesh off your back with each lash and then they brought you back into prison, not to a hospital!); Three times I was beaten with rods, once I was stoned (Note: the brothers thought he was dead and when they took him out to bury him, he revived!), three times I was shipwrecked, a night and a day I have spent in the deep; In journeys often, in dangers of rivers, in dangers of robbers, in dangers from my race, in dangers from the Gentiles, in dangers in the city, in dangers in the wilderness, in dangers in the sea, in dangers among false brothers; In labor and hardship; in watchings often; in hunger and thirsts; in fastings often; in cold and nakedness – apart from the things which have not been mentioned, there is this: the crowd of cares pressing upon me daily, the anxious concern for all the churches" (2 Corinthians 11: 23-28).

Eventually I saw that Paul was the model. He suffered to the uttermost and was even told he would from the day of his salvation. Yet such a one was able to become such a gift to the Body of Christ.

So by the end of this little booklet that talks about our experiencing the God of resurrection, it was abundantly clear that I had no need to fear. Our faithful, loving Father God apportions to each of us so that: "And we know that all things work together for good to those who love God, to those who are called according to His purpose. Because those whom He foreknew, He also predestinated to be **conformed** to the image of His Son, that He might be the Firstborn among many brothers" (Romans 8:28-29).

By the time we finished reading this little booklet, God had so reaffirmed His love to me, and Satan's lies were so exposed, and God's eternal purpose was so fresh in my inner being that I literally and physically and spiritually and psychologically began to heal, really heal, that night straight through two years of physical therapy. While I would never wish on anyone what I went through, I can tell you on this side of this trial, God gained a lot and I will be forever grateful.

In 1999, I decided to go back to entrepreneurship. I had held ever increasing and successful "corporate positions," but I longed to have more time flexibility and the opportunity to directly impact lives. I was expressing such thoughts to my older brother who had spent years in the financial services industry by this time, when he began to outline an opportunity to join him in a small but successful financial services firm called Diddel & Diddel. Mind you, I had helped my older brother through numerous rehabs for cocaine and crack addiction, but he genuinely seemed back in the game and he was a financial genius (if he ever stayed sober long enough).

My brother and I determined we could do much better creating our own company, so we formed Five Star Financial Consulting, LLC. The only problem was I was completely ineffective in controlling my older brothers' repeated and growing excesses. Between his missing key meetings because he was drugging and his poor decision making, grandiose style of living and impaired thinking, he was creating a mess and I was enabling him to the uttermost.

Things came to a head when investors in our small startup company began to realize what was up and together we confronted him and got him into a rehab program. Unfortunately, Rick was still delusional and, after an unsatisfactory completion of that program, created enough other problems that the investors and our board of advisors decided enough was enough. We legally removed him from the company. That was about as heart wrenching as it gets.

God did not close one significant deal in all the time my brother and I worked together, but as soon as he was out of the picture, the Lord blessed us with many, many deals culminating in January of 2006 with $7.2 million to twenty charities in ten states in about fourteen months and we have paid back more than $3 million of debt and payables against a total of $4.5 million.

With an excellent corporate reputation, a diligent and faithful core team and several new products in the works, the future is looking promising. A major lesson I have learned is that every day is a gift. The Lord can do a lot in a single day if our hearts are open wherever we are and whatever we are doing. While as a CEO, I have an economic responsibility to all the shareholders and employees, at the end of the day it is the interpersonal relationships that are eternal. Jimmy Stewart's character in *It's A Wonderful Life* blessed thousands of lives not just with economic help, mercy and compassion, but also with a life of a million little kindnesses. I dream of blessing every human being I touch with the love and compassion of Jesus and His words of love, light, hope and truth.

Our God is very faithful. After tireless months of "saving the company" and trying "to do the next best right thing," I was a little spiritually dry and God knew what I needed. I had previously signed up by faith for a two week mission trip to Russia in October of 2005, but as the time drew near I saw no way. On the other hand, our precious Master showed me, I had no choice and I needed this time away to focus 100% on Him. I have found in business, if you are going to lead with passion and vision, it is critical to invest the time to be spiritually renewed as often as possible.

What I experienced between October and December of 2005 was life changing and historic.

God's love, His incredible forgiveness, His constant cleansing and renewing have never been more real or precious to me as during those two months. Picture me sitting in a Christian meeting in a beautiful new $25 million dollar Bible conference center in downtown Moscow with more than 2,000 brothers and sisters (believers) from more than 38 countries. Then ten brothers walk to the very front where the bread and wine have been prepared for the Lord's Table and, one by one, they begin to pray and praise God beginning first in Hebrew, next in Arabic, next in Russian, next in Ukrainian, next in English, then in

German, French, Spanish, Swahili, and Polish. Every single heart of those 2000 people was knit as one, and I do not believe there has ever been a Lord's Table like that in the 2,000 year history of the Church. This was all happening in the former Soviet Union which used to be the number one atheistic society in the world! There was not a dry eye in the room and God was there in a very powerful way. What could you do but just worship Him for the privilege of being there, knowing that some of the Russian speaking brothers and sisters, had traveled 36 hours by public transportation to come to this one, culminating conference of our time in Russia. Incredible!

It has now been 29 years since that wonderful first prayer. I can surely testify to God's awesome love, care, faithfulness, mercy, and grace. I never dreamed that my own life could have so much meaning. The Lord Jesus has blessed me in so many ways, both spiritually and humanly. In August, my precious wife, and I will celebrate 25 years of marriage; and our two children, are a constant joy and labor of love. My only desire is to faithfully serve my wonderful Savior, Jesus, and to hasten His return by being built up with other believers in Christ in the practical, daily church life and to express Him and glorify Him in all I do and say in business. To Him be the glory forever and ever! Amen!

When I first met Josh he was living in Julian, California, and traveling around the world speaking to thousands of people. He had just finished his book, *More Than A Carpenter*, and its success seemed to be almost instantaneous. In spite of that success, however, Josh retained his interest in speaking to young people. Just talking with him helped me have even more respect for him because he so wanted to be used by God to help kids.

Josh has a great gift for being able to communicate God's unconditional love. Everyone who hears him is energized by the enthusiasm and sincerity in his voice.

It is so difficult for most of us parents to be able to effectively communicate with our kids without their thinking that we are preaching. And as more people heard Josh and realized the gifts God had given him to speak to young people, more and more opportunities presented themselves to him. Today, he speaks to more young adult groups than any other person in the world.

One of his other attributes is Josh's humility. With all of his successful writing of books and articles, and the number of speaking engagements he has worldwide, he has remained humble. It is a blessing to know a man like Josh who is able to communicate God's unconditional love so sincerely. He wants to continue to reach young people for the rest of his life. This chapter is about his own spiritual journey, and much of it appeared in a similar manner in *More Than A Carpenter*.

21 Replacing Restlessness With Love

Josh McDowell

THE FACT THAT I'M ALIVE AND DOING THE things I do is evidence that Jesus Christ is raised from the dead.

Thomas Aquinas wrote, "There is within every soul a thirst for happiness and meaning." As a teenager I wanted to be happy. There's nothing wrong with that. I wanted to be one of the happiest individuals in the entire world. I also wanted meaning in life. I wanted answers to questions such as "Who am I? Why am I here? Where am I going?"

More than that, I wanted to be free. I wanted to be one of the freest individuals in the whole world. Freedom to me is not going out and doing what you want to do. Anyone can do that, and lots of people are doing it. Freedom is having the power to do what you know you ought to do. Most people know what they ought to do but they don't have the power to do it. They're in bondage.

So I started looking for answers. It seemed that almost everyone was into some sort of religion, so I did the obvious thing and took off for church. I must have found the wrong church, though. Some of you know what I'm talking about: I felt worse inside than I did outside. I went in the morning, the afternoon and the evening.

I've always been pretty practical, and when something doesn't work, I chuck it. I chucked religion. The only thing

I ever got out of religion was the twenty-five cents I put in the offering and the thirty-five cents I took out for a milkshake. And that's about all many people ever gain from "religion."

I began to wonder if prestige was the answer. Being a leader, accepting some cause, giving yourself to it, and "being known" might do it, I thought. In the first university I attended, the student leaders held the purse strings and threw their weight around. So I ran for freshman class president and got elected. It was neat knowing everyone on campus, having everyone say, "Hi Josh," making the decisions, spending the university's money, the students' money, to get the speakers I wanted. It was great, but it wore off like everything else I had tried. I would wake up Monday morning, usually with a headache because of the night before, and my attitude was, "Well, here goes another five days." I endured Monday through Friday. Happiness revolved around three nights a week: Friday, Saturday and Sunday. Then the vicious cycle began all over again.

Oh, I fooled them in the university. They thought I was one of the happiest-go-lucky guys around. During the political campaigns we used the phrase, "Happiness is Josh."

I threw more parties with student money than anyone else. But my happiness was like so many others' experience. It depended on my own circumstances. If things were going great for me, I was great. When things would go lousy, I was lousy.

I was like a boat out in the ocean being tossed back and forth by the waves, the circumstances. There is a biblical term to describe that type of living: hell. But I couldn't find anyone living any other way, and I couldn't find anyone who could tell me how to live differently or give me the strength to do it. I had everyone telling me what I ought to do, but none of them could give me the power to do it. I began to be frustrated.

Few people in the universities and colleges of this country were more sincere in trying to find meaning, truth and purpose to life than I was. I hadn't found it yet, but I didn't realize that at first. At my school I noticed a small group of people: eight students and two faculty members, and there was something different about their lives. They seemed to know why they believed and what they believed. I like to be around people like that. I don't care if they don't agree with me. Some of my closest friends are opposed to some things I believe, but I admire a man or woman with conviction. I don't meet many, but I admire them when I meet them. That's why I sometimes feel more at home with some radical leaders than I do with many Christians. Some Christians I meet are so wishy-washy that I wonder if maybe fifty percent of them are masquerading as Christians. But the people in this small group seemed to know where they were going. That's unusual among university students.

The people I began to notice didn't just *talk* about love. They got involved. They seemed to be riding above the circumstances of university life. It appeared that everybody else was under a pile. One important thing I noticed was that they seemed to have a happiness, a state of mind not dependent on circumstances. They appeared to possess an inner, constant source of joy. They were disgustingly happy. They had something I didn't have.

Like the average student, when somebody had something I didn't have, I wanted it. That's why they have to lock up bicycles in colleges. If education were really the answer, the university would probably be the most morally upright society in existence. But it's not. So I decided to make friends with these intriguing people.

Two weeks after that decision, we were all sitting

around a table in the student union, six students and two faculty members. The conversation started to get around to God. If you're an insecure person and a conversation centers on God, you tend to put on a big front. Every campus or community has a big mouth – a guy who says, "Uh... Christianity, ha, ha. That's for the weaklings. It's not intellectual." Usually, the bigger the mouth, the bigger the vacuum.

They were bothering me, so finally I looked over at one of the students, a good-looking woman (I used to think all Christians were ugly) and I leaned back in my chair because I didn't want the others to think I was interested, and I said, "Tell me, what changed your lives? Why are your lives so different from the other students, the leaders on campus, the professors? Why?"

That young woman must have had a lot of conviction. She looked me straight in the eye, no smile, and said two words I never thought I'd hear as part of a solution in a university. She said, "Jesus Christ." I said, "Oh, for God's sake, don't give me that garbage. I'm fed up with religion. I'm fed up with the church. I'm fed up with the Bible. Don't give me that garbage about religion." She shot back, "Mister, I didn't say religion. I said Jesus Christ." She pointed out something I'd never known before. Christianity is not a religion. Religion is humans trying to work their way to God through good works. Christianity is God coming to men and women through Jesus Christ, offering them a relationship with Himself.

There are a lot of people at universities with misconceptions about Christianity. Recently I met a teaching assistant who said in a graduate seminar that "anyone who walks into a church becomes a Christian." I replied, "Does walking into a garage make you a car?" There is no correlation. A Christian is someone who puts his trust in Christ.

My new friends challenged me intellectually to examine

the claims that Jesus Christ is God's Son, that taking on human flesh, He lived among real men and women and died on the cross for the sins of mankind, that he was buried and he arose three days later and could change a person's life today.

I thought this was a farce. In fact, I thought most Christians were walking idiots. I'd met some. I used to wait for a Christian to speak up in the classroom so I could tear him or her up one side and down the other, and beat the insecure professor to the punch. I imagined that if a Christian had a brain cell, it would die of loneliness. I didn't know any better.

But these people challenged me over and over. Finally, I accepted their challenge, but I did it out of pride, to refute them. But I didn't know there were facts. I didn't know there was evidence that a person could evaluate.

Finally, my mind came to the conclusion that Jesus Christ must have been who He claimed to be. In fact, the background of my first two books was my setting out to refute Christianity. When I couldn't, I ended up becoming a Christian.

At that time, though, I had quite a problem. My mind told me all this was true, but my will was pulling me in another direction. I discovered that becoming a Christian was rather ego-shattering. Jesus Christ made a direct challenge to my will to trust Him. I'll paraphrase it this way: "Look! I have been standing at the door and I am constantly knocking. If anyone hears Me calling him and opens the door, I will come in" (Revelation 3:20). I didn't care if He did walk on water or turn water into wine. I didn't want any party pooper around. I couldn't think of a faster way to ruin a good time. So here was my mind telling me Christianity was true and my will was somewhere else.

Every time I was around those enthusiastic Christians, the conflict would begin. If you've ever been around happy people when you're miserable, you understand how they can bug you. They would be so happy and I would be so miserable that I'd literally get up and run right out of the student union. It came to the point where I'd go to bed at ten at night and I wouldn't get to sleep until four in the morning. I knew I had to get if off my mind before I went out of my mind! I was always open minded, but not so open minded that my brains would fall out.

But since I was open minded, during my second year at the university, I became a Christian.

Somebody asked me, "How do you know?" I said, "Look – I was there. It changed my life." That night I prayed four things. First, I said, "Lord Jesus, thank you for dying on the cross for me." Second, I said, "I confess those things in my life that aren't pleasing to You and ask You to forgive me and cleanse me." (The Bible says, though your sins be as scarlet they shall be as white as snow.) Third, I said, "Right now, in the best way I know how, I open the door of my heart and life and trust You as my Savior and Lord. Take over the control of my life. Change me from the inside out. Make me the type of person You created me to be." The last thing I prayed was "Thank You for coming into my life by faith." It was a faith based not upon ignorance but upon evidence and the facts of history and God's Word.

I'm sure you've heard various religious people talking about their "bolt of lightning." Well, after I prayed, nothing happened. I mean nothing. And I still haven't sprouted wings. In fact, after I made that decision, I felt worse. I literally felt I was going to vomit. I felt sick deep down. "Oh no, what'd you get sucked into now?" I wondered. I really felt I'd gone off the deep end.

But in six months to a year, I realized that I hadn't gone off the deep end. My life was changed. I was in a debate with the head of the history department at a Midwestern university and I said my life had been changed, and he interrupted me with, "McDowell, are you trying to tell us that God really changed your life? What areas?" After forty-five minutes he said, "Okay, that's enough."

One area I told him about was my restlessness. I always had to be occupied. I had to be over at my girl's place or somewhere else, talking. I'd walk across the campus and my mind was like a whirlwind with conflicts bounding about the walls. I'd sit down and try to study or cogitate, and I couldn't. But a few months after I made that decision for Christ, a kind of mental peace developed. Don't misunderstand – I'm not talking about the absence of conflict. What I found in this relationship with Jesus wasn't as much the absence of conflict but the ability to cope with it. I wouldn't trade that for anything in the world.

Another area that started to change was my bad temper. I used to blow my stack if somebody just looked at me cross-eyed. I still have the scars from almost killing a man my first year in the university. My temper was such a part of me that I didn't consciously seek to change it. I arrived at the crisis of losing my temper only to find it was gone! Only once in many years have I lost my temper – and when I blew it that time, I made up for about six years!

There's another area of which I'm not proud. But I mention it because a lot of people need to have the same change in their lives, and I found the source of change: a relationship with the resurrected, living Christ. That area is hatred. I had a lot of hatred in my life. It wasn't something outwardly manifested, but there was a kind of inward grinding. I was ticked off with people, with things, with issues. Like so many other people, I was insecure. Every time I met someone different from me, he became a threat to me.

But I hated one man more than anyone else in the world. My father. I hated his guts. To me he was the town alcoholic. If you're from a small town and one of your parents

283

is an alcoholic, you know what I'm talking about. Everybody knows. My friends would come to high school and make jokes about my father being downtown. They didn't think it bothered me. I was like other people, laughing on the outside, but let me tell you, I was crying on the inside. I'd go out in the barn and see my mother beaten so badly she couldn't get up, lying in the manure behind the cows. When we had friends over, I would take my father out, tie him up in the barn, and park the car up around the silo. We would tell our friends he'd had to go somewhere. I don't think anyone could have hated anyone more than I hated my father.

After I made that decision for Christ, maybe five months later, a love from God through Jesus Christ entered my life and was so strong it took that hatred and turned it upside down. I was able to look my father squarely in the eyes and say, "Dad, I love you." And I really meant it. After some of the things I'd done, that really shook him up.

When I transferred to a private university I was in a serious car accident. My neck was in traction. I was taken home, and I'll never forget my father coming into my room. He said, "Son, how can you love a father like me?" I said, "Dad, six months ago I despised you." Then I shared with him my conclusions about Jesus Christ: "Dad, I let Christ come into my life. I can't explain it completely, but as a result of that relationship I've found the capacity to love and accept not only you but other people just the way they are."

Forty-five minutes later one of the greatest thrills of my life occurred. Somebody in my own family, someone who knew me so well I couldn't pull the wool over his eyes, said to me, "Son, if God can do in my life what I've seen Him do in yours, then I want to give Him the opportunity." Right there my father prayed with me and trusted Christ.

Usually the changes take place over several days, weeks

or months – even longer. My life was changed in about six months to a year and one-half. The life of my father was changed right before my eyes. It was as if somebody reached down and turned on a light bulb. I've never seen such a rapid change before or since. My father touched whisky only once after that. He got it as far as his lips and that was it. I've come to one conclusion: A relationship with Jesus Christ changes lives.

You can laugh at Christianity, you can mock and ridicule it. But it works. It changes lives. If you trust Christ, start watching your attitudes and action, because Jesus Christ is in the business of changing lives.

But Christianity is not something you shove down somebody's throat or force on someone. You've got your life to live and I've got mine. All I can do is tell you what I've learned. After that, it's your decision.

If you do decide to follow Jesus, you'll experience what I did – you'll find meaning and happiness, which is what I so desperately desired. And your restlessness, your desire for power and prestige, and your hatred, will be replaced with a love that surpasses all understanding. It's a relationship that changed my heart of hatred into a heart of love, and it changed the people around me as well. It will do the same for you.

The best word to describe Dwight L. Johnson is "passionate." He is passionate in his desire for God, in his love for his wife and sons, and in his never-ending pursuit of deep and lasting friendships.

Dwight understands that men can't thrive or even survive in isolation. They need fellowship, accountability, and relationship. They reveal the nature of God to each other through those friendships. He has been the president and CEO of a large electrical contracting firm, and is president of Christian Catalysts, a ministry organization that specializes in fund raising, sponsorship and promotion of events such as conferences, dinners, athletic tournaments, receptions and other opportunities where believers can network with one another.

Dwight's expertise as a consultant is sought out frequently, as is evident by his membership on many boards for both ministries and corporations. He has played a significant role in the Fellowship of Christian Athletes, Youth For Christ, YMCA, Rotary, schools of business, hospitals, Christian Executive Officers, Prison Fellowship and Promise Keepers. His business consulting is done through Sturgeon Systems, where his expertise is in strategic planning, finance, marketing and sales development.

Dwight has known and advised many leaders in business, education and politics. Those who shared their humanity and fallibility got Dwight thinking about the need for that kind of transparency in a broader arena, which gave birth to his first volume of *The Transparent Leader*. This second volume continues the theme of letting go of the myths of leadership, and allowing the true nature of God's love to shine through each person.

Starting a New Legacy of Love

Dwight L. Johnson

MY FATHER TAUGHT ME ONE OF THE MOST valuable lessons a father could ever teach a son. The problem was that he didn't even know that he was teaching it to me, nor did he know that if I was going to learn the lesson, I would need to do things a lot differently than he had done. My grandfather, David Dwight  Sturgeon, started an electrical contracting business in 1911, Sturgeon Electric, and he and my father built it up to a level where it had a solid reputation in the Denver area. I was the luckiest little guy in the world, because I had a grandfather, whom I was named after, who loved me very much and seemed to have all the time in the world for me. He was my Mom's dad, and we grandkids called him Daddy Dwight or Daddy Dee. And while my dad never had time for any of my athletic events, my grandfather never missed one. It didn't make any difference how busy he was, he always had time for any event I ever did or participated in.

My grandparents had a cabin in the mountains at Pinecliffe, Colorado which was located near the Denver and Rio Grande Railroad train track that kept on going through the Moffitt Tunnel, the longest railroad tunnel in the world. From the time I was four years old until I was fifteen, I was with my grandparents almost every weekend. We would leave Friday afternoon after school was out and stop to get something to eat on the way to the cabin, so Mommy Sturgeon wouldn't have to fix anything for dinner after we got there.

Saturday morning, Daddy Dee and I would go up to the upper pasture and get the horses. We would bring them back down to the corral, feed them, brush them down, saddle them up and go for a ride. Often times Mommy Sturgeon would go with us and we would ride for hours. We would ride down to the old sawmill and get rhubarb so Mommy could make rhubarb sauce or rhubarb pie when we got back to the cabin. Daddy Dee would show me how to cut the rhubarb so I wouldn't hurt the plant, and it would grow again in a month or two.

Daddy Dee would show me how to tie the horses to the hitching post so the knot would hold tight and yet would come loose easily when untied. He would show me how to clean the horses' hooves so they didn't hurt their feet, or he would show me how to put metal shoes on them. Then he would show me how to look for wood ticks on the horses, and when we found them we would put them in a jar of water to kill them.

There were so many things that I wanted to know as a little boy, and he seemed to be able to take all the time necessary to teach me how to do it or to explain the answer to me. Then when he thought I understood what he had said to me or showed me how to do something, he would ask me to repeat it back to him so that he was sure I had learned what he had said to me or showed me what to do. I didn't know it at the time, but he was teaching me some of the most important lessons of my life, and what a blessing it was for me as a little boy to have a grandfather like that, who always seemed to have the time and patience to answer my questions or show me how to do things so I learned how to do them, not just to see how he did them.

After I graduated from the University of Colorado, I

received a commission in the U.S. Navy through the NROTC, and my wife, Betsy, and I were married. When I got out of the Navy in 1962, my dad hired me to do what he did for his father-in-law – to go out and bring in customers. I looked forward to this opportunity because I thought it would give me the chance to be close to my dad. When I was in high school in Denver I was all-city in three different sports, and participated full time with a lot of enthusiasm, but my dad never made it to a single athletic event. He was too busy running the family business. Going to work for him would provide me the link to him that I had missed growing up.

Or so I thought.

Our agreement was that he would be my mentor in the business and spend a minimum of ten hours per week with me, teaching me what he knew. We ended up spending tenhours together in my first six months there – if that. Working in the family business was not what I thought it was going to be.

The first big project I got involved in was when the owner of a large, local mortuary bought an 880-acre mountain above Denver and wanted to build a mausoleum on top of it. He also wanted to build a gigantic cross on the mountain, and hired me to figure out how to do it. I did the calculations, built a model, and got the contract to build the Cross. We turned it on Easter Sunday 1964 – it was 393 feet tall and 254 feet wide. It was the largest lighted cross in the world and still is. Pilots could see it from more than 100 miles away. Nearly all of Denver could see it approximately fifty miles away.

It was a project that appeared to set my course as a successful electrical lighting engineer, but even then dad couldn't compliment me on the incredible success of the project. He didn't even go back to New York City with me when I competed for and won the first place award in the international competition against thirteen other countries for the top lighting project in the world.

But the following year everything changed. The Platte River flood, one of the worst in centuries, took out a significant part of the state, and especially our business. We had about nine feet of water in our building and about twelve feet in various places around our property. The flood took 83 of our trucks and about seventy percent of our small tool and material inventory. It took several weeks and 13,400 man hours to get things cleaned up enough to move back into our building. Even when we did, though, it seemed like my dad never recovered.

He had worked all of his adult life to build this business. In a two-hour span he lost one half of his entire net worth.

In order to try to build the business back up, I co-signed a business loan with my dad. Again, I thought it would help our relationship, but it only seemed to make it worse. The more I got involved in how the company worked, the more he became distant, and even hostile. It got to a point where if he came in the front door, I headed out the back to avoid any conflict with him.

This kind of conflict extended to our board as well. We had eight people on our executive committee, and for three years every vote was 7-1. But since dad was the majority owner of the company, his one vote outweighed the other seven.

Most of us felt that the business should be run a certain way, but the majority owner, dad, disagreed. It seemed as though every day one of the department heads would approach me and ask, "What are we going to do about your dad?"

To make things even more complicated, our business took a turn for the worse, and we started losing money. Debts piled up. Soon after that I was in the hospital with a serious ulcer. My mom knew that my condition had a lot to do with my relationship with my dad, and she visited me in the hospital.

"What are we going to do about this?" she asked.

"I don't know, mom," I said. "I love my dad, but I am vehemently opposed to my boss. They are the same person."

"Let's get you well, first," she said. "Then we'll work on this problem."

After she left that night I had what I can only describe as a moment of spiritual renewal. As a young man I had given my life to Christ through the Fellowship of Christian Athletes up at Estes Park, Colorado at the first summer conference in 1956, but this experience with my health, the family business, and the conflict with my dad showed me that I hadn't really given everything to God. That became clear to me in the hospital. I told God that from that moment on, He would be first in my life and could have everything – *everything!* That's the only way I wanted to live. I also asked God to heal me of my ulcer, which He did. There wasn't even any scar tissue in the X-ray. It was as if the X-rays of when I entered the hospital and the X-rays of when I left were from two different people, which, in a sense, is true!

After I recovered, I worked out a plan to buy my dad out of the business. I went to some of the vice presidents and they took second mortgages on their houses, sold other assets, all to be in the position of buying my dad's interest in the company. We knew there was no way the company would go the way we needed it to go if he was still the majority owner, or involved at all.

At first he agreed to it, but then the day after Christmas, he said the deal was off. He said he didn't want to go out of the business that early in his life – he was 59 – because this was all he really knew.

All along, I kept meeting with a small group of men for

weekly prayer and Bible study. Something I learned during those early days with FCA was that keeping an accountability and prayer group on a regular basis is one of the keys to continued spiritual health. I told the men that I wondered where God was in this ordeal, and one of the men said that God never said things would be easy, but that whatever happened would be the right thing. So the group committed this entire transaction to God, and asked for His direction and intervention. I had a strange confidence when I told the other executives, "I have the assurance that whatever happens, God is in charge and will direct us."

But two people who should have been involved in this from the beginning had been left out – our wives. It's never a good idea to have these kinds of negotiations and conflicts without including the most important people in our lives. So finally, both my parents had a sit-down meeting with Betsy and me that lasted three and one-half hours on a Sunday night. It was very healthy and open, but my dad was a hard guy to read, and when he and mom left, I still didn't know what he would do. If he accepted the buyout offer, he was out of the picture. If he didn't, I was unemployed.

Monday morning my dad walked into the office and said, "Your mother was right last night, and I am sorry. The deal is back on. Let's close it next week." We bought dad out, and at our first board meeting we dedicated the entire company to God. We vowed that we would give all that we possibly could to not-for-profit organizations doing Christian work, and within a few years we had increased the volume of the company 500 percent, and the profit 1,200 per cent.

At first, my dad told many people in town that his son had run him out of the business. That was very difficult to hear. But when I think about how the pressures of his job affected him, I don't think he would have lived much longer if he would have stayed in it, and I found out later that he felt the same way about the pressure.

Four years after experiencing tremendous growth, an electrical contracting company in Michigan contacted me about merging our businesses. We thought this would be the right move to make us more of a national company, so we joined our company with theirs. It was an extremely profitable move for a few years. I began feeling extremely uncomfortable with some of their business practices, though, and told them what I was thinking. Very soon after, I felt pressured to no longer be associated with them. Before long, I was no longer part of that company – I knew a little bit of what my dad probably felt.

I worked in real estate, consulted with companies that could draw from my experience in the business world, but most important, I kept involved in FCA. When we moved to San Diego I got involved with a Christian Executive Officers group, where business people in the area could experience the value of having other believers support them through fellowship, Bible study and prayer. One of the most challenging involvements was when I started a nonprofit Company called Christian Catalysts, Inc., and we were very instrumental in getting one of the early Promise Keepers events in San Diego, along with providing scholarships for more than 200 men to attend.

I was with my father when he died in a hospice facility in Colorado. I loved him very much, but I never had the sense from him that I measured up to his standards. I felt that I could never do enough to please him, could never accomplish enough for him to tell me that he was proud of me.

But I have come to a powerful conclusion in reflecting about my dad. As I grew up, as I went to college, as I went in the Navy, as I returned as his employee, and as I bought him out of the company, I realized that his love for me was

293

conditional. He did the best he could, having come out of the Depression, World War II, and his own hard work of putting himself through the Colorado School of Mines. But he didn't know how to love without strings attached. Dad was one of the best disciplined men I had ever known. He had a tremendous work ethic, he was loyal to his family, his employees, he always felt strongly about putting more back into the community than he took out, and he always provided well for his family and the employees. He truly was a workaholic and expected all of us to be the same. Dad's love was conditional!

The good news is that we have a heavenly Father, though, whose love is *unconditional*. We can't earn it, we can't buy it, we can't even escape it. That's the kind of father I aspire to be, and that is the Father with whom I want to spend eternity. One of the most important things I learned in all of this is the importance of building my priorities of my professional life, my personal life and my family life around Jesus Christ. All other things will fail, but Jesus will never fail.

That cross I designed on that Rocky Mountain is a great symbol. Our lives must be built on the Rock. All other ground is sinking sand.

In my introduction of this chapter, I mentioned that my father taught me a valuable lesson, which was that I needed to do things a lot differently than what he taught me. While he may have been a successful businessman, he was not a good father. He rarely had time for his family, and he did not live up to his word when he said he would do something with one of us kids, or come to our games, or help us understand how to learn from the mistakes he had made, fully realizing that we would make plenty of our own mistakes.

As I grew older, I realized how important it was to have a good father. So I vowed that I would be a better father to my children than my father was to me. I put all of my energy into being a great dad to my kids. And while it is never completely clear how good of a father a person is, one can measure it a little by the letters one's children write, or the notes they get, or the special calls they get when they are least expected after they leave home for college, for jobs, or for their new lives with their spouses.

I have had a very special relationship with my three boys, which is driven in part by the disappointing relationship I had with my own father. Here are some excerpts of what one of my sons, Eric, wrote to me after he had moved away for college:

"I pray for you and mom every night. It is neat to know that I get to have a Bible study with you long-distance every night... Whenever I miss you I look back on that state championship track meet and I picture your smiling, teary-eyed face as I crossed the finish line. What a race! I'll never forget that day, nor the months of effort I put into it. And I'll never forget your encouraging words that kept me going, even when I fell and got back up."

When I read that last line I thought to myself, "Isn't that what we all need? Someone to give us encouraging words when we fall and need to get back up?" Amazingly, Jesus is the One who gave me encouraging words when I was having difficult financial times and it seemed the only place I had to turn was to God, and pray and seek His face. What a blessing it is to have a heavenly Father that we can turn to and get His unconditional love, and direction and encouragement.

"I pray for you constantly, dad," he wrote. "You will triumph in the end!! I am so sorry that you have had to go through this, but God loves you, mom loves you and I love you so much that I just want you to be happy, whatever you do. It's not fair!! But once again, God will triumph. Stay Strong!"

In another letter of encouragement, he said that whether we were rich or poor, it didn't matter to him. What mattered was that love that our family had for one another.

"I look back on all of the things that you have enabled our family to do. You introduced me to our Great Savior. In many ways I feel that I am a lot like you. I have the desire to succeed, to have a family, to see a beautiful sunrise or sunset on a majestic mountain range. Thank you so much for everything you have done for me physically, spiritually, mentally, financially and for just being there when I needed you... I don't know anyone else who has been able to call his dad his best friend. I really look forward to having more times with you and storing them in my memory."

When Eric was in his career, in his mid-20s, he wrote to thank me for a weekend we had just spent together.

"I have not felt that comfortable, easy or restful in a long time. I think that is one of the best aspects of our relationship. No matter where you and I are together, it seems that, if we allow it to, the Holy Spirit really does move through us. I feel so lucky to have done so many wonderful things, been to so many beautiful places and felt so many wonderful emotions. There is not a day that goes by where I don't think of you in some way. Whether it was something you taught me, or what you said, or some special memory that I shared with you – it floods into my head...

"No matter where I go, or what I do, deep down I have a big smile because I am extremely blessed by God, and I am deeply loved by two special people, my mother and my father. I carry your love and support with me everywhere. I don't know where I would be if it were not for your love and influence on me."

Dwight Jr. is the oldest of the three boys and he is 44. He is married and has three children; Shea is seventeen, Emily is fourteen and Adam is eleven. He has a wonderful relationship with his wife Trish and they are truly doing a tremendous job of building a fun loving, well disciplined family unit that prays together, plays together, works together and has a wonderful resolve and love for each other. I am truly amazed and grateful for the terrific job they have done as a family, and in particular in making an incredible contribution to the community they have lived in for the last nineteen years, in the high desert of California in Victorville.

Eric is our forty year old son, and he and his wife Jenny have been married for twelve years, and have a ten year old son, Cooper and a seven year old daughter, Cassie. After living several different places, they have returned to Parker, Colorado where both of them have gotten very involved in their church where Betsy and I were one of twelve couples to help get the church started 24 years ago, Cherry Hills Community Church in Highlands Ranch.

God has such a great sense of humor that he gave us a third son, Stephen, seventeen years after Dwight Jr. was born, and he is 27 years old. He has been a real source of joy, even though, as Betsy constantly reminds me, we don't have the energy now that we used to when the older boys were his same age. Stephen is not married. He has truly proved what it is like to have two generations of children in the same family with the same parents, and has helped Betsy and me realize what a huge difference there is in the two generations.

All three of the boys are strong men of God with incredible commitment of their lives to their Lord and Savior Jesus Christ, and fortunately both of our daughters-in-law are strong women of God, and have built their families around their respective churches and the church communities they serve and live in. We are so grateful for the great jobs they have done in raising their children up in the church, and teaching them that the way, the truth and the life is with their Lord and Savior Jesus Christ.

Several years later Eric wrote me a letter that I wished I could have written to my father:

"In so many ways I want to be like you, to emulate you, to think, talk, act, perform and just be you. I am so proud of you! I am so lucky to have you and mom for parents. I think about how Peter's love for Jesus was so firmly grounded that he was called the Rock. That is where our relationship is as well, firmly grounded on the stability of a solid rock, never weakening, never breaking... I look back on the last fifteen years and see the transformation that you've gone through to be where you are today. God literally had to break you – to make you a broken vessel – for Him to build you back into a powerful tool that God can use, just as He did with King David."

And finally, when he was in his thirties, married to a wonderful woman, with two beautiful children, he gave me perhaps the highest honor a man could experience.

"My wife and I were not able to sleep last night because we were talking about how grateful we were – for such an awesome, loving, living God, the relationship we have with each other, our two incredible children, our wonderful house. As I reflect on this, I wanted you to know how thankful and grateful I am for having such an awesome and loving dad who is not only my best friend, but also my hero.

"Thank you so much for all you have done for me. I am most thankful for what you have instilled in me that has made me who I am today. Thank you for teaching me about our Lord, and what having a personal relationship with Jesus really meant. Thank you for being such a consistent, dependable father. Thank you for always being there for me, whether in the pouring rain or a snowstorm, and for sometimes being the only parent at my games or track meets. Thank you for teaching me what being a father truly meant. You were always such a great role model for me, and now, as a young father, I know what I need to do for my kids to let them know how much I love them. Thank you for always letting me pursue my dreams. Thank you for being such a good sounding board for me. Thank you for trusting in God and me in blessing the second most important thing in my life – my Jenny. Thank you for giving and lifting me up to God and allowing Him to help me become the man I am today. If a man is measured by how he raised his kids and how they turn out, I think you can be pretty proud of yourself. More than anything, though, I want you to know how proud I am of you!

"Dad, thank you for always putting your faith and relationship with Jesus Christ first and foremost in everything in your life. We both know that God does have a perfect plan for each of us, and He won't ever put us into a situation that we can't handle. Thank you so much for breaking out of the mold that was laid before you as to how a father should be. I shake at the thought of where I would be if you had led the same life as grandpa did. I loved grandpa and was truly grateful for him in my life, but you can be so proud of how you loved your boys. What a tremendous legacy of love you have started, dad! It is something you will be known for always."

Could a more significant thing be said by a son to his dad? That he started a legacy of love, despite his own upbringing?

As I reflect back on my life and the mistakes I have made both as a husband and a father, I realize that when we put our faith in our earthly father, we will often times be disappointed, but when we put our faith in our Heavenly Father, we will never be disappointed.

This author may be contacted
for speaking engagements at:

Dwight L. Johnson
Christian Catalysts
P.O. Box 6453
San Diego, CA 92166-0453

Phone or fax: (619) 222-3688
E-mail: dwight@cts.com

Dwight L. Johnson is president of Christian Catalysts, an organization that specializes in fund raising, sponsorship and promotion of special events. Dwight has known and advised many leaders in business, education and politics. He also designed the landmark Cross of the Rockies located 15 miles southwest of Denver, the largest lighted cross in the world.

Dean Nelson is the founder and director of the journalism program at Point Loma Nazarene University in San Diego. He is a journalist who has written for the *New York Times*, the *Boston Globe*, *Christianity Today*, and several other national publications.